Borderline
Personality
Disorder
in
Adolescents

Borderline Personality Disorder
in
Adolescents

**A COMPLETE GUIDE TO
UNDERSTANDING AND COPING WHEN
YOUR ADOLESCENT HAS BPD**

Blaise A. Aguirre, M.D.

FAIR WINDS
PRESS
BEVERLY, MASSACHUSETTS

Text © 2007 Blaise A. Aguirre

First published in the USA in 2007 by
Fair Winds Press, a member of
Quayside Publishing Group
100 Cummings Center
Suite 406-L
Beverly, Massachusetts 01915-6101
www.fairwindspress.com

11 10 09 08 07   1 2 3 4 5

ISBN-13: 978-1-59233-287-8
ISBN-10: 1-59233-287-0

Library of Congress Cataloging-in-Publication Data

Aguirre, Blaise A.
    Borderline personality disorder in adolescence : a complete guide to
understanding and coping when your adolescent has BPD / Blaise A. Aguirre.
        p.   cm.
    Includes bibliographical references and index.
    ISBN 1-59233-287-0
    1. Borderline personality disorder in adolescence—Popular works. 2. Adolescent
psychotherapy—Popular works. I. Title.
    RJ506.B65A38 2007
    616.85'852—dc22   2007024656

Book design by Dutton & Sherman Design

Printed and bound in USA

*The information in this book is for educational purposes only. It is not intended to replace
the advice of a physician or medical practitioner. Please see your health care provider before
beginning any new health program.*

The names and circumstances of certain individuals in this book have been changed to
protect their identities.

To my kids Isabel, Anthony, Lucas, and Gabriel—please always let me know when I don't get it. And for Lauren, who *always* lets me know when I don't get it!

CONTENTS

FOREWORD

THE DIAGNOSIS OF borderline personality disorder in adolescents has a status not unlike that it held for adults 30 years ago—it is widely used by clinicians but lacks the scientific base that entry into the official nosological system requires.

Still, the diagnosis is widely used for adolescents even without such official recognition because clinically experienced adolescent psychiatrists, like their adult psychiatric predecessors, recognize the distinctive problems these patients present: their need for attention, their desperate fears of abandonment, their inappropriate anger and vilification of those who disappoint them, and their suicidal risk when alone.

These patients magnify our own least desirable traits of being too angry or too needy. They are too much like we fear ourselves to be. No other patient group is so easy—and so uncomfortable—to identify with. They leave us all with a conflict—their neediness pulls us to rescue, their anger pushes us to withdraw.

Dr. Blaise Aguirre captures all of this and more. He writes with the sure hand of a clinician who knows his subject from having been personally immersed in it for all of his professional life. His vignettes are instructive and vivid. They evoke the impulse to rush toward or run away from these troubled adolescents. His writing is lucid and engaging, entertaining and educational. This book provides an excellent manual for patients, families, and clinicians. It helps us understand and sympathize with borderline adolescents. It will probably motivate everyone to remain—or become—involved with this desperately needy and usually alienated subset of our population.

The clinical wisdom necessary for their successful treatment is exemplified in this book. That such clinical wisdom exists and is so necessary is in itself a compelling rationale for why the borderline diagnosis should become official for adolescents.

John G. Gunderson, M.D.
Professor of Psychiatry, Harvard Medical School

Director, Treatment and Research Center for Borderline Personality Disorders, McLean Hospital

INTRODUCTION

RECENTLY, MY COLLEAGUES AND I had a family meeting with a teenage girl from Connecticut and her parents. She had been admitted to McLean Hospital for treatment of bipolar disorder even though she had all the classic symptoms of borderline personality disorder (BPD): fears of abandonment and emptiness, self-injury, overidealizing and later devaluing her boyfriend, suicidal thoughts, reactive mood swings, and impulsivity.

The girl's parents wondered why she wasn't getting any better despite all the medication she had been on. We reviewed her symptoms and pointed out that she met criteria for BPD but not bipolar disorder. The father, a prominent psychiatrist who worked with adult patients, became very upset and asked for a meeting without his daughter.

"How," he asked after she left the room, "can you make the diagnosis of BPD in a child? Giving her that diagnosis means years of misery and hopelessness for her and for us. You forget I am a psychiatrist. I know borderlines. They're impossible!"

Years ago, I would have agreed with this father. Years ago, I myself saw firsthand the devastating suffering of a close friend who struggled with the disorder. I was a medical student at the time, and though I tried to find help for her, there was little useful treatment or understanding of BPD. My friend found no peace or hope that she would ever get better. Like many others who have relationships with people who suffer from this disorder, I found I didn't have the strength to maintain our relationship, and we fell out of touch. But my friend's intense suffering made a lasting impression. Despite—or perhaps even because of—my inability to help her I developed a profound interest in this difficult and little-understood disorder.

A decade and a half later, in May 2000, I joined the staff at McLean Hospital, the largest psychiatric affiliate of Harvard Medical School, to work on its thirty-bed, adolescent residential psychiatric unit. I soon discovered that there was great disinclination to make the diagnosis of BPD in adolescents for fear that it would label these teens with one of the most feared, stigmatizing, and difficult-to-treat disorders in psychiatry. To make matters worse, of all the conditions in psychiatry, BPD has one of the highest suicide rates, with up to 10 percent of patients committing suicide.

From the beginning, I felt an ethical obligation to diagnose adolescents with BPD when appropriate, regardless of the early reluctance of some colleagues.

Despite being cautioned against making the diagnosis of BPD, I found that, for the most part, neither the patients nor their parents shied away from the diagnosis. The stigma of BPD was the clinicians' issue, not the patients'. In fact, the more parents read about BPD in adults, the more it seemed to fit the clinical picture of their children. Parents were frustrated, however, that there was so little information on the condition in adolescents, and they often ask for something to read on adolescent BPD. Sadly, there was scant literature, despite the fact that many of the adolescents who come through psychiatric hospitals like McLean have BPD or traits of BPD. Furthermore, I was frustrated that our early attempts at treatment in adolescents did not appear to reduce their misery. No amount of medication or talk therapy seemed to help. But soon after my arrival at

McLean, some of our clinicians started to practice a form of treatment known as dialectical behavioral therapy (DBT), and these sometimes highly self-destructive adolescents would dramatically reduce their self-destructiveness.

It took me a few more years to fully understand and accept the promise of DBT, but after seeing the outcomes I completed an extensive training in the therapy. It is a powerful and comprehensive treatment that helps patients, families, and the therapists who work with emotionally intense BPD, self-injurious, and suicidal kids. In 2007, the McLean Hospital Adolescent Dialectical Behavioral Therapy Center opened.

NEW THERAPY, NEW AWARENESS FOR A RARELY RECOGNIZED YET COMMON DISORDER

It has always been a fairly straightforward matter to explain the use of lithium for bipolar disorder, or Prozac for depression, because these conditions have been talked about and written about for years. But it has been much harder to explain the use of DBT for BPD. Most parents have never heard of BPD, let alone DBT, when we tell them of it. DBT is an excellent therapy, but sadly it is neither understood, nor talked about, nor written about! It is because of this glaring gap that the idea came about to collect the stories of the adolescents I work with along with my colleagues at McLean and put them together with the adolescent BPD research and treatment approaches currently available.

My hope is that with this book parents will have a more comprehensive understanding of BPD. This condition is widely recognized by the adult psychiatric community but only recently recognized in adolescence, despite compelling evidence that BPD has its roots firmly planted in childhood and adolescence.

The right diagnosis guides treatment, and so I hope that therapists, too, will find accounts in these pages that resonate with their clinical experience. Beyond this, I hope that therapists will take on the challenge of working with these kids.

One of the kids I have worked with for a few years recently had a very difficult time and became angry and self-destructive. She used emotional regulation skills, a coping mechanism I discuss later in the book, to rapidly calm herself down. In her next session, she asked me why I would ever want to work with not only one, but a group of kids who are as needy, demanding, and potentially lethal as she was! The answer to this is complex. Some of it is remembering my friend's suffering and some of it is that I find many of these adolescents to be insightful, empathic, caring, and funny much of the time. Also, because these adolescents cannot tolerate their misery, many are truly committed to their therapies and to creating lives worth living. But most of all, new insights into BPD and the promise of DBT have made the outcome of the condition far more promising than it has ever been.

I remember that when I first started to work with people with BPD I would often end up feeling as hopeless and defeated as I had with my friend. But after years of this work, I realize that it is not about how *I* feel. My feeling inept and hopeless for an hour or so pales in comparison to the years of pain and emptiness my patients with BPD have felt. To be able to recognize that their anger, frustration, rage, and suicidality is often a reflection of their feeling alien and alone and say, "OK, I get it. I can handle that," helps kids with BPD feel they are understood, and the healing can begin. This, too, liberates me to persevere in the work of helping children live lives worth living. Increasingly seeing kids live such lives is reason enough to continue in this effort.

CHAPTER ONE

What is Borderline Personality Disorder?

PSYCHIATRIC DIAGNOSES APPEAR to be like cultural fads that come and go. There was a time in child and adolescent psychiatry when everyone had post-traumatic stress disorder (PTSD), and then everyone had bipolar disorder, then Asperger's syndrome, and surely the next big diagnosis will come and go.

Part of the perception of these problems as fads stems from problems in diagnosing psychiatric disorders and the general absence of accurate diagnostic tools and procedures. Without such tools, any single behavior might be "claimed" by people researching a particular diagnosis. For instance, agitation with anger might be a part of bipolar disorder, or a symptom of PTSD, or a reaction in BPD. The complexity of the brain and its functioning does not yield its inner workings or disruptions as easily as do the illnesses of other organs. An x-ray, a blood test, and a blood pressure cuff can confirm a broken leg, diabetes, or high blood pressure respectively. Despite powerful imaging machines and a better understanding of gene and neural functions, we are still far from making diagnoses for most psychiatric disorders based on anything more than a description of behavior and functioning.

In that light, there is something particularly elusive about borderline personality disorder (BPD), especially in adolescents. It seems to overlap with many of the behaviors of normal adolescence and also with PTSD, bipolar disorder, and attention deficit disorder (ADD).

BPD is all of those conditions at once and then none at all. Yet sitting with adolescents with BPD is unlike sitting with any other group of kids. It is as distinct as being with someone with autism or Down syndrome, but trying to capture what makes it so is difficult at best. Adolescents with BPD don't have the social deficits of autism, the disheveled appearance of depression, the disorganized thinking of psychosis, the grandiosity of mania, or the cravings of addictions. Yet frequently, the scars on their arms bear testament to lives of misery and inner pain. When adolescents with BPD feel understood, they lighten up and talk profoundly and insightfully of their struggles and desires. But when they feel threatened or abandoned, they shut down or rage as if all their insights were nothing more than illusions.

Yet, adolescents with BPD are not alone. About 2 percent of the general population suffers from BPD. That equates to about six million Americans. And BPD affects not only those afflicted but also those family members and friends who care for them.

According to the American Psychiatric Association and statistics from the World Health Organization, 10 percent of mental health outpatients and 20 percent of psychiatric inpatients have BPD. Of those diagnosed, 75 percent are women.

The greatest tragedy of BPD is that up to 90 percent of people with the disorder will attempt suicide, and up to 10 percent will complete suicide. (We do not have statistics on suicide attempts or rates specifically in adolescents, and these data are desperately needed.) It is a well-established finding that suicidal thinking is found almost universally in people with BPD. Many people with BPD cite the hopelessness and pain of the suffering together with the loneliness and constant fear of abandonment as reasons to want to die. All of the adolescents with BPD admitted to our adolescent unit at McLean Hospital were admitted either after a recent suicide attempt or for having persistent suicidal thoughts, among other symptoms, such as severe self-injury.

CHARACTERISTICS OF BPD

BPD in adolescents is typically characterized by the following five features:

- Adolescents with BPD often display **behavioral dysregulation**. They commonly injure themselves (frequently in the form of cutting themselves), usually trying to better regulate their emotions. Other forms of self-injury include burning, branding, picking at scars, piercing, head banging, and punching walls. Adolescents say the self-injury either takes away the emotional pain and transforms it into physical pain or that when they are feeling emotionally numb or dead, self-injury makes them feel alive or at least "something." Researchers are looking to see whether self-injury releases naturally occurring brain opiates that might provide a temporary sense of well-being.

    Impulsivity is another behavioral problem, and parents will often describe how the adolescent appears to be "acting without thinking." This can include sexual promiscuity and substance abuse.
- Adolescents with BPD typically suffer from problems in their interpersonal **relationships** with sometimes profound fears of abandonment, which can lead to chaotic relationships as they try to grapple with this fear.
- They frequently have difficulty regulating their **emotions** and can appear for treatment with problems controlling their anger, or very reactive moods. They can appear perfectly happy one moment; quickly become explosive, weepy, or agitated; and then appear to calm down just as quickly.

- There is often **cognitive dysregulation** in that an adolescent with BPD can have paranoid and irrational beliefs. A common belief is that they are not loved, or that they will be abandoned, despite no evidence to support either belief. This fear can become all consuming, with adolescents believing that they will end up alone for the rest of their lives.
- Finally, there is **self-dysregulation** where adolescents are often confused about their own identity, feelings, and values. Although normal adolescents sometimes share these features, adolescents with BPD and their families recognize that they are at times so devoid of a sense of self that they take on the characteristics of people around them, almost appropriating others' identities. Adolescents with BPD also sometimes describe profound loneliness, emptiness, or boredom.

Further, adolescents with BPD show unstable relationships with their parents and "close" friends. They have intense anger, most often in response to problems in relationships. They describe feelings of emptiness and fears of being abandoned or misunderstood by the people they love most. They often recognize that they feel things more deeply and for longer than most of their peers. BPD can be diagnosed in adolescents when maladaptive and self-destructive traits are persistent, pervasive, and worsen over time.

While by nature, the personality of adolescents is still developing and changing over time, the above symptoms—when coupled with self-damaging impulsiveness such as reckless sexual encounters, binge eating, substance abuse, reckless driving, and self-injury—are not characteristic of a typically developing teen.

MULTIPLE MEDICATIONS AND DIAGNOSES

Time and again young people appear for treatment with variations of the symptoms just discussed. Their stories are frequently similar in that they

DYSREGULATION DEFINED

Throughout this book, I use the psychological term "dysregulation." Dysregulation means an inability to or difficulty in regulating or controlling behavior or emotional states.

Emotional dysregulation. People with borderline personality disorder (BPD) often display marked emotional sensitivity, feeling things "quicker" and for longer periods of time than other people and then taking a long time to return back to a "normal" mood state.

Behavioral dysregulation. Those with BPD have difficulty in regulating their behavior and often display extreme and destructive impulsive behaviors, such as attempts to harm themselves; recurrent suicide threats; binge eating, drinking, or drug use; episodes of promiscuity; and gambling or spending sprees.

Cognitive dysregulation. People with BPD can display episodes of disorganized and paranoid thinking to the point that they might lose all touch with the world around them and dissociate, a state in which a person's thoughts, feelings, and memories are disconnected from their current or actual experience. They appear to have a hard time regulating their thought processes, especially under stress, and they can resort to extreme, black-and-white thinking, all-or-nothing thinking, marked self-doubt, and indecision. They can have repeated thoughts that people do not like them, and this can bring on profoundly debilitating self-loathing.

Self-dysregulation. This inability to maintain a stable sense of self is common in people with BPD. It is not unusual for adolescents to say that they have no sense of self, feel empty, and do not know who they are or what they want. They often have difficulty expressing their needs, feelings, likes, and dislikes to others, and they can be easily influenced by the opinions and actions of those around them. They tend to be very concerned with outward appearances and frequently compare themselves and their situations to that of others.

often have had multiple diagnoses (most commonly a mood disorder such as bipolar disorder—formerly known as manic-depression—PTSD, or ADD). They often have been on multiple psychiatric medications, which have had little or no effect on their behavior.

Many psychiatric disorders have a disturbance in one or two of the previously mentioned areas. But when one person has a disturbance in all five areas, this is a diagnostic category in itself—even if for no other reason than that no one treatment type can treat all the problem areas and further, that a comprehensive treatment approach is needed.

Consider the following stories from parents seeking help for their children.

"My daughter Katrina is twelve, and she will be thirteen in June. She has been in therapy for about five years with everyone you could possibly think of. She has been evaluated by top doctors, and she has been on medication, all kinds of meds to control her behavior, even though I thought she was still too young to be on meds and thought therapy was the goal. In any case, none of the meds worked at all. She's defiant, constantly angry, and very disrespectful to her peers, parents, and grandparents. It has begun to spill out to other than family members, such as her teachers. I am at my wit's end and don't know what to do anymore. I cannot find a program anywhere or people who know about her problems. I don't think an outpatient program is for her best interest now. I almost think it's too late, although I am trying to stay positive. I am afraid of the future."

"My fourteen-year-old daughter has a four-year history of treatment for mental illness. She started with cutting her arms and her thighs and talking about death, and then she developed more extreme mood swings, mostly when she was angry at her friends or me. Her diagnoses have included BPD, mood disorder not otherwise specified, and attention deficit hyperactivity disorder from three different psychiatrists in our city. Then we took her to university hospital mood disorder clinic, and she was

diagnosed with cyclothymia [a condition characterized by repetitive periods of mild depression followed by periods of normal or slightly elevated
mood]. She continues to have impulsive, aggressive, unstable mood
swings with an intense lack of self-worth. Currently she is hospitalized
in our city's acute care psychiatric hospital, which is able to provide only
'safety net' treatment."

"I have a daughter who has been in seven different hospitals for the
past three consecutive years. Presently, she is in residential care, but they
want her sent to another hospital. She has many diagnoses from many psychiatrists and many med trials. She will be seventeen in two months and
time is running out. [Many parents of mentally ill adolescents worry about
their children turning eighteen because their legal status changes, too; the
law now considers them adults with far broader legal rights, including a
stronger right to refuse treatment.] She is a client of the department of
mental health. We are terrified for when she turns eighteen."

A NEW THERAPY BRINGS NEW HOPE

There is hope for adolescents like those described here. A treatment called
dialectic behavior therapy (DBT) has changed the prognosis of adolescent
BPD, and the promise of this relatively new treatment means that far
fewer adolescents will suffer from the ravages of BPD or develop full-
blown adult BPD.

Although DBT was originally developed for adults with BPD, it has
been adapted to the needs of adolescents who suffer from early symptoms
of BPD. For example, parents are included so that skills can be extended
to the home, the language of DBT is simplified and made more developmentally pertinent to adolescents, and further, the therapy is adapted to
address the dilemmas of the parent-child interaction. At McLean Hospital,
we teach the DBT skills in a classroom setting and assign homework. In
this way, it feels more like school, making it a more familiar way to learn.

DBT is composed of the following four major treatments, all of which will be explored in depth later in this book.

- Weekly individual psychotherapy
- Group skills training
- Phone consultation/coaching with the patient
- A support system for therapists who treat people with BPD

DIAGNOSING BPD IN ADOLESCENTS

BPD remains a controversial diagnosis in adolescence, even though the *Diagnostic and Statistical Manual of Mental Disorders-IV* (*DSM-IV*)—the American Psychiatric Association–published manual that covers all mental health disorders—allows for the diagnosis of BPD in adolescents. The *DSM-IV* is the manual physicians, psychiatrists, psychologists, therapists, and social workers use to diagnose mental illness.

Clinicians give two major reasons for not making the diagnosis in adolescents. First, clinicians say that it is difficult to distinguish between BPD symptoms in adolescence and normal adolescent behavior. Second, clinicians say that the adolescent personality has not fully developed and that giving someone such a diagnosis means unfairly stigmatizing the adolescent. Most clinicians wait until a person is eighteen years old before making the diagnosis.

Other clinicians who treat adolescents tell parents that they simply cannot diagnose an adolescent with BPD or that the kids will grow out of the behavior. Still other clinicians say that they didn't want to say anything to the parents about BPD for fear of upsetting them, and that being diagnosed with bipolar disorder or attention deficit hyperactivity disorder (ADHD) will "look better," because they are so much easier to treat.

But here is the problem with not making the diagnosis as early as clinically evident. BPD is a complex and serious psychiatric disorder.

If left untreated, a person with BPD has a one in ten chance of killing themselves. People who suffer from BPD can feel profoundly miserable, so much so that they would rather die than tolerate their suffering. Not diagnosing BPD or misdiagnosing it as something else prolongs the suffering of the children and their families. This can contribute to a cycle of multiple hospitalizations and at times unnecessary or unwarranted medication trials.

Two things are absolutely clear. First, adults with BPD almost always recognize that their symptoms and suffering started in childhood or adolescence. Second, some adolescents have symptoms that are so consistent with BPD that it would be unethical to not make this diagnosis and treat them accordingly.

Clinicians who are unwilling to make this diagnosis in adolescents do so in the face of recent research, which has determined the conditions necessary for BPD's development are found in the genes of the baby, in the temperament of the young child after birth, and in the environment in which the child is nurtured. I will discuss the causes of and contributing factors to BPD in depth later in the book.

BORDERLINE SYNDROME COMES OF AGE

It is enlightening to look at the history of BPD. The psychiatry books of the 1950s reflected the view that adolescence was a time of such emotional turmoil that it was difficult to decide whether a teen's behavior reflected a psychiatric illness that required treatment or normal adolescent development and that any strange behavior would subside. Treatment was not recommended.

In the 1970s, psychiatrist James Masterson, M.D. (a pioneer in the area of personality disorders), challenged this view when he treated a series of adolescents whose behaviors would be recognized as BPD today. He termed these adolescents as having borderline syndrome. He noted these patients had a cluster of symptoms that included mood swings, terrible fears of abandonment, and self-destructive behaviors. Unfortunately, psychiatry at the time had not had the benefit of current research and Dr. Masterson concluded that the adolescents' parents almost universally had borderline syndrome themselves.

If it was believed that many of these behaviors would burn themselves out—but on the other hand, if the child had it the parents had it—perhaps that is why therapists often decided to wait for people to turn eighteen before diagnosing them with BPD. Many psychiatrists had acting-out adolescents of their own; surely they did not want to be labeled with borderline syndrome themselves. Putting the diagnosis off until age eighteen allowed for the hopeful resolution of this adolescent turmoil until the parents could be absolved of any guilt or diagnosis.

So let's agree that adulthood begins at eighteen. What do these young people look like the day before they turn eighteen, and the day before that? I have seen kids as young as thirteen with such behaviors, and even in their younger days they were described as being emotionally intense and anxious children.

The enduring nature of the behaviors, the lack of clear boundaries between normality and illness, and the patient's perception of the symptoms as being a part of them, and not necessarily something that is happening to them, make BPD-type symptoms and behaviors more difficult to conceptualize than the more typical, episodic mental disorders, such as bipolar disorder and major depression.

Even though researchers have very different ideas as to what causes BPD, with some looking at it from a genetic perspective and others feeling that it is a problem of poor parenting, most experts agree that BPD has its roots in childhood.

This is critical. Comprehensive treatment must be started when the symptoms first appear to stop them from becoming an entrenched pattern of maladaptive and disruptive behaviors. At times it seems that clinicians focus only on the immediate problem. For example, a patient with BPD may complain of feeling empty and so, rather than looking at the whole picture, the clinician diagnoses depression and prescribes anti-depressant medication. This is especially unfortunate because while medication has a clear role in the treatment of BPD (especially in reducing anxiety and treating other co-occurring psychiatric conditions), medication plays a lesser role in treating BPD than for treating most other major mental illnesses.

The recent surge of research reports dealing with personality disorders such as BPD in adolescents suggests that the reluctance to make the diagnosis in adolescents may be waning.

In this book, I hope to make a clear case for making the diagnosis in adolescents. But if after the stories, the arguments for the diagnosis, and the research have been presented there is still doubt, I argue that the degree of self-destructiveness, despair, self-loathing, and suicidal behaviors in adolescents who don't respond to conventional treatment needs a more careful evaluation. The need for early and effective treatment is critical.

A Parent's Story

The research in this book would make little sense if it didn't resonate with adolescents who suffer from BPD, and with their parents. Because of this many parents and some patients have kindly allowed for their stories to be included in the book. However, to respect their privacy and with their agreement, I have changed all identifying details while retaining all clinical details.

The following is one mother's experience with her daughter with BPD.

"As a baby, Miranda always wanted to be held. No matter what we were doing, as long as my husband or I held her, she was fine.

She seemed to have a hard time sleeping through the night until she was about two, but as soon as I picked her up and rocked her, she would go right back to sleep. That seemed okay with us, though.

"When she started preschool at about three and a half years old, she would get so upset that I was leaving her that she would throw up. It wasn't just in the beginning of the school year, it happened throughout the year, probably three to five times a month, and I would have to take her home with me—school rules. Her pediatrician said she was fine, that it was a ploy and it was working, so she kept doing it. The next year, she didn't go to preschool.

"As she got a little older, her temper tantrums seemed to be completely out of control, nothing like with any of the other kids whom I saw. And it seemed as if the smallest thing would set her off, like if I wouldn't let her have a snack before dinner. She would throw herself on the floor and kick and scream bloody murder. She did this until she was about six or seven! As she got older, it seemed like there was a lot of emotional trauma happening with her at school over friends. She either loved her friends or hated them. We thought it was girl stuff; our two sons didn't seem to have those same issues with their friends. She seemed to go 'through' friends a lot. She still does now at seventeen.

"I also noticed that she always seemed to act or behave like whomever she was a friend with, that is laughing like them, speaking like them, etc. I asked her why she does this, and she doesn't think she does. We thought she seemed almost desperate to have friends, causing her to do anything to be accepted by them, which has gotten worse as she gets older.

"I started taking her to different therapists when she was about ten because she just didn't seem 'normal' to me compared with all of the other little girls that I knew, and I felt really sad for her having such a hard time emotionally. I thought if I understood her better and we could figure out why she always seemed to feel 'empty,' then I could help her. She gained about thirty pounds when she was eleven, and we fought about her weight. It broke my heart that she never seemed to have enough to eat and was always sneaking food when she thought no one was watching. The doctors said that it was my issue, and she was fine. At about this time she started to tell 'stories' to get what she wanted so she didn't hear 'no' as much. Her temper tantrums were becoming less frequent, but more volatile when they happened.

"At about age twelve, she discovered the 'power' she had over boys by using sex. We didn't want to believe this. Our older son tried to tell us. He was really angry that his little sister was a 'slut.' She would offer complete strangers a 'blow job' if they would be her friend. That really broke our hearts; we figured she had to be hurting inside to act like that. We got even stricter with her after that; she never went anywhere without one of us or another adult. We even stopped sending her to overnight camp. Life got tougher. She started sneaking out in the middle of the night to meet up with boys—people she was meeting on the Internet, we found out later.

"One time, there were two cars filled with guys from a neighboring town, and they came and picked her up one night. I was awoken by a phone call from 'Tyndall' looking for his boys because his new sneakers were in one of their cars and they were at our house to see my daughter—this was at 1:30 in the morning and Miranda was thirteen. When she finally came in that morning, she was mad at me for finding out. Shortly after that, she tried to run away to Philadelphia to live with a bunch of guys who were going to help her become a 'famous singer.' Her dog alerted me that she had left; that dog is obsessed with her. The police came, and we were able to find her at the bus terminal as she was getting off of the bus.

"I had her escorted to a behavior modification program in upstate New York. She was there for twelve months, and she made the same mistakes over and over again so she was never able to move up in levels to complete the program. It was almost like she forgot every time she was corrected for breaking a rule and losing points, because a week later she would do it again. She did start to behave like a robot, albeit one without a memory. That was where we learned a lot of the gory details of her past indiscretions. She kept a journal while she was there that is just amazing; there was so much emotion poured onto the pages that it made me cry to read it and feel her some of her pain.

"When she came home, she was so beautiful and sweet. She said she finally believed that we loved her and she was really happy. Life was nice for about nine months, and then slowly it started to be just like it was before with the lying, stealing, and sneaking out. We couldn't believe it. And the temper tantrums were back worse than ever because not only was she out of control emotionally, she started punching herself in the head over and over every time really hard, and we couldn't stop her. And if we would slap her to try and snap her out of it, we were 'beating' her up. If we spoke in an angry voice, we were 'screaming' too loud, and she had to block her ears. According to her, we all hated her, her life was miserable, and she hated us and wanted us out of her life. She started to break things and punch holes in the walls and also started threatening to 'shoot' me, if she had a gun. And these rages would happen if we said no to what she was asking. It didn't matter what it was, as soon as we said no, she would freak out.

"Two weeks before her seventeenth birthday last year, she was arrested at school with drugs and asked not to go back to school for the rest of the year. She was angry at the school for catching her; it was their fault. She was not remorseful in the least, which didn't surprise us; she has never seemed to be remorseful for anything that she does, because it is always 'everyone else's fault.'

"She started to see a psychologist on her own; she thought it would help get her out of the trouble she was in. I thought that maybe she would get something out of it since it was her decision to go, and at first the psychologist thought that she was a spoiled brat, which is something that we had been hearing her whole life, and we didn't spoil her at all. Then as time went on, the psychologist thought that maybe she had bipolar disorder. She sent us to a clinician who specializes in treating adolescents with this disorder. We started going to her every four weeks for about six months, trying different meds until we found some that seemed to help.

"It was around this time that I went to the bookstore to get some books on bipolar disorder, but nothing I read seem to fit. I stumbled upon a chapter in one book that talked about misdiagnosis and borderline personality disorder. It described Miranda to a T. Then I bought the book *New Hope for People with Borderline Personality Disorder* by Neil R. Bockian, Ph.D. I was amazed how much it described Miranda. She seemed to have seven or eight of the criteria listed in the *DSM-IV* for BPD. So I called the psychologist, and she said that you can't diagnose an adolescent with BPD and that I shouldn't think of that because she will probably out grow a lot of her behaviors. I called the clinician and told her what I thought, and she said, 'Oh yes, she does have BPD,' but she didn't say anything because she didn't want to upset us! I was so angry. The more I read about BPD, the more I feel comfortable with this disorder because knowledge is power and I can handle Miranda so much better now that I know more. Her clinician is also more comfortable with it now. (The psychologist told me she went to a seminar about BPD and is trying to learn more about it.)

"Her clinicians have recommended that Miranda be on some kind of an emotional individualized education plan (IEP) at school because of her issues, but the school doesn't want to do anything for her because she is a 'bad' kid. We are fighting them right now. I was told that without a letter stating what Miranda had, they were not going to do any further testing on her. The clinician didn't want to write that she has BPD because it would look bad for Miranda, so she wrote that she has bipolar and ADHD, with borderline personality disorder traits. She didn't want Miranda to be stigmatized!

"I have now read several books about the disorder, and the one thing I keep thinking is, if only I knew even half of what I now know when Miranda was younger, it could have made all of the difference in the world for her. None of the psychologists whom we went to even hinted at any kind of a disorder. They all seemed to feel that Miranda was fine, just a little 'bratty.' I asked her to read the chapter on what the disorder is about and its symptoms in the book *Borderline Personality Disorder Demystified* by Robert O. Friedel, M.D., and she was amazed how much it described her also. Better late that never; she will be eighteen next week."

CHAPTER TWO

How to Diagnose BPD
in Adolescents

BECAUSE OF THE LACK OF information about adolescent BPD, there are no formal criteria for diagnosing it in teenagers. The *Diagnostic and Statistical Manual of Mental Disorders-IV* (*DSM-IV*) describes BPD as a pervasive pattern of instability in relationships, self-image, and affects, and marked impulsivity beginning by early adulthood, which present in a variety of contexts, as indicated by five or more of the criteria that follow. I have added notes in italics to show how the criteria might pertain to adolescence; my notes are not part of the official *DSM-IV* criteria.

1. Frantic efforts to avoid real or imagined abandonment.
Adolescents with BPD who are hospitalized often appear for treatment after a break-up with a boyfriend or girlfriend. They usually have considered or attempted suicide and recognize the despair or fear of being left by a loved one. The fear of abandonment is not simply that some loved person will leave, but rather it's a profound sense that someone essential to their well-being will absolutely never come back. I remember struggling with this concept when one young woman told me: "OK, imagine that you are a six-year-old at Disney World, and your parents suddenly

disappear, and you cannot find them, and there are all these strange people around you. It is like that. The dread is terrifying, and when I fear being left, it is exactly that fear."

It is the fear of being left without a rudder on a boat, in the middle of a huge ocean, without anything certain or secure. The fear can be so consuming that even if there is no basis to the fear, children will protect themselves against an imagined abandonment by acting in a way that forces the parents to remain near, by doing things such as saying that they feel suicidal.

2. A pattern of unstable and intense relationships characterized by alternating between extremes of idealization and devaluation, called "splitting." Parents describe how at one moment their children tell them that they are the best parents in the world, and at another, they are the worst parents ever. This behavior occurs repeatedly and tends to be reactive. Adolescents with BPD similarly divide staff on psychiatric units into good and bad staff, and these designations can easily change. Another example is children asking parents or staff members for something and then going to other parents or staff members if they don't get what they wanted in the first place. Parents and staff members often find themselves taking sides, which often leads to conflict between them. This is considered to be a reflection of what goes on in the person with BPD's sense of self. Sometimes they feel all bad, and other times they feel all good. This tends to lead to all-or-nothing or black-and-white thinking. The problem becomes integrating the good-self and bad-self into a complete person, or recognizing that we are all composites of "better" and "worse" qualities.

One of our former patients emailed McLean Hospital to let us know how she was doing. As you'll read in her message that follows, the relationship quickly switches from a fulfilling one to a meaningless one. The torment of the doubt about whether people care comes and goes rapidly in BPD, and this can be terrifying to an adolescent. The former patient also acknowledged in her email that because of treatment she had become more self-aware.

"So things with my boyfriend are so good. I have accepted that he gets me even though he doesn't know a lot about my disorder, and that that's the way it's supposed to be. Maybe it's better because it's not that intense. Maybe we are supposed to ride in the car silent together with a little talking on the side. I do wish he knew my ideas though. I will work on that. I have gone crazy here in Florida. I think he wants to talk to me when I get back. He called a couple times, but I think it's just how he wants it to be, nothing bad. But there is still me giving in on some independence but him not at all because he does his own thing 100 percent. And also it's kinda like how he wants the relationship to be.

"Damn! It switches so fast from I know he loves me to what the heck I mean nothing to him. And I think some of that is justified now. Will you give me advice on how not to be so self-absorbed? My best friend, who I do not like except that she tells me things, told me that I talk about myself a lot (she said it when she was drunk), and now I can't stop thinking about it. Now if I say something about myself . . . well I am constantly catching myself. My dad has always called me selfish my whole life and says that I think only of myself, and I think that it's true when it comes to my family but what if not? What if I treat everybody that way? And even so, even in my head I'm constantly thinking about the good things or the bad things or events that all have to do with me. I don't know how to stop. What a mess."

3. Identity disturbance: markedly and persistently unstable self-image or sense of self. Adolescents with BPD have a hard time defining a stable sense of who they are. They often describe being able to define themselves most easily by depending on whom they are with—"I am a very different person with different people or groups of people." This criterion is not that helpful in diagnosing adolescents with BPD because adolescence is generally a time of defining identity, so identity issues are common in adolescents without BPD as well.

Many parents with kids with BPD say that they have no real sense of who their kids are. Parents often compare their kids without BPD to their kids with BPD and say that they always had a sense of who their kids without BPD were, whereas, their adolescents with BPD seemed to change identities "with the wind." "She wants to pretend that she is a 'rich girl' who couldn't be bothered with middle class people," complained one parent, or "she tells us that she is going be the next Paris Hilton" and then acts completely like what she reads about Paris Hilton in the magazines, or she acts "like a happy, fun, loving girl all the time, when deep down she is miserable." Other parents have said that their children will change to be images of whoever the children's best friends happen to be at the time.

Adolescence is a time when popular culture can have a profound influence on behavior, but in these cases it is an extreme version of itself, and the kids at some level truly internalize the idealized characteristics of the people they are trying to copy. They often complain that this is because they have no identities of their own.

4. Impulsivity in at least two areas that are potentially self-damaging— such as excessive spending, sex, substance abuse, reckless driving, and binge eating. In younger adolescents with little money or access to cars, extreme spending and reckless driving are unusual. However, sexual promiscuity, drug abuse—including sharing psychiatric medication— eating problems, and running away from home are quite common. Further, younger adolescents might go for drives with older drivers who are reckless. Another example of potentially self-damaging impulsivity is "hooking up" with older adults whom they have met on the Internet.

5. Recurrent suicidal behavior, gestures, or threats, or self-mutilating behavior. In adolescents, we most commonly see cutting of the wrists and other parts of the body, burning themselves, scratching, and drug overdoses. (See Chapter 3 for more information on cutting.)

6. Affective instability due to a marked reactivity of mood (e.g.,

intense episodic dysphoria [which is a type of "low grade" depression, or a low-mood state that is not as severe as depression], irritability, or anxiety that usually lasts a few hours and only rarely more than a few days). Adolescents describe (and parents agree) how they can feel perfectly normal one minute and the next they are "pissed off" or angry or depressed, and that this change in mood is a reaction to something that happened between them and someone else, generally a parent, close friend, boyfriend, or girlfriend. The mood is reactive in that it is a reaction to a clear precipitant. This type of moodiness does not, in my clinical experience, reliably respond to mood stabilizing medication. (See Chapter 9 on dialectical behavior therapy [DBT] for more information.)

7. **Chronic feelings of emptiness.** Adolescents also describe this as feeling lonely or bored.

8. **Inappropriate, intense anger or difficulty controlling anger (e.g., frequent displays of temper, constant anger, and/or recurrent physical fights).** Fights often occur most predictably with people with whom the adolescent with BPD is closest, and the fights might not be witnessed or experienced by casual acquaintances. Many adolescents and parents feel that although this criterion does not apply, that it would apply if the feeling were something other than anger. They say that their children have, for instance, inappropriate intense jealousy, or intense self-hatred. That's why any inappropriate intense emotion should be considered.

9. **Transient, stress-related paranoia or severe dissociative symptoms.** Dissociation is a psychological state in which certain thoughts, emotions, sensations, or memories are separated from the rest of the person. It frequently occurs in people suffering from post-traumatic stress disorder (PTSD). Although sexual and other abuse is neither necessary nor sufficient to cause BPD, people with BPD have often suffered abuse, and some go on to develop PTSD. In clinical practice, we identify dissociation when patients talk about their traumas. They appear to be almost narrating from a book,

Generally parents are not too concerned when a two-year-old has a temper tantrum. At that age, children have a sense of what they want, but they do not have the words to ask for it.

Temper tantrums, which are also called rage episodes, in adolescence however, are a source of serious disruption in a family. Rage episodes can terrify a family and wear them down to the point of exhaustion. Some adolescents with BPD say that they don't remember what happened during the rages but that they feel strangely calm after the episodes. For the family, though, there is seldom a sense of calm. Although many times adolescents and parents say that the eruption came out of nowhere, kids often recognize that there was a gradual build of irritability, and that when triggered by an interpersonal conflict, the rage eruption took place.

Irritability itself can wear parents down to the point that they give in to the children rather than put up with the anger outbursts. The children then learns that rage works to get the parents to give up. It is this "learned" anger, and not the actual irritability itself, that parents must address.

In some cases, rage episodes have become out of control, and adolescents with BPD have assaulted family members, teachers, peers, and even police officers. One young adolescent we admitted to McLean Hospital bit her mother hard on the chest to the point of bleeding. In other cases, adolescents with BPD turn their violent anger on themselves in the form of self-injury. In still other cases, adolescents with BPD destroy property, threaten homicide, or barricade themselves in rooms. Some adolescents with BPD describe being so angry that they have jumped from moving cars or run into traffic. In my clinical experience, these have never been planned events, but rather sudden and explosive episodes.

Preventing Rages Before They Happen

The first step is prevention. Recognizing early signs of irritability or potential conflict can help the parent intervene at a point where the pre-frontal cortex is still functioning. The pre-frontal cortex is the part of the brain that allows a person to weigh actions versus consequences. Many studies have shown that if the adolescent gets into a rage state, the brain goes into a more primitive form of functioning. This is the "fight-or-flight" response where a person sees a perceived threat and must then either fight the threat or run away from it. Clearly recognizing early signs that things are not going well is vitally important to both the adolescent and the parent.

The second step is to teach the child the skills necessary to get grounded or calmed down before the irritability goes any further. Some simple but effective techniques are breathing deeply, counting backward, using pleasant imagery, listening to music, going for a jog—techniques that any person might use to reduce stress.

If children do in fact rage, the single most important rule is that the parents must make sure that angry outbursts never work. Adolescents must know that they will never get what they want by angry reactions. There is no exception to this rule, no matter how violent the temper reaction. If safety is a real concern because of threat of injury to self or others, parents should call the police or emergency medical technicians (EMTs), whichever is appropriate.

Parents should never give in to yelling, threats, throwing things, or even violent aggression, no matter how distressing or embarrassing it may be at the time. This prevents the possibility of rewarding, and encouraging, more anger reactions, or teaching the adolescents that all they need do is to escalate such behavior.

An important corollary to the first rule, however, is that adolescents need to learn that although angry reactions do not work, there are more socially appropriate behaviors that might work.

For example, Michael Hollander, Ph.D., a psychologist and dialectical behavioral therapy (DBT) expert, is a consultant on our unit at McLean Hospital who frequently interviews families in crisis. Kids tell him that they had their tantrums because they were right about some point. Dr. Hollander then asks, "Do you want to be right, or do you want to be effective?" Most kids recognize that they want to be effective to get their needs met. Learning how to be effective is important for both adolescents and their families.

continued on the next page

Finally if there is going to be a consequence for a rage episode, parents should be both calm and realistic when deciding on the consequence. In the heat of an argument, a parent might say, "Young man, you are grounded for a month." Generally this consequence is hardly ever carried out because the teen might behave well and the parent does not have the emotional resources to maintain such a rigid consequence. Empty consequences teach children that there is never any substance behind a parent's threats.

It's important to avoid using guilt or manipulation as a response to an adolescent's unwanted behavior (such as rage, tantrums, or self-injury). This is in part because manipulation is often a behavior a parent is trying to end, and guilt is an emotion that already paralyzes an adolescent with BPD.

Adolescents with BPD often experience tremendous guilt because they feel that they are not good enough, or they feel guilt for the hurt they cause other people because of their own "evil."

with little of the feelings that would usually be associated with such traumas.

Given the tremendous amount of research into BPD since the publication of the *DSM-IV*, many experts believe these criteria fail to capture the full picture of BPD. As we will see later, research is taking place into all aspects of BPD functioning, including impulsivity, anxiety, shame, anger, attachment, genetics, and relationships—that will more clearly define some of the terms, and it will also probably establish various subtypes of BPD. Although this research will reverse the *DSM-IV* criteria in future *DSM* editions, at this time the criteria are a fair and universally accepted starting point.

One other point should be made clear. Many people argue that the *DSM-IV* does not allow for the diagnosis of BPD in adolescents. In fact, the *DSM-IV* allows for the BPD diagnosis in adolescents when ". . . maladaptive traits have been present for at least one year, are

THE PERSONALITY DISORDERS

The *DSM* divides personality disorders into three groups called clusters They are:

Cluster A. The disorders in this cluster are broadly seen as being "odd" or "eccentric" and include the following:

- **Paranoid personality.** Marked by a distrust and suspiciousness of others, such that their motives are interpreted as malevolent
- **Schizoid personality.** Characterized by a pattern of detachment from social relationships and a restricted range of expression of emotions in interpersonal settings
- **Schizotypal personality.** Distinguished by a pattern of social and interpersonal deficits marked by acute discomfort with, and reduced capacity for, close relationships as well as by cognitive or perceptual distortions and eccentricities of behavior

Cluster B. The disorders in this cluster are broadly seen as being extremely emotional or erratic and include the following:

- **Borderline personality.**
- **Antisocial personality.** Marked by a pattern of disregard for and violation of the rights of others
- **Narcissistic personality.** Evidenced by a pervasive pattern of grandiosity (in fantasy or behavior), need for admiration, and lack of empathy

Cluster C. The disorders in this cluster are broadly seen as being anxious or fearful and include the following:

- **Dependent personality.** Characterized by an excessive need to be taken care of that leads to submissive and clinging behavior and fears of separation
- **Avoidant personality.** Distinguished by pattern of social inhibition, feelings of inadequacy, and hypersensitivity to negative evaluation
- **Obsessive-compulsive personality.** Marked by a pattern of preoccupation with orderliness, perfectionism, and mental and interpersonal control, at the expense of flexibility, openness, and efficiency

persistent and all-encompassing, and are not likely to be limited to a developmental stage or an episode of an axis I disorder."

To explain further, the *DSM-IV* is the manual physicians, psychiatrists, psychologists, therapists, and social workers use to diagnose mental illness. It spells out specific diagnostic criteria, such as for depression, anxiety, and personality disorders. A psychiatric diagnosis is made at five levels or axes. The first level is known as axis I. Axis I includes all the mental health conditions except personality disorders and mental retardation. Personality disorders and mental retardation are identified on axis II. (We'll talk about axis III, IV, and V later in this book.)

So for instance, a psychiatric diagnosis might read:

Axis I: major depression

Axis II: borderline personality disorder

CAUSE FOR OUTSIDE HELP

Even though many adolescents with BPD appear for treatment with the criteria I've discussed, some of these criteria can overlap with normal adolescence. So why are adolescents referred for treatment?

The following snippets are from a few typical emails from parents asking for help with their adolescents whom they suspect have BPD. In some cases we don't have enough information, but in others the parents' descriptions appear consistent with adolescent BPD.

"I have a fifteen-year-old daughter. She has recently started cutting herself and may have depression. None of the medication has worked."

"My son has had problems since he was thirteen. He was diagnosed with bipolar disorder, but he seemed to fit BPD more. He spent his teen years in and out of hospitals, residential programs, special classrooms, etc, and made our family's life a living hell. I have tried so hard to do the right thing for years, but his rage toward me has worn me out."

"My daughter got a diagnosis of ADHD and bipolar disorder. They

DEFINING TERMS

Some of the concepts regarding BPD problems or BPD functioning vary between researchers. Here's the way that I define certain ideas.

For the purpose of this book, I define **emotions** as mental states that arise spontaneously and generally as a response to certain stimulus, rather than through conscious effort. They are often accompanied by physiological or visceral changes, such as agitation or excitement. Examples of emotions are joy, sorrow, jealousy, hate, and love. They tend to be brief in duration, lasting from moments to a few days at most. Adolescents with BPD tend to attach powerful judgments to their emotions, or the behaviors of others. Unfortunately for many people with BPD these judgments tend to become "true" in their own minds. For instance, one young woman with BPD told me that she often felt as if she hated her mother. She judged this feeling as an "evil" feeling and so felt in turn that she *was* evil.

I define **affect** as a generalized feeling that by some is considered more persistent than an emotion but less so than a mood. Affect is the external, observable manifestation of an emotion. Affect is often described using terms such as labile (which means, for instance, observing the patient change from weepy to happy to angry in a short period of time) or flat (which means the general absence or reduction of expressiveness) or expansive (which means a lack of restraint in expressing one's feelings, frequently with an exaggeration of one's significance or importance).

In the context of this book, I use **mood** as a more prolonged state of emotional being, a more characteristic or habitual state of feeling. It is a feeling state that a person would generally recognize as their usual state of being or feeling. Examples are an irritable state, a happy state, or a depressed state of being.

Many people use these three terms interchangeably. Also, In many cases of BPD, by my definition of "mood" a person with BPD would not have a typical "mood" state. Instead, and especially if people with BPD are in crisis, they live in an almost persistent state of reactive emotions with very little stability. Parents describe that there children's "moods" are constantly changing.

tried several medications, which helped a little with the mood but not with her rage. Everywhere else she is loved—her teachers, classmates, sports coaches, but at home we are either loved one minute or are hated if she doesn't get her way."

"My fifteen-year-old daughter has attempted suicide four times, and I think she's heading down the road to number five. Cutting, sex, impulsive spending, drinking, and drama are all part of her story."

"My fourteen-year-old nephew has created so much trouble for our family, and he has caused a lot of strain and tension in the household. He throws unbelievable temper tantrums."

From these emails and from the phone calls and interviews with adolescents with BPD, it is clear that we need more adolescent-specific diagnostic tools. In thinking about the criteria to use in future diagnostic tools, we need to consider the behaviors that lead these adolescents and their families to seek help.

Adolescents with BPD have disturbed thinking patterns, and they are often paranoid that they are being constantly judged by their friends and others. They almost always seem to be in crisis, whether with friends or family, or at school. They can be rational and calm one moment, and the next moment explode into frightening rages in response to some perceived rejection or criticism. They often tend to ascribe maliciousness to the motives of others. Other than the classical cutting seen in many adolescents with BPD, the types of self-injury we see include carving to form heavy scars; burning with lighters, matches, and heated metal; branding; picking at old scabs; self-biting; and extensive body piercing.

Although the *DSM-IV* criteria for BPD includes a poor sense of identity, I do not recall ever having a parent worried that his or her adolescent had a poor sense of identity. The typical call for help is because of self-harming behavior, excessive sensitivity, and moodiness that happen when adolescents experience the following:

- Don't get their way
- Display episodes of rage
- Show extreme overidealization and devaluation of friends and families
- Abuse drugs
- Are promiscuous
- Attempt or contemplate suicide

These behaviors need to be prominent in future screening tools for adolescent BPD.

CHILD AND ADOLESCENT PERSONALITY TRAITS AND THE DEVELOPMENT OF BPD

When we ask the parents of adolescents with BPD when they first became aware that there was something wrong or that they needed help for their children, some say they noticed a significant change in behavior when their child reached puberty. They attributed the difficult behavior to the hormonal changes associated with puberty. Many parents, however, say that they recognized that their children were different from other children soon after birth.

Adolescents with borderline personality symptoms are often described as having been more colicky or less cuddly, of making less eye contact, of being sadder and more upset, of having more temper tantrums, and of being more difficult to soothe than other children. These symptoms do not necessarily mean that such a baby will go on to develop BPD, but if the symptoms persist and worsen over time, they may indicate that something is wrong.

I am certainly not advocating that young children be diagnosed with BPD. However, if it is clear that a child has marked emotional regulation problems, and that these difficulties cause social and educational damage to the child—and family stress at home—then addressing these problems as early as possible by providing the child with skills to deal with them is critical.

Even if children were never going to go on to develop worsening problems, learning problem-solving skills at an early age will benefit them for years to come. For instance, relaxation techniques such as deep breathing exercises, physical exercise such as taking a fast walk or jog, or grounding exercises, such as counting slowly to five after being asked a question rather than impulsively blurting out an answer can go far to lessen the effects of stress and anxiety.

Acquiring these skills when young is like learning a new language earlier in life. The earlier children are introduced to these skills, the greater the chances are that they will become truly proficient in using them.

SEEMINGLY DIFFICULT TO DIAGNOSE AND TREAT

Parents of adolescents with BPD often say that their children were diagnosed with attention deficit disorder (ADD) or bipolar disorder, but that these diagnoses did not seem to completely explain their children's behavior.

Or parents say that all the medication in the world did not appear to reduce their children's symptoms. Medications have a clear role to play in many psychiatric conditions that affect children and adolescents. There is well-researched evidence for medication use in mood disorders, attention deficit hyperactivity disorder (ADHD), and anxiety disorders, but the parents we see at McLean Hospital are not simply describing mood or anxiety symptoms in their kids, but serious self-injury, impulsivity, and desperation in their children's lives.

For example, the child's behavior might have started to affect relationships. For instance, some parents feel that they can no longer trust their children, or that their children are outright liars. Other parents worry about going to sleep at night for fear that their children will kill themselves. Children feel that their parents don't understand them and slowly isolate themselves from their parents. Some adolescents feel that they have to threaten self-harm in order to get the attention of their peers. These chaotic interpersonal interactions will ultimately leave the children feeling lonely, misunderstood, and at times suicidal.

The usual kinds of treatment will not work with BPD. For instance, when adolescents with BPD are simply diagnosed as depressed, psychotherapies that link their current depressive symptoms to conflicts that originated in their earlier years are not effective in reducing the self-injury or self-loathing that these kids exhibit. Treatment approaches such as DBT and cognitive behavior therapy (a form of psychotherapy that emphasizes the important role of thinking in how people feel and what they do but does not include the validation strategies of DBT) are much more useful in this age group at dealing with the broad spectrum of disruptive behavior. Medication in many of these cases hardly seems to have an effect, and it is further unclear what consequence medications have in the developing adolescent brain, particularly when medications are not indicated.

PONDERING PERSONALITY TRAITS

In a 2006 publication that looked at social, emotional, and personality development in children and adolescents, the authors felt that the following personality traits in adolescents were likely to be important in the development of BPD.

- They noted that children and adolescents vary in their experiences and expression of **trust** of others, **anger**, **rage**, and other intense emotions. Poor trust in others and high levels of anger are more likely to be important for the development of BPD than not having those traits.
- They explored the concept of **agreeableness**, where children can range on a spectrum of being highly agreeable to being antisocial. Low agreeableness—as shown by children being spiteful, hostile, manipulative, and defiant—is more likely to be associated with the development of BPD than being agreeable.
- There is the idea of **conscientiousness**, which is comprised of the capacity for attention and the capacity for self-control. Being less con-

scientious is more likely to be associated with the development of BPD, and as we will see in later chapters, the capacity for attention is affected by the functioning of the frontal lobe of the brain.

• Children and adolescents who are by nature nervous and who worry excessively about things are often also more anxious, tense, easily frightened, and insecure. Many people who go on to develop BPD often describe a childhood filled with excessive worries and insecurities.

These personality traits are simply building blocks of the whole person, but it is now possible to imagine that these building blocks—under the right environment and with the right biological pressures—can develop into a more maladaptive and enduring way of functioning.

A NOTE ON BIPOLAR DISORDER

When adolescents with BPD are referred to our unit, they are most commonly diagnosed as having bipolar disorder (formerly called manic depression), and typically a type of bipolar disorder called bipolar not otherwise specified (NOS). Bipolar NOS is a mood disorder that fits no other category and includes fast cycling between manic (highs) and depressive (lows) symptoms.

Bipolar disorder, just like BPD, occurs in adolescents, but the two are not the same illness. They are two very different entities whose main similarities are a change in mood states. Confusing the two leads not only to a serious misdiagnosis, but also an errant treatment approach.

Bipolar disorder is a mood disorder that involves one or more manic episodes alternating with major depressive episodes. A manic episode is a period of time where an elevated, expansive, or notably irritable mood is present, lasting for at least one week. A major depressive episode must either have a depressed mood or a loss of interest or pleasure in daily activities consistently for at least a two-week period.

So as you see, the manic and depressive episodes each last for at least a

MY CLINICAL VIEW ON BPD SYMPTOMS

My composite view of adolescents with BPD is based on years of working with this group. The following symptoms broadly capture the majority of what I see clinically as adolescent BPD, although I think that many of the symptoms are accurate for adults as well. Not all of these symptoms have been validated by scientific research, but they are almost always seen in adolescents with BPD and are frequently part of their histories. It's important to bear in mind that the adolescents I work with have ended up on a residential unit, and so they may represent a more extreme version of BPD.

Many of the adolescent patients with BPD see themselves as loathsome, evil, or contaminated by some toxic poison, and they believe that they contaminate others with this poison. They feel that they should not get close to people despite wanting desperately to be close. They describe feelings of emptiness and of being intolerably alone. This pain can be so unbearable that self-injury or suicide is frequently seen as the only way out of their pain. This profound sense of hopelessness and self-hatred seems to be unique to patients with BPD. In fact, I cannot remember a patient with this combination of symptoms who did not have BPD.

The adolescents with BPD tend to have trouble regulating their daily rhythms in activities such as sleeping, eating, exercise, studying, playing, and resting. One remarkable symptom is a marked lack of a sense of continuity of time. For example, patients have told me that what appeared to be terribly hurtful fights that occurred only a week ago are nearly forgotten and instead remembered as if they had taken place months or years ago.

At times the chaos is so enduring that many of the kids with BPD have great difficulty in consistently performing at school (or work) despite being intelligent and apparently able.

Their relationships tend to be chaotic, unstable, and rapidly changing, and their views of others tend to change dramatically, often depending on their own moods. These mood states tend not to last long and are often reactive to interpersonal conflict or fear. At times, there can be reactive aggression or

continued on the next page

impulsive aggression toward the people who are closest to them. The adolescents frequently complain that they are misunderstood (often by their parents). And in fact, many parents recognize that they don't really understand their adolescents. Adolescents with BPD fear rejection or abandonment to the point that that when they sense loss, it can be remarkably devaluing of their formerly over-idealized person (friend, parent, teacher, therapist, etc.)

People with BPD can appear to be incredibly attuned to non-verbal communication by significant people in their lives to the point that parents and others remark on just how remarkably intuitive their kids suffering from BPD appear to be. My personal theory is that this capacity is due to the triggering of "mirror neurons" in their brains (which will be reviewed in a later chapter). However, it is also true that given the amount of abuse that BPD sufferers have frequently experienced and the abandonment they often fear, it is possible that this ability to read non-verbal cues is an adaptation to protect themselves from further abuse or to look for facial and other clues that they might be abandoned once again.

Arguments of adolescents with BPD with others tend to be "all-or-nothing" and "black and white" in nature, and one of the most difficult aspects for a parent, clinician, or loved one to deal with is a dynamic where the adolescent pushes the other person away while demanding help or responding both with anger and by desperately seeking help, as in the title of the BPD book by Jerold Kreisman, M.D.: *I Hate You, Don't Leave Me.*

Most adolescents with BPD have a poorly defined sense of who they are—much more so than the normal identity challenges of adolescents—and they tend to describe themselves as if they are the people who they are most close to at a given time, usually a peer group. This pattern of changing self-identity continues as they move from one group to the next. They also sometimes complain of being a "false-person" or that they are "wearing a mask" because who they are in public does not match their inner selves.

Other than these core symptoms, there is frequent drug use, although even this appears to be qualitatively different from other adolescent drug use in that it often appears to be in the service of getting away from their own internal misery. If there is promiscuity, it also appears to be in the service of wanting to escape the misery of loneliness rather than some rampant and wanton display of sexual indulgence.

Clearly more comprehensive and definitive diagnostic tools are necessary. I am certain that such tools will be developed and also we will become so much more sophisticated in the use of brain imaging, genetics, and brain chemistry (which deals with the brain chemicals that allow the brain to function) that together with the clinical history, our level of confidence as to the diagnosis will be very high.

week. In BPD, however, the mood states tend to last only a few hours. Also, the moods tend to be highly reactive, which means that they are triggered as a reaction to a situation, usually an interpersonal conflict.

So while some people have bipolar disorder, and other people have BPD, still other people have both. In Chapter 7, we will look at the co-occurrence of BPD and bipolar disorder.

REACTIVE ATTACHMENT DISORDER

Some clinicians have wondered whether BPD is a variation of reactive attachment disorder (RAD).

The *Diagnostic and Statistical Manual of Mental Disorders-IV* (*DSM-IV*) defines RAD of infancy or early childhood as follows:

A. Markedly disturbed and developmentally inappropriate social relatedness in most contexts, beginning before age five years, as evidenced by either (1) or (2):

1. Persistent failure to initiate or respond in a developmentally appropriate fashion to most social interactions, as manifest by excessively inhibited, hypervigilant, or highly ambivalent and contradictory responses (e.g., the child may respond to caregivers with a mixture of approach, avoidance, and resistance to comforting, or may exhibit frozen watchfulness)

2. Diffuse attachments as manifest by indiscriminate sociability with marked inability to exhibit appropriate selective attachments (e.g., excessive familiarity with relative strangers or lack of selectivity in choice of attachment figures)

B. The disturbance in criterion A is not accounted for solely by developmental delay (as in mental retardation) and does not meet criteria for a pervasive developmental disorder.

C. Continued discounting of a child's needs and wellbeing, as evidenced by at least one of the following:

1. Persistent disregard of the child's basic emotional needs for comfort, stimulation, and affection

2. Persistent disregard of the child's basic physical needs

3. Repeated changes of primary caregiver that prevent formation of stable attachments (e.g., frequent changes in foster care)

The American Academy of Child and Adolescent Psychiatry adds that RAD can be difficult to diagnose, but that most children with RAD have had problems or severe disruptions in their early relationships. Further, many had been physically, sexually, or emotionally abused or neglected. Also, others had had multiple traumatic losses or changes in their primary caretakers.

Although it is a stretch to make RAD a childhood version of BPD, it is possible that some traumatized and neglected children with RAD could go on to develop BPD given the common pathway of trauma, abuse, and neglect in many cases of BPD.

Reprinted with permission of the American Psychiatric Association

CHAPTER THREE

The Typically Developing Adolescent

M ANY PARENTS AND CLINICIANS dismiss concerns about worrisome adolescent behavior, feeling that the behavior is just a part of normal development. Parents might argue that they themselves were wild as teens and turned out OK.

The critical difference is that like typical adolescents, adolescents with BPD may drink, drive recklessly, use drugs, and defy their parents. However, adolescents with BPD often use drugs, self-injure, and rage against their parents as a way of coping with profound misery, emptiness, self-loathing, and abandonment fears. Though adolescents with BPD go through the same challenges and changes of normal adolescent development as any other child, recognizing the meaning or purpose of the behavior is critical.

Although the behavior of two kids may be identical, it may be far more concerning for one than for the other. For instance, we sometimes get kids who come in who say that they have cut themselves once or perhaps twice. When asked why they did this they might say that it is because their friends were doing it. They will say that it hurt, they don't want to do it again, they cannot understand why their friends do it, and that it didn't do anything for them. Other children might cut themselves in an identical manner, saying that they had read about it online as a way to relieve misery, felt a profound sense of relief, want to do it again, and did not feel that it hurt that much. These children would be far more worrisome than the first group. If they learn that cutting is an effective way to deal with their emotions, cutting will increasingly become part of their repertoire. The more they practice a behavior, the more it gets hardwired in the brain as a problem-solving skill.

STAGES OF TYPICAL ADOLESCENT DEVELOPMENT

Before looking more closely at adolescents with BPD and the theories of BPD development, we should review the typically developing adolescent.

Following are ways adolescents grow and mature physically, emotionally, mentally, socially, and sexually into adulthood.

AGES TWELVE TO FOURTEEN

During the late middle school and early high school years, parents are often confused by the developmental changes in their teenagers. These children begin to move toward independence, and during this time adolescents often struggle with a sense of identity. They tend to feel awkward or strange about their bodies, especially during the marked changes that come with the onset of puberty. Many parents and patients with BPD identify this as the first time that they started to self-injure.

Teens in general tend to focus on self, alternating between high expectations of their capabilities and poor self-esteem. They focus on clothing style, which is often influenced by their peer groups as well as popular culture, such as the music industry. Typical adolescents are frequently moody. Up until this age, children tend to see their parents as generally right, but now the kids start to realize that their parents are not perfect, and they show less overt affection and at times rudeness toward them. Almost all adolescents,

WHAT TO DO WHEN YOUR TEEN CUTS

Some teens have told me that they started cutting years before their parents ever found out. Parents sometimes say that looking back they "should have known" that something was wrong, but most parents say that they had no idea their children were injuring themselves.

Self-injury can occur as a fad. Most often this happens when someone in a group starts to self-injure and others follow. However, for most adolescents self-injury is very painful and so they soon stop the behavior. The adolescent who cuts is someone typically described as very sensitive. They generally recognize that they feel emotions quicker than other people, that they feel these emotions deeper or more intensely than others, and that it takes longer for them to get their feelings back to normal.

Signs of Adolescent Self-Injury

Some of the more obvious signs that adolescents are hurting themselves are frequent or unexplained scars, cuts, bruises, and burns. These are usually on the extremities, particularly the arms, but can be on the legs, thighs, chest, abdomen, or back.

When parents see these cuts, teens often give implausible explanations for the injuries, such as that they were scratched by a dog or a cat or they fell.

Other signs include the consistent wearing of long-sleeved clothing, isolating behavior after a fight, excessive time spent in the shower, isolation from friends, and increasing substance abuse. These all could be signs of possible self-injury as well as symptoms of other concerns, such as major depression, anxiety, an eating disorder, or substance abuse. The hoarding of sharp implements such as razor blades, pins, needles, knives, and scissors would be very concerning and a huge red flag of self-injury. Also because many teens 'ritualized' cutting behaviors involve clean blades, antiseptic lotions, or cleaning solutions and clean dressings, a teen suddenly buying quantities of these might also be concerning.

Remaining Calm

Most adolescent self-injury doesn't require medical treatment nor does

continued on the next page

it mean the teen is contemplating suicide. However, some adolescents have done terrible damage to themselves. I have seen kids who have cut almost every bit of exposed skin, others whose cuts always need stitches, others who target arteries so that they bleed more and yet others who have sliced their tendons. Some young women specifically target their breasts. One young woman told me that if she had not had breasts she would not have been sexually abused.

Certainly the first exposure to such self-injury is terrifying. Although it is generally difficult to be calm under these conditions, a calm approach allows for clearer and more effective planning.

Parents usually do not have medical training and so when presented with self-injury the initial step is to address the teen's medical needs first by dressing the wounds or going to the hospital or doctor's office. Because it might be unclear as to what the teen used to self-injure, and if the cut is bleeding, the adolescent should receive a tetanus shot if he or she hasn't had one recently.

If the teen is in a therapy, such as dialectical behavior therapy (DBT), which specifically targets self-injury then follow the treatment plan as prescribed.

What Actions Do Not Work

Some parents act horrified, which is understandable, but because many cutters have a negative self-image, and negative body image, they can be very sensitive about their wounds. I have had kids tell me years later that they wish that they had never cut, that the scars always remain as a testament to their past, and that when friends or intimate partners are curious about the cuts it can be difficult to talk about.

It is easy for parents to judge the self-injury behavior or the teen. More important, more effective, and more therapeutic is to work hard on understanding what is going on emotionally for the adolescent. We have found that rather than promoting self-injury, teens who know that others go through similar situations and use similar coping skills helps them to not think of themselves as alien, and that they can be helped. Sadly, somewhere between 150,000 and 360,000 adolescents in the United States self-mutilate.

> Just telling a kid to stop the cutting behavior will not work. Generally the cutting helps the adolescent to regulate their emotions and unless there is another behavior that can replace the cutting, they will not stop. This is why a skills-based approach is essential to adolescent self-injury.

whether BPD or not, complain that their parents interfere with independence, but in times of stress they tend to regress to more childish behavior. There is also frequent rule- and limit-testing, both at home and school.

It is typical during this stage for adolescents to be mostly interested in the present, with limited thoughts of the future. At times when I absent-mindedly ask a child in this stage how he imagines himself in ten years, he'll answer "I don't know, I'm only 13!"

This time is also one of increasing interest in sexuality, and most typically they display shyness, easy embarrassment, modesty, and an increased interest in sex. There is generally a move toward heterosexuality and fears of homosexuality, and they are frequently preoccupied with concerns regarding their physical and sexual attractiveness to others.

There also tends to be frequently changing relationships. Adolescents change their relationships for many reasons. These include factors such as changing from middle school to high school, changing and shared common interests such as sports and extra curricular activities, an increasing move to interest in the opposite sex after puberty, and a greater curiosity and interest in experimentation.

Teens have become more sexually active and experiment with more partners than before. The reason for this is also complex. An interesting study has suggested that adolescents who rely heavily on television for information about sexuality will have high standards of female beauty and will believe that premarital and extramarital intercourse with multiple partners is acceptable. They are also unlikely to learn about the need for contraceptives as a form of protection against pregnancy or disease. Another interesting response I have heard from many teens who perform oral sex on multiple partners is that they do not believe that oral sex is sex. Sadly, they often cite former President Clinton for this assessment.

Although many parents refuse to accept that it is normal, experimentation with sex and drugs is very common. For adolescents with BPD this is particularly true, however as stated earlier, the reasons behind the behavior are different. Often they use sex as a way of holding onto partners who might otherwise leave them or as a way of coping with the fear of abandonment.

AGES FOURTEEN TO SEVENTEEN

As teenagers grow, they move toward independence. They are more self-involved, alternating between unrealistically high expectations and poor self-concept, and more strongly complain that their parents interfere with independence. They continue to be extremely concerned with their physical appearance and use images portrayed in popular culture as the ideal, which is most concerning especially for young women, since emaciated models cover popular fashion magazines.

By now, they frequently have a lowered opinion of their parents, and they often withdraw emotionally from them, while redoubling their efforts to make new friends. They place a strong emphasis on the peer group and many of the friendships formed in this stage can last a lifetime.

They can exhibit periods of sadness especially as the psychological loss of the parent takes place. I am often struck by children's answers about what it is that has changed in their relationships between them and their mothers or fathers. I remember a young girl who told me that she used to go fishing with her father, and a teen who said he used to watch the early Saturday morning cartoons with his dad while his mother was sleeping. Parents are often surprised, given how withdrawn and disdainful their adolescent has been, that their child is nostalgic for these times.

HOW TO COPE WITH AN "EMOTIONALLY INTENSE" YOUNGER SIBLING

The mother of an eighteen-year-old boy with BPD told me that she was beginning to see some of the "same emotional intensity" in her ten-year-old daughter.

She wondered whether her daughter, too, could have BPD, and if there was anything she could do to handle her daughter's anxiety and outbursts.

Even though from what the mother told me there was no indication that the child had any psychiatric problems, using strategies to deal with such intensity is helpful at many levels. It teaches the child at an early age that there are ways to deal with being very upset, and it helps the family feel less hopeless about the situation. In some cases, such a low tolerance of stress can become problematic if left unchecked and can morph into a broader problem, so using the following strategies might prevent the child from spiraling out of control.

- Recognize behaviors that signal that the child's stress level is rising, such as increased irritation, frustration, or annoyance.
- Provide activities that are soothing, such as a warm bath, massage, quiet music, or familiar stories.
- Help the child learn to recognize cues that signal that intensity is rising. Doing routine, yet simple mindfulness exercises will teach him or her to monitor his or her mind and body. An easy example is teaching slow breathing techniques while watching the body relax. Also, find a quiet space that a child can always use when he or she needs a time-out or as a place to calm down.
- Avoid escalating the intensity of the child be reacting intensely in return to the child's behavior.
- Work with the other kids in the family about not escalating their sibling's anxiety during these moments. Help them recognize that this leads only to chaos and a prolonged situation. Including them in the mindful practice exercises can make it a fun family routine.
- Finally after an outburst, give calm, clear, brief feedback and the commitment to continue to find ways to help the child and family as a whole.

Teens in this age range often spend much time in the examination of their inner experiences, and they often keep diaries. They also tend to be more goal-directed and have a better sense of what they want to do with their lives.

At this age, relationships, both intimate and not, take on greater importance. Teens are increasingly concerned about their own attractiveness, and they show a clearer identification of their sexual orientation. They exhibit increasing tenderness and are less afraid to be vulnerable toward the opposite sex. They express feelings of love and passion, and the kids I see often tell me that they imagine that their current boyfriends or girlfriends are the people that they will be with for the rest of their lives.

Drug and alcohol experimentation is extremely common at this age. Interestingly, there is increasing evidence that teens of this age have consciences that can consistently differentiate between right and wrong.

Ages Eighteen Plus

By the time adolescents reach their eighteenth birthday, they normally show increasingly independent functioning and a far more consistent and cohesive sense of identity. They show a more developed ability for examination of inner experiences.

In adolescents with BPD, this ability for examination of inner experiences seems to develop much earlier than in typical adolescents. It is perhaps because adolescents with BPD suffer as they do that they begin to examine their lives at an earlier stage.

Also at this age, typically developing adolescents show an ability to think ideas through, which is a reflection of a maturing frontal lobe, the part of the brain that deals with executive functioning, or decision-making. Their conflict with their parents begins to decrease. Adolescents at this age begin to show an increased ability for delayed gratification and compromise as well as increased emotional stability, which again may represent maturation of the brain.

SPOTTING SUBSTANCE ABUSE IN YOUR TEEN

Parents often wonder how to know whether their adolescent is using drugs. Certainly the smell of marijuana on clothes or alcohol on the breath is a pretty clear sign. Short of drug testing, there is no fail-proof test, but there are many signs that should warn parents that substance abuse could be an issue.

At school, work productivity might have declined and grades might have slipped or even dropped dramatically. The adolescents might seem to lose their motivation to complete work, or they might be disinclined to do anything other than being with their friends. Teens might miss school altogether, or walk off campus during breaks or free periods. They might also drop out of their usual activities such as sports or music. At some times this is simply because they would prefer to do drugs than do the activity and at other times because the drug use has severely affected their ability to participate in these activities.

In relationships the children might suddenly change friends, and be secretive about these friends. Often they don't want the parents to meet the friends and refuse to invite them over.

At home the teens might become more moody and irritable, might begin to take less care of their physical appearances, and become increasingly secretive in their behavior.

They might spend more solitary time, such as by going to the basement, keeping their bedroom doors locked, not responding when called, or taking a long time to answer. They can appear hostile and defensive when questioned about apparently unimportant matters.

Parents have told me that a sure sign that their child is doing drugs is when money begins to disappear from their purses or wallets, or when valuables go missing. These are often sold to pay for a drug habit.

Sudden changes in sleep habits, and being overly exhausted despite apparently adequate sleep, might signify the use of tranquilizers in particular.

In relationships, adolescents at this age show increased concern for others, and in their romantic relationships they express deeper feelings of love and passion. These relationships tend to last longer than the experimental relationships of earlier adolescence. Adolescents at this age gain a firmer sense of their own sexual identity and an increased capacity for tender and sensual love.

Older adolescents show increased self-reliance and place a greater importance on their own role in life and a greater emphasis on personal dignity and self-esteem. At times social traditions regain some of their previous importance, and parents will at times offer a silent prayer of thanks as their child returns to their religious or cultural roots.

After this, a typically developing adolescent is on adulthood's door, and his or her personality has almost fully developed.

TYPICAL BPD SYMPTOMS IN ADOLESCENCE

I have never met an adult BPD patient who did not have symptoms in either childhood or adolescence.

If we look at the previous description of typical adolescent development and we artificially contrive an adolescent by plucking out some of the descriptors of typical adolescence, we can create a hypothetical child who exhibits periods of sadness as the psychological loss of the parent takes place, struggles with sense of identity, is frequently moody, has self-perception alternating between high expectations and poor self-esteem, is extremely concerned with the appearance of his or her body, shows a tendency to return to childish behavior, particularly when stressed, experiments with drugs and sex with frequently changing relationships, and is self-involved. Given this picture, it is easy to see why normal adolescence could look like emerging BPD.

In this hypothetical child, and using the criteria in the *Diagnostic and Statistical Manual of Mental Disorders-IV* (*DSM-IV*), abandonment fears (criterion 1), identity issues (criterion 3), impulsivity with drugs and sex (criterion 4), and affective instability (criterion 6) are clear, so then only one more criterion is needed to meet adult criteria for BPD. Throw in some existential suicidal thoughts, which are common in adolescents, and there we are. Given this, it is easy to see why many mental health care professionals are reluctant to make the diagnosis of BPD in adolescents.

Given that BPD occurs in an estimated 2 percent of the population, 98 percent of adolescents will not have BPD. Concerning and occasional behaviors, such as drug use, come and go in adolescents. However, when those behaviors persist in the context of broad emotional problems in an adolescent, clinicians must recognize the possibility that a personality disorder could be developing.

USING METAPHORS AND ANALOGIES TO COMMUNICATE

Like many people who work with adolescents with BPD, I initially found that the adolescents' experience of my interactions with them was confusing, and they complained that I simply wasn't getting it.

After working on becoming more flexible in my approach, I also found that one technique that they found useful was my explaining a perspective or thought to them in a metaphor. Many of my initial attempts at metaphors failed; however, some began to resonate, and I have used the following metaphors fairly repeatedly over time.

Two Beans in Two Pots

A bean pod is split open, and two beans are removed. One bean is dropped into a pot full of rich, well-composted soil, watered regularly, and given plenty of sunlight. The other bean is dropped into a pot full of poor soil with few nutrients. It receives little water and is kept in the shade.

The first bean grows into a full, green, vigorous plant. The second develops into a spindly twig of a plant.

HOW TO MAKE PARENT-CHILD COMMUNICATION WORK

Effective communication between parents and their teen is essential to get through the developmental challenges of adolescence. This is true not only for the typically developing teen but for the teen with emerging BPD symptoms as well. Old patterns of communication will probably have to change to fit the growing needs and capabilities of the child. Multiple studies have shown a relationship between a child's overall well-being and parent-adolescent communication.

The first step is to create an environment or expectation that allows for the free and safe interchange of ideas. All family members should feel free to bring up questions, worries, achievements, and perceived failures. Set aside time daily for family to be able to share, even if this is just a few minutes. On weekdays, a shared dinner might do it. On weekends, a drive to a sports game or a walk in a park could provide the time necessary for a teen to share. Over time this will allow for discussion of the sensitive issues that arise during adolescence, such as sexuality, relationships, and drug or alcohol use. Studies have shown that adolescents who openly communicate with their parents are less likely to abuse substances.

It is important for the teen to know that their perspective is both recognized and valued, although not necessarily shared. This helps build self-esteem in the adolescent and the understanding that people can have varying points of view, and, at times, disagree amicably.

Effective communication involves both listening and speaking. Listening with curiosity and interest is most effective. Parents should ask for clarity if they don't understand, or at least not assume that they understand what their adolescent is saying. Asking clarifying questions can help achieve this, although many teens and parents get frustrated at the "twenty questions" in which communication has broken down and a parent asks multiple questions to find out information. The teen tends to answer these with "maybe," "no," "yes," "I don't know," or a grunt.

Teens also often get frustrated when advice is offered without being asked. Even therapists fall into this trap. Often adolescents want to work a situation out by themselves or just know that they have been heard. Also, as the times change, so do behaviors. This is true of all generations. For instance, at the turn of the twentieth century children and adolescents were far more likely to adhere to rules and wear school uniforms, they were—and famously—to "be seen but not heard." At the end of the twentieth century, children were encouraged to express themselves, wear whatever they wanted to school, and question authority. Kids often do *not* want to hear about what it was like in their parents' time, and so it is important to listen with as little judgment as possible, trying to recognize and understand the culture of the times. Being judgmental, or not recognizing that one is being judgmental, will often shut the teen down, and not allow for the full understanding of a situation.

Here is the question: Which of the two is the perfect plant?

Answer: They both are. Neither of the plants could have expected to grow into anything other than that which they grew to be. Both are perfect given their individual conditions. How could they have turned out to be anything other than that which they are?

The point to this is that at any moment in our lives we are the sum total of everything that has come before us. We can in no way have expected to be anything other than what we are.

Now different from the plant, once we realize this we can try to do something about it. If the weak plant had legs, perhaps it could go look for better conditions.

So the person with BPD can look at the relationships that get them into trouble, the drugs that complicate their lives, and the emotions that overwhelm them, and by better understanding these conditions in their lives, work toward changing them.

The Over-Watered Plant

Imagine a potted plant sitting by a sunny window, which after time appears to be wilting. The concerned gardener notices and recognizes that it needs water, and so he waters the plant, which appears to do better. After a few days the plant again looks a little soft and so again the gardener waters the plant. This time it does not seem to change the plant, so the gardener tries more water. The plant's leaves are now beginning to fade or turn yellow. The gardener continues to water the plant, but to no avail. The problem is that the plant also needs fertilizer. The gardener has surely given the plant all the water it needed and more, but what the plant needed was some nutrients. The plant could not talk, and the gardener did not know.

How does this relate to BPD? Many parents feel as if they have given their child everything they could possibly have given them. Although historically clinicians blamed parents for "causing" their child's BPD, we now recognize that there is a combination of factors that go into the development of BPD. Many parents have truly done the best that they could.

Many kids recognize that their parents have given them all the love and material things that they could have asked for, but that all along they still felt lonely and misunderstood. What they did not get from their parents was feeling fully understood by them. It is both true that the child could not express this need, and that the parents understandably would find it difficult to divine such a need. When, despite all the love in the world something still feels off or not right, it is important for parents to wonder whether they are missing something.

The Emotional Puppet

Imagine being a puppet but instead of being attached by strings and being forced to move at the will of another, it is your emotions that are tied to your interactions with people. In the same way that a string pulled on a puppet instantly moves that part of the puppet, in people with BPD certain interactions pull at different emotions. A fight with a boyfriend elicits a sudden fear of abandonment, a disagreement with a parent leads to sudden rage, a slight by a friend leads to sudden anger, feeling misunderstood by a therapist leads to sudden suicidality, and so on.

People with BPD have tremendous difficulty in controlling their emotions and frequently feel that other people cause them to feel the way they do. The problem with this way of seeing things is that they will remain emotional puppets for the rest of their lives. Taking control of their emotional selves is essential in healing. Recognizing that certain interactions do not necessarily need to lead to certain destructive emotions and working on skills that help recognize and change or overcome these automatic responses liberates the BPD sufferer from this emotional bind.

The Dog and the Rainbow

How does a rainbow appear to a dog? Most dogs see the world in black and white. A dog may either not see the rainbow, or not care, when to its owner, it is a beautiful apparition.

I use this metaphor when parents wonder how it is possible that an adolescent could be so self-loathing, so desperate to die, and so full of anger despite being intelligent and beloved.

Parents frequently have a difficult time with the idea that they don't understand their adolescent with BPD. The adolescent often feels profoundly misunderstood by his or her parents.

Adolescents with BPD often see things differently from others, including their parents. Parents are often validated in their position by other adults around them—"Oh yes, she is so beautiful, or so smart, or so wonderful," when all that the adolescent feels is disgust, self-hatred, and loneliness.

Being Dropped in a Remote Village

Parents and their adolescents with BPD frequently feel that the other is not listening to them. The problem is that they are frequently not speaking each other's language. The language of BPD comes from emotions, the language of parental responsibility from logic.

Imagine that you are dropped into a village in a remote part of the world and you are surrounded by people who do not speak your language. To survive, you either have to teach them your language, or you have to learn theirs. There is no other way to get your needs met or to understand theirs.

So in BPD, if there is a clear lack of understanding, parents need to speak their child's language of emotional need, and the adolescent needs to learn the parents' language of "rational" thinking.

The Chameleon

Many adolescents with BPD recognize that they act differently with different people, but some acknowledge that they have absolutely no sense of self without another person being present. Their identity is derived from the relationships.

It is as if they are a chameleon but rather than their skin changing color in order to blend in with their surroundings, their identities change to blend in with the person or people they are with. As blending with its surroundings is essential for the chameleon for its survival, so is assuming the characteristics of the people around them for those with BPD to help them to form identities, albeit temporary until the person or group changes.

Fair Skin and the Sun

Some adolescents with BPD argue that their behavior is all their parents' fault—that if their parents had been more supporting and understanding, they would not have started the self-destructive, self-injurious, and suicidal behavior. Some of our patients at McLean request we have their parents admitted to the hospital and let the kids go home.

Being in this situation is like having fair skin and having to deal with the sun. One way is to protest that the sun burns your skin every time you are exposed to it, and vow that you are never going to go outside during the day, divorcing yourself completely from the sun. The other option is to recognize that the sun is what it is and even though you cannot change it, you can do things to protect yourself. Putting on sunscreen and a long-sleeved shirt, wearing sunglasses, and staying out of the sun during the hottest part of the day are important strategies to recognize and practice. So it is in practicing interpersonal skills with your family.

The Kenyan Runners and the Biosocial Theory

Over the past twenty years, runners from Kenya have come from seemingly out of nowhere to win almost one-third of all international marathons. They are the record holders of most long-distance runs. This is remarkable for such a relatively small country.

How do they do it? Research has shown that when the family trees of these runners are traced back in time, most of the runners come from a handful of families or clans. So they have some genetic variation that allows their muscles to move faster, their lungs to deliver more oxygen to their legs, and a variety of other benefits. Further, they live at high altitude, which naturally forces their blood to carry more oxygen.

But many people in these families are not great runners, and many other runners around the world also have great genes and the body types that could make them champions.

Here is where the social piece comes in: It is not enough to have the genes; lifestyle matters. Many of these kids had to run around barefooted on hard playgrounds during recess and walk or run home from school, sometimes carrying heavy backpacks, sometimes up hills. They don't play video games or sit around watching TV all day. They are motivated to win the prize money, which may not be huge to everyone, but it is to them. They have a different attitude about suffering and can tolerate the pain of running distances at high speed.

So you have a biological component, coming together with an environmental and social component to "create" a great runner. So it is with BPD. Not all children in a family have BPD, despite similar living environments, and not all emotionally dysregulated children develop BPD. The biologically vulnerable child has to be in the right social environment for BPD to develop.

CHAPTER FOUR

How to Stop BPD Teens from "Manipulating" Others

C AROLINE WAS A FIFTEEN-YEAR-OLD whose parents forbade her from seeing her boyfriend, a young man who had introduced her to cocaine. Her parents spoke to his parents and agreed that neither child could visit the other and that both sets of parents would enforce this ban. Further, the children could not email, instant-message, or telephone one another.

One evening Caroline asked her mother if she could go visit a friend and do her homework at her house. Caroline's mother checked with her friend's mother who assured her that it would be fine. Caroline's mother took her to her friend's house and said she would pick her up after a few hours. During the visit, Caroline's boyfriend showed up at the house, and they both used cocaine. Caroline had used her friend to organize the rendezvous, and had used her mother to transport her to the meeting with her boyfriend. Caroline argued that her mother had never said anything about meeting up with her boyfriend at somebody else's house.

"She is so manipulative," her mother said.

I hear this assertion about nearly all of the patients with BPD who come to us for treatment. The charge is made both as a judgment and an accusation, as if not needing further explanation. Many parents and siblings of adolescents with BPD say that they end up feeling manipulated constantly by the child, and eventually the label of manipulative sticks.

A father told me about his fourteen-year-old "going on 20" daughter: "Boys were always attracted to her. All she had to do was look at them, and they would come running. She could get them to do whatever she wanted, like take her places in their cars, especially the older boys. Or she would get them to do her homework. She would pit them against each other, to let them think that they were the ones. But eventually the boys would get discouraged, and she would move on to a new group. She manipulated them so easily."

The idea that people with BPD are manipulative is so widespread that it is important to spend time examining it. Consider, for example, the following definitions of "manipulate" from *Merriam-Webster's Collegiate Dictionary, Eleventh Edition*:

> "To control or play upon by artful, unfair, or insidious means, especially to one's own advantage."

and

> "To treat or operate with or as if with the hands or by mechanical means, especially in a skillful manner."

Generally when someone with BPD is accused of being manipulative, the implication is that the person used shrewdness, deviousness, and cunning to get what he or she wanted at the expense of another. But the concept of manipulation also includes the idea of the skillful use of the environment or the ability to adapt and change in order to survive. For example, babies learn that when they cry they get fed and held. Or a young girl learns that when she smiles sweetly at Daddy, he buys her the doll she wants. Or a boy realizes that if he learns how to skateboard, he will more readily be accepted into a group of friends. These are all examples of skillful use (whether conscious or not) of understanding the environment and adapting to it to get needs met.

The reality is, we are constantly manipulating others and our environment for our own well-being. In many cases, such as the previous examples, these manipulations are either mutually beneficial or don't cause others to feel that they have been taken advantage of.

In BPD, the concept of manipulation takes on a sinister connotation. In large part, it is because many people feel that the gains in the transaction between adolescents with BPD and their parents are all in favor of the adolescents. It is also because on further reflection, parents often feel that they should never have "caved" in, and they feel duped.

MANIPULATION AND BPD

Marsha Linehan, Ph.D., the developer of dialectical behavior therapy (DBT), has spoken frequently about her dislike for the word "manipulative" as commonly applied to patients with BPD. She has pointed out that this implies that they are skilled at managing other people, when precisely the opposite is true. I personally think that this is a well thought out perspective and agree with its core sentiment, even though in my earlier clinical practice, I concurred with the more sinister or "malicious-intent" definition of manipulation.

The fact that therapists, parents, or others may feel manipulated by the adolescent does not necessarily imply that this was the adolescent's intention. It is more probable that the adolescent does not have the skills to deal with the situation more effectively. Usually their "manipulative" behavior is an impulsive action driven by fear of abandonment, loneliness, desperation, and hopelessness—not maliciousness. It is an ultimately maladaptive attempt to get others to care for them, which initially has that effect, but leaves caregivers feeling burned out in the long term.

Here's an example: James was a sixteen-year-old boy whose parents were separated. He was admitted to our unit for suicidal thinking, which he said was because he was profoundly alone. His relationship with his parents appeared to have a major impact in his life. He told us that they had a fair relationship with each other, but that their separation was still fresh enough in their minds that they were affected if the other was dating another person. James loved clothes and his parents had agreed on a monthly clothing allowance for him. However, whenever he felt that his parents were not buying him what he wanted, he would say something like, "Well, dad's new girlfriend bought me this shirt the other day." This would get his mother upset and her impulse would be to buy him whatever he wanted, despite the agreement, as she felt that she needed to prove that she was a more loving parent than her ex-husband's new girlfriend.

James's mother recognized that she was doing the wrong thing by buying him clothes. James's father said James was simply manipulating his mother. What probably happened was that at some point in the past James had said something about his father's girlfriend. His mother had become upset and bought James clothes. Whether conscious or not, James now linked talking about his father's girlfriend with his mother becoming upset and buying him things. His behavior (talking about his father's girlfriend) was rewarded (his mother bought him clothes). Pointing out this pattern of behavior and teaching the parents about learning theory (which we'll talk about in more detail later) helped the parents change their own behavior. James's father was a little more mindful of when he invited his girlfriends over to the house, and his mother learned not to respond when James mentioned his dad's girlfriend.

The point is that James had learned to get a desire met. He loved his mother and at no point did his thought process appear to be: "OK, I know mom gets upset when I talk about dad's girlfriend. All I have to do is talk about her and I will get what I want, even if mom is terribly upset afterward."

Many parents feel, however, that their children calculate exactly what they are going to do in a premeditated way by preying on the parents' own vulnerabilities. Worse for parents is when their kids threaten to tantrum in public or have an angry outburst to get their parents to do what they want. Parents often give in rather than endure the behavior. All that this does is teach children that they can get their way by behaving or threatening to behave in a certain way.

Here's what one mother told me.

"When my daughter turned fourteen, she became increasingly impossible to live with. She would rage, hit, spit, and throw things if she didn't get her way. In self-defense and to keep her from hurting herself, I would at first just try to hold her until she would become quiet. Later I was too terrified and I would just leave the house and listen to plates being thrown about. Then, just as soon as it had started, maybe fifteen minutes later, she would come out all happy and as if nothing had happened. Sometimes she would see me shaking and crying, and she would say that she was sorry. Sometimes I would just give in to her, even if I didn't think it was right because I was so afraid of her tantrum. I would always feel so manipulated by her."

From my perspective, given the behavioral dysregulation this adolescent with BPD displayed, her awareness of herself and her mother during her out-of-control behavior is so distorted that what appears to be a manipulative intent cannot be, as she could not possibly be considered "skillful" during these moments. In this case it was clear that the mother was both traumatized and terrorized by her child. The child required long-term residential treatment, and the mother went into therapy for herself.

Explaining manipulation, here's what one bright adolescent told me.

"My parents think I am so manipulative. I am not aware of it. They tell me they feel manipulated, but I don't spend my time consumed by thoughts of how to get back at them. Everything I do, I do to survive, to belong and to be heard. I can learn how to do things better, but my actions are not some preplanned way to get people to hate me. It's ridiculous."

The term "emotional blackmail" is sometimes used instead of manipulation and implies some sort of devious, planned intent. While this may be true for some people, people with BPD who appear to be "blackmailing" usually act impulsively out of fear, loneliness, desperation, and hopelessness, but rarely malice, and the thing that they want most is to be understood.

BEHAVIOR AND CONSEQUENCES

To further examine the connection between manipulation and BPD, let's take a look at three concepts that are relevant in understanding behavior in general: classical conditioning, operant conditioning, and extinction.

Classical Conditioning

The first concept is that of classical conditioning. Classical conditioning forms an association between two stimuli.

Many people remember the example of Pavlov's dog, which would salivate when a bell was rung. In this example, the dog learned to associate the sound of a bell (a stimulus that originally had no meaning to the dog) with the presentation of food (a stimulus that had a lot of meaning for the dog) some time later.

So, classical conditioning happens when a person learns to associate some signal that has no intrinsic value to the person with an event that has tremendous meaning to the person based on how closely in time the signal and event are presented.

In BPD a self-injuring adolescent might learn to associate going to the drug store (a stimulus that originally had no meaning to the teenager) with the availability of a razor (a stimulus that has a lot of meaning to the teenager). For an adolescent with BPD, the razor would have a lot of meaning if it is the tool they use to cut themselves in order to relieve stress.

Operant Conditioning

Another concept is operant conditioning, which happens when an association is formed between a behavior and a consequence. There are the following four possible consequences to any behavior:

MANIPULATION: WHAT PARENTS CAN DO

Whether we define an adolescent's manipulation as an active and conscious behavior used to get his or her way at any cost, or an adaptive behavior that comes about because it is the only effective way he or she knows how to do something, parents clearly don't "like" manipulation!

The manipulative adolescent needs to be given the opportunity to identify unfulfilled needs, which they are trying to meet through their manipulative behavior. Once these needs are identified, it is important to explore alternative, less alienating methods of having his or her needs satisfied.

When I ask parents why they think their child is manipulative, or what the purpose of the manipulation is, the answers fall into the following general themes:

- The child simply wants to be liked by everyone and so will do whatever he or she thinks will get the other person to like him or her.
- The teen fears forming close relationships only to be abandoned and manipulates situations so the other person won't get close.
- The child simply wants people to feel guilty, or that by having people feel sorry for them, people will pity them and take care of them.
- Some parents feel that they are pitted against each other as the teen capitalizes on parent disagreements about how the child should be handled. They describe behavior such as "sucking up," whining, begging, or being profoundly earnest in their requests.
- Parents feel at times that the manipulation is a method to seek revenge and that the teen does this by pitting people against each other.

There is no instant way to stop behavior that we don't like, but it is crucial not to reward the manipulative behavior by giving in to it. The "manipulator" will simply learn that such behavior is rewarded and continue acting this way.

Parents, on the other hand, need to consider their parenting styles. Some parents say "no" simply just to dominate or control their adolescent without a broader perspective on the situation. This

continued on the next page

typically happens when a parent is exhausted or at a loss for knowing what else to do, but at times parents know no better.

Allowing for a dialogue to explain a decision sets a precedent for how things will be approached. It also allows children to know that they had a say in the discussion even if they don't get their way.

Another technique is for parents to explain how they see the behavior as manipulative. For instance, if the adolescent says, "Jen's mom is the nicest mother in the world. She lets her kids stay up until midnight and have sleepovers with boys," a parent might feel jealous of the other mother, or feel that they would like to be the best mother in the world. Saying instead that it is okay to ask to stay up late at night, or have a sleepover, even if the answer is no, is more effective for the parent in the long term.

If the point of the adolescent's comments was to make the parent feel guilty and shame him or her into allowing the later bedtime or sleepover, it is important for parents to point out that they feel as if they are being manipulated and that this behavior will not be effective.

If parents sense manipulation, they should ask their teen what it is that they are really asking. A statement such as, "Being honest takes courage, and it helps us trust you, whereas, being sneaky or deceptive creates a lack of trust," can be useful. The child then needs to be rewarded for taking the courage to be honest. This does not necessarily mean giving into the teen's request. The reward is recognizing the honesty and promising a willingness by the parent to continue to work hard at understanding where their teen is coming from.

Another situation is when an adolescent asks for something that the other parent has already vetoed. A statement such as, "That's between you and your mother (or father). Leave me out of it," makes manipulation less likely to occur. If a parent sets a rule and the adolescent challenges it, saying the other parents has allowed a certain behavior, then saying that until the issue is clarified with the other parent that the current rule sticks, allows for clarity and less possibility of future manipulation.

Parents should generally not have disagreements or arguments about rules or child-rearing issues in front of the adolescent. Nor should they sabotage the other parent's authority in any way. If parents do argue, children then know which parent is on "their side" and consistently go to that parent to get their needs met. The "agreeable" parent can then be stuck in a situation where the child now demands to be allowed to do some high-risk activity, does not know how to say no, and ends up feeling manipulated.

Careful, considerate parental teamwork can help reduce the chance of manipulative behavior.

- Something good can start or be presented
- Something good can end or be taken away
- Something bad can start or be presented
- Something bad can end or be taken away

For animals, consequences must either be immediate or clearly linked to the behavior to have an effect on the behavior. For instance, one cannot expect a dog to stop barking if the punishment or reward comes a week later. The dog would have no context and would more likely pair the punishment or reward with its most recent behavior. For humans, the consequence doesn't have to be immediate or even clearly linked to the behavior to have an effect on the behavior. As humans are verbal, we can explain the connection between the consequence and the behavior, even if they are separated in time. For example, you might tell your adolescent that he can borrow your car later because he had a good report card, or you might tell him that he is grounded because you found drugs in his room. He will be able to understand how the behavior affected the consequences.

For our purposes, adolescents with BPD might learn to associate a tantrum or a rage episode (behavior) with getting what they want (consequence). Parents learn to associate giving in to the adolescent (behavior) with not having to endure the threat (something bad might start). Both parents and adolescents are "rewarded" for their behavior.

Extinction

Another concept is that of extinction (or reducing an unwanted behavior) and the extinction burst (which is a temporary increase in the unwanted behavior before it is reduced). Behaviors that are followed by something positive tend to be either maintained or strengthened. If, for instance, cutting makes a person with BPD feel better, the person will tend to continue, or even increase, the cutting behavior.

In another example, a child who receives attention from a parent every time she throws a tantrum learns that to get the parent's attention, all she has to do is tantrum (as in operant conditioning above). If parents recognize this cause-and-effect, they can change their behavior so that they do not reinforce their child's tantrum by—for example, not paying attention to the tantrum. Without this reinforcement, the behavior should eventually die out (extinguish).

When a person is trying to kill a behavior, it's important to understand two things. First, the person trying to kill the behavior must be able to control the reinforcer (the "something good"). If the person cannot control the reinforcer, they will not be effective in controlling the behavior.

For instance, if parents consider rewarding their adolescent for consistently doing his homework by letting the adolescent watch an extra hour of TV, but the adolescent is able to watch TV whenever he wants, the parent does not have external control of the reinforcer. On the other hand, if the parents offer the adolescent $10 every week for doing his homework, the parent has far more control of that reinforcer. Obviously not being able to control the consequences for a behavior would make it difficult to change that behavior.

Second, the behavior must be expected to increase before it gets extinguished. This is called an extinction burst. We often see that a person will try the behavior at an increasing rate and intensity to get the desired response. It makes sense to them because the behavior has worked before.

If we wanted to reduce a person's cutting, for example, extinction would not be a suitable method to choose because the reinforcement (the temporary form a relief the person who cuts feels) cannot be externally controlled; if the person cuts herself, the reinforcement will inevitably follow, that being the temporary sense of relief.

However, if the reinforcer can be externally controlled and prevented from rewarding the behavior—such as a parent deciding not to pay attention to his or her child's tantrum—then initially this can result in an "extinction burst." The child realizes that the expected reinforcement—the parent paying attention to them—is not forthcoming, so he repeats the behavior. If still there is no reinforcement—the parent still ignores the behavior—the child may raise the level of the behavior, in this case, throwing more intense tantrums. If the reinforcement is rigorously withheld, no matter how much worse the behavior becomes, the behavior should then begin to lessen, slowly at first and then more rapidly.

If, however, as the behavior worsens during the extinction burst the parent cannot tolerate the worsening tantrum and gives in by paying attention to the raging child, the child learns that all he or she has to do to get attention is simply to escalate the tantrum. From then on it is likely that the tantrums will be worse than they were originally.

It is very important that a parent not try to use extinction of a behavior if they are not going to be able to follow through on what they need to do to extinguish the behavior.

EFFECTIVE RESPONSES TO MANIPULATION

As human beings, we are constantly manipulating our environment and relationships. Manipulation is not the exclusive domain of the adolescent with BPD, even if the effect of this behavior is that it leaves parents and caregivers feeling manipulated. Yes, kids with BPD rage. The kids learn that it is a reliable way to get their parents' attention. Obviously it is not an effective way, although without learning other ways, it is the only way they know.

Therapists also teach parents of kids who don't have BPD to ignore tantrums, which is the most effective way to end this pattern of behavior. (Obviously if the child poses a risk to himself, a parent needs to intervene, however. Simple tantrums will end with parents not paying attention.)

Parents also need to reward effective behavior from their children, so that when a child advocates for her needs without a tantrum, a parent needs to recognize how much more effective this approach was.

Some parents have argued that spanking or punishing their children for such behavior is just as effective. Although in many cases this is true, parents often find that as the child grows and gets bigger, it becomes much harder to use punishment. Some kids will fight back or simply disregard the punishment. In my experience when parents understand the behavioral principles behind classical and operant conditioning and apply them consistently, they become far more effective in dealing with their children's behavior.

CHAPTER FIVE

Discovering the Many Causes of BPD

T IS AN INTERESTING PARADOX that the brain, which has discovered so much about so many things, knows so little about itself, including all the mental health disorders.

BPD is no exception. As we gain knowledge and understanding and harness the promise of more powerful research tools, the causes of BPD will prove to be a complex combination of genetic makeup, how these genes express themselves under conditions of stress, the environment (including family interactions), brain maturation, development, and psychological constitution or temperament. It is unlikely there is a single cause for BPD, but rather that it is a product of the accumulation of risk factors expressing themselves in a vulnerable individual.

I'll make this clearer by pointing to specific research that looks at each of these areas. Though most of this research involved adults, much of it points to trauma or other factors in childhood or adolescence.

BRAIN STRUCTURES AND BPD

"When we adopted James as a six-month-old, the adoption agency told us that he had a skull fracture, but that he didn't have any neurological problems. But now he is impulsive, angry, and manipulative. Do you think that it is possible that he had a brain injury that is causing all his problems?"

This was what the parents of a seventeen-year-old boy with BPD wanted to know. Unless a child develops typically and then displays behavior changes after a head trauma, there is no easy answer as to whether a head injury in infancy, such as James experienced, caused the behavior changes. However, because the brain ultimately controls the behaviors and symptoms found in BPD, a basic understanding of brain anatomy is useful.

Some researchers believe the behavioral problems of BPD lie in the abnormal functioning of two main regions in the brain—the frontal lobes and the limbic system—and in one network—the hypothalamic-pituitary-adrenal axis. We'll talk about each in turn.

The Frontal Lobes

The frontal lobes are the part of the brain entrusted with executive function. This includes the ability to accomplish the following:

- Recognize future consequences resulting from current actions
- Choose between good and bad actions
- Hold and weigh opposing viewpoints
- Override and suppress unacceptable social responses
- Determine similarities and differences between things or events

One theory of the development of BPD is that if a child is traumatized (physically, sexually, or emotionally) in childhood, this can lead to damage of the frontal lobes, which in turn leads to diminished executive function. People who have had accidents or trauma that have damaged their frontal lobes often display irritability, impulsivity, and angry outbursts.

The Limbic System

The limbic system is a part of the brain that is often referred to as the "emotional brain" because it controls many of our emotions and motivations, particularly those that are related to survival. It is also the part of the brain that controls the "fight-or-flight" response. The two main parts of the limbic system are the hippocampus and the amygdala. The hippocampus is mainly responsible for learning and memory. The amygdala plays an important role in emotions, such as fear, anger, and those related to sexual behavior.

These two brain regions are the most important to know when trying to understand BPD. The frontal lobes and the limbic system are generally in constant communication. The problem is that during highly emotional states the frontal lobes—which govern decision-making—shut down, and the limbic system—which is involved in emotions—takes over.

This reaction works against people with BPD, or any person for that matter. In BPD for instance, stopping to think what the future consequence of repeated self-injurious behavior, such as cutting, will be during an episode of feeling overwhelmed and self-injuring is nearly impossible. Techniques aimed at both recognizing and reducing high emotional states are essential in BPD therapy. Using them, the adolescents with BPD can spend more time in their frontal (rational) brains, and as a consequence train them to better deal with conflicts.

THE HYPOTHALAMIC–PITUITARY–ADRENAL AXIS

Hypothalamic-Pituitary-Adrenal (HPA) axis is a complex group of nerves that acts between the hypothalamus (which controls body temperature, hunger, thirst, and body rhythms), the pituitary gland (which secretes hormones including oxytocin—considered important in attachment between mother and child), and the adrenal glands (which are responsible for stress regulation through the functioning of the hormones cortisol and adrenaline).

The interaction between these three organs, which takes place by way of neurotransmitters and hormones, governs reactions to stress, controls early attachment between mother and infant, and regulates mood and sexuality.

Many studies have shown that this nerve network does not function properly in people with BPD, so some treatments are targeted at these problems. For example, some people with BPD who become stressed can take medication that partially blocks the effects of adrenaline, which can reduce stress.

What the Brain Reveals about BPD

In 2006, researchers from the University of Freiburg in Germany looked at all the published studies on neuroimaging and BPD. They noted that neuroimaging had become one of the most important tools for investigating the biological causes of BPD.

All the studies regarding imaging and BPD found abnormalities in the limbic system and frontal lobes, which the researchers considered to be consistent with the idea that problems in these areas of the brain led to BPD symptoms.

People often ask me whether any such brain scans or blood tests will "prove" that a person has BPD or at least show that the person has "something wrong with her brain," as one parent put it. The short answer is that there are no current tests that will diagnose BPD. The longer answer is that researchers are looking at information from various types of scans to see whether they can detect differences between the brains of people with BPD and those without BPD. So far, these scans have shown what researchers hypothesize—that the frontal lobes and limbic system play an important role in BPD.

The types of scans used are the following:

Magnetic Resonance Imaging (MRI): This scan produces three-dimensional pictures of the brain using magnetic fields and computer technology.

Positron Emission Tomography (PET) Scan: A PET scan examines the level of activity in the various areas of the brain by measuring the brain's use of glucose.

HOW EMPATHY WORKS IN THE BRAIN

Empathy is the ability that allows people to feel the emotions that other people feel, understand their motives, and see things from their points of view. This quality is of particular importance to people with BPD as there are times that they seem to be profoundly empathetic, intuitive and aware of others' emotional states.

But how does empathy work? It turns out that certain brain cells respond not only when a person performs an action such as crying, but also when they watch another person perform an action such as crying. Because the brain cells reflected what others were doing, these brain cells are called "mirror neurons."

Imagine that you are crying or smiling in front of a mirror. The reflection would be that of you doing the same thing.

In people with BPD, it is as if these mirror neurons are magnifiers, so that people with BPD often pick up tiny changes in another person's facial and behavioral changes.

The problem is then that they make assumptions about what those changes mean that may not be correct. For example, someone with BPD might see another person frown—which is then reflected in his or her own brain—and they interpret this as meaning that they are not liked.

More recent experiments have shown that mirror neurons not only respond for physical actions, but for emotions and sensations as well. So when we see someone crying, our mirror neurons respond and we can feel their sorrow and not simply have to imagine what they are feeling.

Mirror neurons have been considered to be faulty in other mental disorders besides BPD, such as autism and Asperger's, where people with the condition have a very difficult time reading social cues. Also mirror neurons might explain how children develop what's called a theory of mind. A theory of mind is a child's understanding that other people have minds similar to their own.

Single Photon Emission Computed Tomography (SPECT) Scan: A SPECT scan is a test that can provide information about blood flow to the brain and the metabolic activities in the brain. It is used frequently in patients with epilepsy to help pinpoint the area in the brain involved in producing seizures.

Electroencephalogram (EEG): This test measures the electrical activity in a person's brain.

Computed tomography (CT or CAT) Scan: This type of imaging scan uses x-rays that shows the internal structure of a person's brain.

How BPD Brains Are Different

Researchers have made the following findings as a result of the imaging scans described above:

PET scan studies. In a 2003 study, researchers noted that the brains of violent criminal offenders, murderers, and aggressive psychiatric patients showed that their frontal lobes had lower brain activity. They also noted that impulsive-aggression was a clinical characteristic of BPD, associated with assaultive and suicidal behaviors. They scanned the brains of thirteen impulsive patients with BPD with a history of aggression and found that the frontal lobes of these patients similarly had low brain activity.

PET scan studies have also found that patients with BPD have smaller amygdalas and smaller hippocampi compared to people with no BPD. Again, these findings are consistent with the theory that changes in the hippocampus and amygdala are associated with BPD.

MRI studies. In 2003, researchers from the University of Freiburg measured the size of the limbic system and the frontal lobes in patients with BPD. Using MRI measurements they found that women with BPD had smaller hippocampi and amygdalas than the women without BPD.

EEG studies. A 1998 study by researchers at the Free University of Brussels in Belgium noted that epilepsy and brain abnormalities contribute to BPD. They looked at fifty-eight EEGs in twenty patients with BPD and found that 40 percent of patients with BPD had abnormal EEGs although none of the patients with BPD had epilepsy. They also found that giving these patients with BPD an anti-seizure medication did not change the EEGs.

SPECT scan studies. Given all these findings, it is not surprising to find that using SPECT scan, researchers have found abnormalities in the frontal lobes and limbic systems of patients with BPD.

The bottom line of all these studies is that people with BPD have abnormalities in these two areas of the brain. Whether these abnormalities cause BPD, or if having BPD leads to these abnormalities, remains to be seen.

PARENTING AND ATTACHMENT

The concept in psychology of temperament is generally thought of as that part of the personality that is genetically based—the innate, inborn aspect of a person's personality. For example, parents will describe how their children were different from one another and recognize these differences as early as the first year.

There is, and has been for many years, an ongoing debate over the importance of nature versus nurture in the development of personality traits and temperament. Some have stated that though personality traits are acquired patterns of thoughts and behavior over time, temperament is hard-wired. There are studies that support the idea that personality is completely genetic or in-born and others that show that environment plays an important role. The reality is that while we might not know for specific individuals just how much their genes or environment play a role in their developing personality, it is surely a combination of both factors.

For instance, in the following case one might argue for a predominantly genetic or hard-wired temperament. This is part of an email from a family member looking for help.

BRAIN CHEMISTRY AND BPD BEHAVIOR

Studies have shown that the following brain chemicals (also known as neurotransmitters), hormones, and blood fats can be abnormal in people with BPD:

Acetylcholine. This brain chemical appears to be involved in learning and memory and also has been shown to regulate mood. High levels of acetylcholine cause a depressed mood in people whether or not they had depression before. This effect appears to be even more intense in patients with BPD. Giving patients with BPD a chemical that increases acetylcholine in the brain produces significantly more depressive symptoms than giving this chemical to patients who do not have BPD.

Adrenaline. This hormone, which is also known as epinephrine, also acts as a brain chemical. It is extremely important in the "fight-or-flight" response, as it signals the heart to pump harder to get ready for action, although in excess adrenaline can lead to terrible anxiety. Some psychiatrists use medications that block the effects of adrenaline to lower the anxiety of people with BPD.

Cholesterol. Some studies have shown an association between low or lowered cholesterol and impulsivity, aggressive behaviors, and suicide. One study found this blood fat to be low especially in suicidal BPD patients, and that the lower the cholesterol, the more the suicidal thinking.

Corticotropin-Releasing Factor (CRF). This hormone acts on the adrenal glands leading to the release of adrenaline. Like cortisol, it is also commonly released in response to stress. Studies have found that low CRF levels are associated with the degree and severity of childhood trauma.

Cortisol. This hormone is also known as the "stress hormone" because it is secreted in high levels during the body's "fight-or-flight" response during stress. It has been found in studies that low cortisol levels are found in people with posttraumatic stress disorder. This finding has also been found in patients with BPD and a history of trauma.

Dopamine. This brain chemical regulates movement, emotion, attention, motivation, and feelings of pleasure. Researchers often cite as evidence of dopamine problems in BPD by pointing to the beneficial effect of drugs that block dopamine in some patients with BPD.

G protein. This chemical switch in the brain allows messages to pass from one nerve cell to another. One study has found that people with a gene variation of the G-protein are much more likely to self-mutilate, which is a behavior commonly found in people with BPD.

Leptin. This hormone produced by fat cells suppresses appetite and encourages the burn of fat stored in adipose tissue. One study found this hormone to be especially low in suicidal BPD patients.

Serotonin. This brain chemical affects emotions, behavior, and thought. Many studies have shown that low serotonin levels are associated with impulsive aggression and depression in patients with personality disorders. Low serotonin levels have also been found in people who attempt or complete suicides.

"My cousin (a mother of five children) has a very aggressive pancreatic cancer. Her nine-year-old daughter, Charlie, has been diagnosed with borderline personality disorder (her maternal grandmother and two maternal aunts also have the disorder and were treated at many hospitals well into their adult lives). The family hasn't told Charlie about the cancer—so she's just about to have her world blown apart. Her current therapist does not specialize in BPD and has had no success with her 'storms,' which go on for hours every day and always seem to occur after she has had a fight with her mother, father, or one of her siblings. Her family says that she is beginning to show the kind of behavior that her grandmother and her aunts showed when they were children, and they want to prevent things from worsening now, especially as her mother is going to have to tell her about the cancer and that she will probably die."

Clearly, there are factors in this child's life that are of great concern and need to be the focus of treatment, but there is also a strong genetic component for BPD and getting the child into a treatment with a clinical

WHAT MAKES UP TEMPERAMENT?

The following nine traits are associated with temperament:

- Activity level: The child's general state of activity
- Distractibility: The level of concentration and attention displayed when a child is not particularly interested in an activity
- Intensity: The level of a child's reaction to an event
- Regularity: The predictability of a child's biological functions, like appetite and sleep
- Sensory threshold: How sensitive a child is to physical stimuli, such as sound, touch, smells, taste, and temperature
- Approach/withdrawal: A child's characteristic response to a new situation or strangers
- Adaptability: How easily the child adapts to transitions and changes, like switching to a new activity
- Persistence: The amount of time a child continues in activities in the face of obstacles
- Mood: The tendency to react to life primarily in either a positive or a negative way

team experienced with BPD and family systems at this point will clearly be of help for the girl and the family.

THE EFFECTS OF ATTACHMENT

In addition to temperament, a lot of research and thinking is taking place now on attachment deficits in the childhood of adults with BPD. Attachment is essentially the tendency to seek closeness to another person and feel secure when that person is present. It is the emotional tie that endures over time that binds a person to another, and in this particular context, a child to its mother, father, or other early caregiver.

A fundamental theory of attachment is that sensitive and attuned responding by a parent to an infant's needs will result in secure attachment, and that the lack of such sensitive response will result in insecure attachment. Whether poor parent-child attachment is one cause of BPD, or disrupted brain wiring leads to poor attachment, remains to be seen. Poor attachment, nevertheless, is an almost universal finding in borderline research.

Consider the following case of attachment being traumatically disrupted at a young age.

The father of an otherwise very likeable fifteen-year-old girl told us that his daughter had always had "problems." She had been admitted to our adolescent inpatient unit for severe self-injury, suicidality, and profound abandonment fears.

He told us that even as a young child she had more severe temper tantrums than any child he had ever seen. He recognized that the problems started very soon after his first wife, the mother of the girl, had died from an aggressive form of cancer. He rapidly remarried a woman whom he thought would be a good mother to his then one-year-old daughter.

Instead, his new wife had no time for the girl. She was distant and cold toward the child, and he described how soon after his daughter had potty-trained, his new wife would scold and at times spank the child if she soiled her diaper. He acknowledged that he was frequently away from home on business and that in retrospect his daughter would have terrible tantrums whenever he would go away. His wife felt that the girl was behaving terribly and that he should simply leave on his trip without recognizing the bad behavior. He noted that the girl was terrified of using the potty for fear that she would have an accident and that her stepmother would punish her.

The new couple then had another child of their own, and this child was treated like "treasure." His new wife never took to his daughter and by the time the girl was twelve she had started cutting herself. The mother refused to come into any family therapy, and the girl alternately hated her father for having remarried and loved him for being the only one who could possibly help her.

THREE DIFFERENT THEORIES ON BPD

The importance of childhood experiences in the development of BPD cannot be overstated. Many studies have looked at how people with BPD function interpersonally. These studies were all originally carried out in adults, but increasingly they are being conducted in children and adolescents.

At McLean, we are looking at the ramifications of early childhood events—such as trauma, abuse, and loss of a parent—and other attachment issues in our adolescent patients with BPD.

The current research in children comes from the following three theoretical perspectives:

Object-relations theorists. This theory emphasizes the importance of mental representation of the self and of others. Researchers from this perspective study the mental representation that a child has for its mother. A mental representation is the image or picture that a person has of another person. Such an image includes all the individual qualities of the other person.

Researchers have studied the concept of "rejection sensitivity," that is, the expectation that a significant other is intentionally trying to hurt the person. Rejection sensitivity includes problems in understanding others' motivations, and how patients with BPD represent significant others in their minds.

Attachment theorists. These researchers look at early child-caregiver attachment; they have linked BPD to preoccupied and fearful, disorganized, and unresolved attachments between children and significant others.

Cognitive-behavioral theorists. This group has linked BPD to interpersonal skills deficits or that patients with BPD never learned adequate and adaptive interpersonal functioning and so tend to isolate or rage in response to stressful interpersonal conflicts.

Again, given the complexities of BPD, it is probably true that all of these considerations play a role in an at-risk or vulnerable individual.

What the Attachment Theorists Have to Say

Peter Fonagy, Ph.D., is a professor of psychoanalysis at University College London and a clinical psychologist in child and adult analysis at the British Psycho-Analytical Society. He has researched borderline psychopathology, violence, and early attachment relationships, looking at the early attachment experiences of children and the affect these experiences have on later functioning, particularly as these experiences pertain to BPD.

Dr. Fonagy defines attachment as the emotional connection that infants and children develop toward their parents and others who care for them. Attachment refers to a set of behaviors and emotions that can be observed in infants.

One of the fundamental questions Dr. Fonagy has explored is how deprivation, neglect, abuse, or early trauma affects the development of personality and further how then to avoid such early trauma or its effects. Dr. Fonagy's key assumption is that any person's social behavior can be understood in terms of the mental models of social relationships that the person thinks up. Mental models are representations in the mind of real or imaginary situations. They are an explanation in someone's thought process for how something works in the real world. Examples of imaginary situations are a child's explanation of how Santa brings presents at Christmas, or how the tooth fairy leaves money under a pillow. Real situations are for instance how a child perceives his mother or her father to be or how they imagine their relationships with their parents is. Dr. Fonagy believes that these representations, which are constantly evolving and modifying, are most strongly influenced by a child's experiences with his or her primary caregivers.

Dr. Fonagy developed the concept of "mentalization," which he defines as the capacity to think about your own thoughts and feelings as well as those of others. For example, an attuned mother might infer that her crying infant is hungry from the infant's cry alone. The infant need not (cannot) tell its mother that it is hungry for the mother to "mentalize" or understand the infant's "mental state."

Another way to define the ability to "mentalize," is that it is the capacity to understand and manipulate other people's behavior in terms of their mental states. This capacity is a major ingredient in successful social interactions. An example might be a spouse returning home from work and slamming the front door shut. His wife, knowing him, might infer his mental state by observation rather than being told that he had a crummy day at work.

Dr. Fonagy suggests that parents' ability to be aware of their own feelings increases the likelihood of their child's secure attachment. He believes the opposite is true, too: If a parent is not able to be aware of his or her own mental state or feelings, in turn, his or her child will have a harder time developing his or her own capacity to do so. In essence, the parent's modeling empathic behavior integrates such behavior into the hardwiring of the child's developing brain.

In addition, he suggests that individuals who experience early trauma might protect themselves by blocking their capacity to empathize with others.

This is to avoid having to think that their caregiver might wish to harm them. Some characteristics of severe BPD may be rooted in the inability to understand other people's intentions and behavior accurately. An example might be a child's inability to recognize genuine caring and empathy in another person and feel instead that the other person poses a threat and so he or she strikes out in anger.

The Mother-Child Bond

The quality of maternal care has been repeatedly shown to predict infant security. The parent's sensitive responsiveness is considered to be the most important determining factor of whether an infant feels secure. Studies have shown that negative parental personality traits are associated with child insecurity. Negative parental traits include, for example, rigidity, black-and-white thinking, being non-empathic, externalizing blame onto others (especially the child), and *always* believing that *all* their actions are in the best interest of the child.

Dr. Fonagy suggests that the parents' empathy and sensitivity to their children makes it easier for the children to empathize with others and that this is made all the easier by a secure attachment.

Parents who can accurately reflect what their children are feeling and thinking are termed "reflective caregivers." Say an infant begins crying and his mother attempts to soothe him. The infant perceives in his mother's behavior not only her reflecting what he feels, which he infers to account for her behavior, but he also perceives in his mother's stance an image of himself as someone who can think and elicit reactions.

If the infant's mother's reflective capacity allows her to accurately capture the infant's intentions, he will eventually internalize the idea that he is a real thinking person in the mind of his mother. If his mother cannot do this, then he may think of himself only as a physical person rather than as a person with a mind of his own. Another way to think about it is that if a mirror did not reflect who you are, or reflected a constantly changing image, then you would only recognize yourself by the body that you can actually see rather than an image represented in a reflection.

Dr. Fonagy states that the fundamental need of every infant is to find his mind, his intentional state, in the mind of his mother, and that this allows for "containment" or internalization of this concept of himself. If he cannot do this, he develops no stable mental sense of himself and this leads to a desperate search for other ways of containing his thoughts. This in turn leads to intense feelings, which the child finds difficult to manage.

Dr. Fonagy suggests that the search for other ways of mental containment could give rise to many pathological solutions, including taking the mind of the other, which for our hypothetical infant would make things worse if the mother did not have a reflective capacity.

He believes that this lodges an alien person in the child's self, a representation that the child cannot make its own, as it does not feel right. Developmentally, the child then tries to separate from this and establish its own autonomy. However, and tragically, he finds that this is an impossible task as his own sense of self is centered on a mental state with confusing representation of his own emotional states. Inevitably, it leads to the question "Who am I?" a question that is not easily answered and ultimately leads to the profound core identity issues that plague many adolescents with BPD.

Dr. Fonagy points out the apparent paradox that as the child searches for his own sense of self, he becomes increasingly one with his mother as her representation is the only one he has. He is unable to consider himself as a separate thinking individual, due to her incapacity to reflect that he is a unique thinking individual.

Dr. Fonagy feels that this accounts for the phenomenon seen in patients with BPD of swinging between the struggle for independence and the terrifying need for extreme closeness.

During adolescence, the child is increasingly required to become separate from his parents and an individual, but a crisis arises for the adolescent with BPD. He cannot tolerate this demand and becomes self-destructive and suicidal—what he perceives to be the only feasible solution to an otherwise insoluble challenge.

Disturbed attachment may have a significant role in the development of BPD, but together with all the genetic and neurological findings, studies have shown that up to 87 percent of patients with BPD who required hospitalization for their symptoms had a history of severe abuse/neglect and that 81 percent of those patients had abuse at the hand of their parents. The issue of trauma is significant because studies have shown that childhood trauma affects the functioning of the frontal lobe, which is implicated in the pathology of BPD. Nevertheless, the role of parenting is important to look at.

Types of Attachment

John Bowlby, M.D., was a British psychoanalyst who postulated that there was a universal human need to form close emotional bonds. This core concept was the fundamental basis of his attachment theory. Despite his training as an analyst, Bowlby felt very strongly that psychoanalysis put too much emphasis on a child's fantasy world and far too little on actual events, and that attachment could be observed. He described attachment as a "special type of social relationship, between infant and caregiver, involving an affective bond."

Mary Ainsworth, Ph.D., was an American psychologist who imported Bowlby's attachment theory to the United States. She described the concept of the "strange situation," which goes essentially like this:

1. The mother and infant enter a room.
2. The child plays with toys while the mother is present.
3. A stranger enters the room and the mother leaves.
4. The stranger tries to comfort the child.
5. The mother returns and the stranger leaves.
6. The mother comforts the child and then leaves for a second time.
7. The child is left alone for three minutes.
8. The stranger enters and interacts with the child.
9. The caregiver enters and picks up the child and the stranger leaves.

Ainsworth observed three patterns of attachment and termed them **secure, anxious avoidant**, and **anxious ambivalent**, and later a fourth category termed **disorganized** was added.

Secure attachment is characterized by a child who explore his environment freely while his mother is present, engages with strangers, is visibly upset when the parent departs, and is happy to see his mother return. Early secure infant-mother attachments provide children with greater social skills.

A child who avoids or ignores his mother, showing little emotion when she leaves or returns characterizes **anxious-avoidant attachment**. The child does not explore his environment much, regardless of who is there. He tends not to treat strangers all that differently from his mother and shows little emotional range, regardless of who is in the room.

A child who is anxious of exploration of the room and anxious of strangers, even when the parent is present, characterizes **anxious-ambivalent attachment**. When the mother departs, the child becomes extremely distressed. The child is then ambivalent when mother returns, both seeking to remain close to mother but resentful that she left.

The later-described **disorganized attachment** is defined by the lack of a particular style or pattern for coping. Children with disorganized attachment experience their caregivers as either frightened or frightening. Interactions with others are experienced as erratic, so these children cannot form regular styles of interaction. Children with disorganized attachment are often hostile and combative, and they are often considered "problem children" during their school years.

Ainsworth and her fellow researchers noted that the anxious-avoidant and disorganized children sought attachment, but that they experienced anxiety as a consequence of attachment. The researchers noted that both groups of children experienced anxiety at the disappearance of their mothers and were difficult to soothe upon reunion. The disorganized children appeared to be particularly ambivalent upon reunion with their mothers, both approaching and avoiding contact.

In a 2006 study, the researchers wanted to look at adult social attachment and evaluate that attachment as it pertained to childhood maltreatment and current symptoms in forty outpatients with BPD. The researchers found that this BPD group had significantly greater attachment impairment and fearful attachment, and further, that among BPD patients attachment-anxiety was specifically associated with sexual abuse, whereas attachment-avoidance was associated with other maltreatment types. The researchers concluded that BPD was characterized by adult attachment disturbances, that these attachment problems were strongly related to childhood maltreatment, and that the diverse problems of patients with BPD might arise from attachment problems.

Issues of Early Attachment

Karlen Lyons-Ruth, Ph.D., of Harvard Medical School at the Cambridge Hospital has spent a career looking at how very early attachment between infant and caregivers pertains to later personality development. This has included looking at the relationship between the quality of early attachment and care on borderline symptomatology in adults.

Regarding attachment, Dr. Lyons-Ruth has stressed the significance of the mother-child interactions that lead to the capacity of emotion regulation in the infant. She theorizes that disruption in the "attachment-exploration balance" interferes with a child's development of cognitive and social skills. The "attachment-exploration balance" is the idea that if an infant is to competently explore her environment, she must be confident that her mother will be there if a threat arises. A child who is not confident that this will happen will focus on the attachment relationship with her mother rather than exploring the environment around her. The fear that her mother might not be there if a threat arises is consistent with later abandonment fears in patients with BPD. Dr. Lyons-Ruth has reported on the consequence of disrupted attachment from infancy to age twenty, exploring the interplay of early attachment problems, later abuse, and genetic factors in the development of BPD and other disorders.

In 1991 Dr. Lyons-Ruth and her colleagues reported a number of studies that demonstrated that maternal and family risk factors such as child abuse, parental stress, and mothers' depressive symptoms consistently produced children who had difficulty in forming secure attachments to their caregivers.

A 2004 review of thirteen attachment studies with patients with BPD found that every study concluded that there is a strong association between BPD and insecure attachment. The types of attachment found to be most characteristic of BPD subjects are unresolved, preoccupied, and fearful attachments. The review showed that in each of these attachment types, patients demonstrated both a longing for intimacy and a concern about dependency and rejection. The authors concluded that the finding that adults with BPD have insecure attachments is consistent with the finding of disturbed interpersonal relationships in people with BPD. They also concluded that people who have insecure attachment are vulnerable to developing BPD.

ON GENES AND INHERITANCE

Many parents feel that they are to blame for their child's BPD, that they either did something wrong in their parenting or passed on a bad gene. Further, few adoptive parents are aware that serious behavioral and personality problems can occur in adopted children. When such problems manifest themselves, parents are often guilt-ridden, believing that they are to blame.

Symptoms of BPD—in particular inappropriate anger, mood swings, paranoia/dissociation, impulsivity, and intense, unstable relationships—are more common among the relatives of borderline patients than among patients with other personality disorders. It appears that BPD traits—rather than BPD itself—are more common in the first-degree relatives of BPD patients.

Family and twin studies of BPD suggest that while BPD itself might not be inherited, some behaviors such as impulsivity, suicidality, mood instability, and aggression do appear to be inherited. For instance, many parents recognize that they were moody as children, for example, but not as moody as their child. Some parents admit that they had suicidal thoughts but never acted on such thoughts.

It will probably be true that given the incredible variation of BPD behavior, the underlying cause of the disorder will include many genes as part of the complex puzzle. No gene study has found that there is one gene that causes BPD, however, studies do point to the fact that variations of genes can be strongly associated with certain behaviors. These gene variations, when put together with brain anatomy and the effects of the environment on an individual, will represent a more complete answer.

GENE VARIATIONS

Before we look at the research, a word about genetics: Genes are the basic biological building blocks that make us who we are. They are composed of even smaller building blocks known as DNA. Genes are what give us our physical characteristics, such as hair color and eye color.

Genes are not all alike, and different or alternative forms of a gene are known as **alleles**. Variations in all inherited characteristics, such as eye color, are due to different alleles. Researchers have tied particular variations in behavior (such as impulsive aggression) to a particular allele or gene variation.

At McLean Hospital in Belmont, Massachusetts, John Gunderson, M.D., and his fellow researchers have initiated a large study to look at the genetics of BPD. His group has divided BPD patients into three subtypes based on the major problems each group displays. The first group has marked mood swings, the second group has behavioral problems such as self-injury, and the third group has interpersonal problems such as difficult relationships. The researchers are studying whether any of these subtypes has a stronger genetic component than the others. The study hopes to provide results that will help us to further classify BPD and to develop a gene bank (where DNA is collected and stored) for future BPD research. One study of BPD found a variation in a gene that affects the functioning of dopamine, the brain chemical that regulates movement, emotion, motivation, and feelings of pleasure. Patients with BPD with this gene abnormality tend to be more depressed than those without it.

Another genetic finding is that people who have the variation of a certain gene that controls brain switches, known as G-proteins, were more likely to self-injure or self-mutilate.

Yet another study found that a variation in a gene involved in the production of the brain chemical serotonin leads people who have that gene to make more suicide attempts than those who do not. Finally another gene study confirms that a different serotonin gene variation is associated with aggressive behavior in adolescents.

Gene studies are still in their infancy as they pertain to human behavior, but slowly, as the effects of genes are better understood and more of these gene variations are discovered, the impact of genes on the development of BPD will become clearer.

THE ROLE OF PARENTING

The mother of a seventeen-year-old with BPD who had moved out of her parents' home after her she had had an abortion once told me:

"I'm so sad that my family is broken. My daughter hasn't spoken to her dad or me in months. He gets angry at how she treats me. My two younger children are also angry with her. I'm tired and depressed, and I don't feel like I have any fight left in me. I want my daughter to be happy. I want to reach out to her and help her with her pain. I failed her as a child, and now I'm failing her as she becomes an adult. I am worried about what will happen to the other kids as well."

Getting into a "blame game" is not helpful in the treatment of adolescents with BPD or their families. There is often plenty of blame being thrown around by various people when it comes to BPD, and it is easy to get caught up in the "bad parenting" argument. In many cases, parents did the best they could. It should be clear by now that BPD has many risk factors and underlying causes.

Having said that, parenting *can* play a role—sometimes a big role—in the development of BPD. Understanding the role of parenting helps us to recognize the risk factors and further help the family change whatever contributing parenting style might be pertinent.

A recent study recognized that inadequate parenting and traumatic experiences could negatively affect mood regulation. The researchers found that people who perceived their parents as having poor parenting styles had a harder time describing their emotions and had increased levels of depression. However, a positively perceived maternal parenting style was found to help adolescents express emotion, even if sexual abuse had also taken place.

The researchers concluded that the perception of one's parenting appeared to be of significance in the development of an inability to express emotions. They further found that optimal parenting of one parent could protect against the development of alexithymia (which is the inability to describe emotions, or how a person is feeling, in words) when the parenting of the other parent was perceived as non-optimal.

Another core concept in the bio-social theory of BPD is the "invalidating environment." The term refers to a situation in which the personal experiences and responses of a child are discounted, or "invalidated," by his parents or the significant others in his life. The child's personal communications are not accepted as an accurate indication of his true feelings. Also it is implied that, if the feelings were accurate, they would not be a valid response to circumstances. To combat this, in therapy, parents learn to recognize that despite having a different experience to an event, their child's experience can be just as valid as their own experiences are.

OTHER FACTORS IN THE DEVELOPMENT OF BPD

If it were only bonding issues or low serotonin levels that influenced BPD development, a few parenting classes and a serotonin-boosting drug would be all that was needed, but many other life events affect the emergence of BPD, including substance abuse, trauma, maltreatment, and sexual abuse.

Substance Abuse

A 2005 study by Dawn Thatcher, Ph.D., and colleagues looked at adolescent alcohol use and other adolescent characteristics as predictors of adult BPD symptoms. The researchers recruited 355 adolescents with a history of alcohol abuse and 169 adolescents without any history of alcohol abuse into their study.

Six years later, they measured symptoms of BPD in the now young adults. They found that the group of adolescents who abused alcohol and also had other psychiatric disorders were more likely to develop adult BPD than those adolescents with psychiatric disorders without alcohol abuse.

Trauma, Maltreatment, and Sexual Abuse in BPD

Many studies have shown that the majority of people diagnosed with personality disorders have a history of trauma, abuse, and maltreatment. This is particularly true of people diagnosed with BPD. Also, adults with BPD and a history of childhood and adolescent physical abuse are twice as likely to develop post-traumatic stress disorder (PTSD) as those without BPD or an abusive history.

Clinicians who treat BPD are often on the lookout for childhood abuse, and upon finding it, tie it in as *the* cause of BPD in a patient. This assumption is strongly supported in the BPD literature, which shows that the majority of individuals with BPD have suffered emotional, physical, and sexual abuse. Research shows that up to 75 percent of patients with BPD have been sexually abused, and it is important to recognize that many do suffer abuse. However, a significant minority has not suffered childhood sexual abuse. John Gunderson, M.D., of McLean Hospital has pointed out that sexual abuse is neither necessary nor sufficient to *cause* BPD.

Research has also found that sexual abuse by a parent is significantly related to suicidal behavior, and both parental sexual abuse and emotional neglect are significantly related to self-mutilation.

The following four risk factors pertaining to abuse have been found to be significant predictors of a BPD diagnosis:

- Female gender
- Sexual abuse by a male non-caretaker
- Emotional denial by a male caretaker
- Inconsistent treatment by a female caretaker

Of patients with BPD who were sexually abused, more than 50 percent report being abused both in childhood and in adolescence, on at least a weekly basis, for a minimum of one year, by a parent or other person well known to the patient, and by two or more perpetrators. More than 50 percent also report that their abuse involved at least one form of penetration and the use of force or violence.

It stands to reason that the severity of reported childhood sexual abuse is significantly related to the overall severity of BPD and general functioning.

Despite trauma and abuse being neither necessary nor sufficient to produce BPD, these events are sadly found all too commonly in BPD patients, and they clearly affect the development and course of the disorder. Trauma can affect brain development, which was earlier shown to contribute to BPD. So too, can trauma lessen the body's chemical stress response, which has also been shown to contribute to BPD.

Childhood Mental Disorders

Before looking at childhood mental disorders and how they might contribute to the development of BPD, let's consult the *Diagnostic and Statistical Manual of Mental Disorders-IV* (*DSM-IV*) to clarify the concepts in this section.

The manual contains the criteria clinicians use to diagnose mental disorders. A diagnosis is made by categorizing the conditions on the following axes:

BPD AND THE PERCEPTION OF PAIN

People with borderline personality disorder (BPD) may have a different tolerance for pain than the general population.

Consider this description of a fifteen-year-old boy by his mother:

> "My son cut [himself] all over his body, and it never seemed to hurt him. When he was a baby, he would bang his head and that didn't seem to hurt him either. When he was twelve, he broke his leg skiing, and he hardly complained."

Like this boy, people with BPD appear to tolerate pain, or even not experience pain, when compared to people without BPD, according to many studies. For instance, people with BPD have lower pain ratings during cold temperature tests (where people place their hands in freezing cold water) than people without BPD.

A 2004 study by researchers at the University of Freiburg in Germany noted that approximately 70 to 80 percent of women who met criteria for BPD reported less pain perception during self-mutilation. The women applied brief heat pulses generated by a laser to the skin, and the researchers found that patients with BPD had significantly higher heat pain thresholds and lower pain ratings than those without BPD.

Later, in 2006, these same researchers performed MRI brain scans of women with BPD who self-inured. They found that women with BPD had less brain activity in the pain centers of the brain, which they felt accounted for their reduced pain perception.

- Axis I contains the clinical disorders, such as major depression
- Axis II includes the personality disorders (such as BPD) and mental retardation
- Axis III refers to medical conditions (such as asthma or diabetes)
- Axis IV contains the social stressors (such as difficulties at school or work or problems with the law)
- Axis V refers to a number from one to one hundred that quantifies how well a person is functioning

From my perspective, the distinction between Axis I and Axis II is not that clear. All psychiatric conditions ultimately emanate from some aspect of brain function (or dysfunction) even if how that dysfunction came to be remains in question.

Almost all the kids referred to our unit at McLean Hospital have had a previous diagnosis of attention deficit disorder (ADD) or bipolar disorder. Childhood mental disorders, such as ADD, attention deficit hyperactivity disorder (ADHD), or bipolar disorder might increase the risk that the affected child develops a personality disorder when he or she grows up. This can happen in various ways.

First, the disorder itself could directly influence personality development. For example, a child who is depressed might feel that she is worthless, and over time this belief could become a core belief she has about herself.

Second, the symptoms and behaviors of a condition might lead to a response by others, which could affect personality development. For instance, a hyperactive child might be physically punished or abused by a parent or might receive differing responses to his behavior, sometimes getting punished, sometimes being ignored.

Third, it is possible that the childhood mental disorder is simply a manifestation of personality problems in the first place.

Australian psychiatrist Joseph Rey, M.D., one of the foremost researchers of personality development in adolescence, has conducted various studies over the years. His group found that 40 percent of patients who were diagnosed with a "disruptive disorder" (such as ADHD) during adolescence were later diagnosed with a personality disorder. By contrast, only 12 percent of patients who had "emotional (or mood) disorders"— such as depression—had a personality disorder. When he continued to follow this group of kids into adulthood, he found that having a personality disorder was associated with poor functioning. Issues included problems with the law, a poor work record, early cohabitation, social isolation, and problems in interpersonal relationships.

Other research has found that personality disorders are more than twice more common in individuals who had an Axis I diagnosis in adolescence than those who had not, and further that the more Axis I diagnoses that a person has, the more likely they are to develop a personality disorder.

The Effect of Contemporary Culture

Does modern American culture contribute to the development of BPD? Eating disorders and self-injury appear to be predominantly Western phenomena. Research shows that when other societies are exposed to Western culture, previously unseen and sometimes maladaptive behavior quickly arises in these societies.

The argument for implicating contemporary culture in BPD is that the high level of family dysfunction and divorce in our society today means that parents are less reliably present. Making matters worse, many two-parent families have both parents working full-time. Childcare is then sometimes subbed out to a network of nannies and day care centers, rather than parents or extended family being the primary caregivers. In situations when frequently changing caretakers are involved in the lives of young lives, it stands to reason that consistent and predictable adult figures are less reliably present.

The problems created by an inconsistent family environment are further worsened by our culture promoting a "false-self" with emaciated cover models, beauty over brains, and sex without commitment. (The "false-self" occurs when a person is forced to comply with external expectations, such as being polite or looking attractive, or being demure when such expectations might be inconsistent with who they really are and how they would ordinarily act or feel. Over time, living in a perpetual "false-self" state can become extremely unhealthy as the person loses their sense of genuine self.) Yet another concern is that generally our culture caters to the need for instant gratification and quick fixes, and disdains the idea of people looking for long-term help. One catch phrase is "better living through chemistry," or the idea that taking a pill can make things better. Although this is certainly true for many conditions, it does not work for many others. Telling people with BPD that there is a simple answer or to "snap out of it," invalidates their experience but worse, is not the answer. Many of these cultural factors combine with family environment and individual biology to set up the conditions for the development of BPD.

Online Dangers

No doubt the Internet is an innovation that has changed society's behavior Never before has so much information been available to so many people— allowing an individual to readily influence the behavior of some other random person.

The Internet clearly presents incredible benefit to society, but on it lurks many dangers, and adolescents with BPD could be particularly vulnerable. Online sexual predators, dangerous information about drugs and suicide methods, friendships created without context, the formation of instant peer groups, and rapidly disseminated anonymous bullying are just a few of the dangers.

In April 2006, the American Psychological Association published a series of articles entitled *Children, Adolescents, and the Internet.*

The association noted that between "75 and 90 percent of teenagers in the United States used the Internet to email, instant message (IM), visit chat rooms, and explore other sites on the World Wide Web," and that, "a lot of time on the Web can have both negative and positive effects on young people, i.e., the sharing of self-injury practices by some and the improvement of academic performance and health awareness by others."

Another recent study found that the use of friend-networking sites, such as myspace.com, increased the number of relationships that an adolescent has. The study also found that the frequency and tone with which adolescents received feedback on their profiles affected their self-esteem. Positive feedback enhanced adolescents' self-esteem and well-being, whereas negative feedback decreased their self-esteem and well-being.

The Internet may be particularly important for adolescents who feel marginalized. It provides a venue that they perceive to be low-risk for finding others who share their differences (both perceived and real) and for exchanging information that may be difficult to share in person. Further, the Internet offers anonymity. Adolescents can hide behind assumed identities.

Sadly, adolescents with psychological problems are much more likely to share personal information on the Internet with total strangers than those without such problems. For example, studies have shown that females between twelve and twenty years of age populate most self-injury message boards and chat rooms. They log on to ask for and share information related to cutting and other self-injurious behavior. It's true that the chat rooms provide social and emotional support for isolated adolescents, but they also normalize cutting, other self-injurious behavior, and other potentially lethal "problem-solving" options.

The following message was recently anonymously posted on an Internet chat board.

"Thanks guys. I sign in to chat room whenever I'm going nuts. Even my friends don't get it. It's nice to chat with some of you. It helps me to understand and I relate to what some of you guys have been through. This BPD is a horrible thing to be diagnosed with and I do feel alone most of the time. Someone said cutting, but I don't cut. Instead I burn myself and feel empty most of the time, but burning helps sometimes. I have been in the hospital and in emergency rooms throughout my life and have isolated most of my family and friends. I really want to find some people who share my diagnosis. I'll be back soon."

In their article "The Virtual Cutting Edge: The Internet and Adolescent Self-Injury," researchers looked at the role that Internet message boards played in creating communities centered around self-injury. They found that in 1998 there was one message board, with nearly 100 members, that dealt with self-injury. By 2005 there were 168 boards with nearly 10,000 members. The boards provided anonymous forums yet places where people felt they were understood.

An important question is: What happens to the emotionally vulnerable child who is hooked into the Internet or an electronic lifestyle that provides little structure or consistency? Who do they turn to when they are having a hard time? Internet chat rooms are an impersonal substitute for friends and family. The Internet is not filled with people who understand the situation or know the total misery of a person asking for help. One of the major fears of people with BPD is abandonment. In a chat room, for example, it is easy to simply log off when the conversation gets too intense. This can trigger abandonment fears if a person with BPD is seeking help and the Internet peer logs off. One sixteen-year-old girl told me that whenever she would tell a support peer on a cutting board that more than cutting, she was thinking of suicide, the person would simply not respond or disconnect. She felt abandoned by someone she didn't really know. "I was cyber dumped," she said.

Cyberspace Society

Of course, the Internet does offer benefits, even to adolescents with BPD. Because chat rooms and blogs can, in theory, be a place where less socially skilled adolescents share experiences anonymously, they also can be a place for adolescents to practice social interaction.

Researchers have found that such online exchanges decrease social isolation among adolescents and helps them connect with peers as well as explore their identity. This helps to explain how the Internet can be a virtual peer support group for adolescents under stress, where they can express their feelings and exchange information about modes of coping.

In one study, the authors read 406 message boards to investigate how adolescents solicited and shared information related to self-injury. As previously mentioned, they noted that females aged twelve to twenty visited these bulletin boards the most.

The main reason for joining a chat board was to find social support and reprieve from isolation. But despite the community a chat board can provide, online boards can not only normalize but also encourage self-injurious and potentially lethal behaviors.

The authors found that the Internet message boards (which number in the hundreds) provided a powerful vehicle for bringing together self-injurious adolescents.

Self-injury is not the first behavior that has spread because of and through the media. In the 1980s, anorexia nervosa became widespread soon after it was exposed by the mass media as a problem. This was aggravated by portrayals of feminine beauty by increasingly emaciated fashion models.

Many of the adolescents we treat talk about how the Internet has provided a community that they needed. One told me that it was because she had posted that she was going to kill herself that night that she was saved from an overdose when a peer poster, "a sponsor" as it was explained, talked the girl into telling her mother that she had taken an overdose of pills. Some adolescents, though, say that the idea of hurting themselves would never have occurred to them had they not read about it online.

Besides using self-injury as a coping skill, many other online discussions are worrisome, including drug use, sexual behavior, purging of food, and normalizing suicidality. Another popular topic of adolescent discussion is frustration about parents who, they claim, don't understand them.

Although it is increasingly difficult to monitor and restrict Internet content and access, parents and caregivers need to know that it is a powerful source of information for adolescents. Some online resources are invaluable, but others are biased, misinformed, and potentially lethal. An adolescent needs a forum, whether in therapy or with a parent, to be able to question what she is reading or being told. For parents, the single most important ability to acquire is to be curious without being judgmental. It's a skill that requires tremendous practice.

Increased Competition and Achievement Expectations

Another component of contemporary life that contributes to the development of BPD is the pressure and stress put on students (by themselves and institutions of higher learning) to perform and compete. Many clinics report that they are seeing a marked increase in self-injury in response to stress.

When the pressure of stress becomes overwhelming, many emotionally intense kids turn to cutting themselves. The reasons they cut vary, but here is what kids say cutting does for them. "It makes me feel real, alive, feeling something. It makes me stop feeling numb." "I can control the pain, not like what people did to me." "It makes me feel pain on the outside instead of the inside." "It makes me feel calm." "I cut myself because I hate myself. I deserve the pain for being such a terrible, disgusting person."

Some kids who self-injure recognize that they do it because it makes their families pay attention. Some parents feel that their kids are cutting themselves to manipulate the parent into "caring" or into "feel guilty," but I have not seen kids who cut themselves for this reason.

A 2006 study by Cornell University researchers defined self-injurious behavior as "inflicting harm to one's body without the obvious intent of committing suicide, and which includes behaviors such as cutting, ripping or pulling skin or hair, biting, bruising and breaking one's own bones." Researchers surveyed 3,069 undergraduate and graduate university students, including 2,875 students at Ivy League schools. They found 17 percent of all students—20 percent of women and 14 percent of men—reported that they

A 1994 Japanese study compared the BPD symptoms of thirty-three American and nineteen Japanese female outpatients. The researchers found that patients with BPD in Japan presented with the same symptoms—including fear of abandonment, self-injury, hopelessness, and emptiness—as American BPD patients, which speaks to the universality of the syndrome and says that it is not a uniquely American phenomenon.

had self-injured. Self-injurers were more likely to be female and to have had eating disorders. The students further reported that the first incident of self-injury occurred between ages fourteen and fifteen. About half of the Ivy League students who harmed themselves said they'd experienced sexual, emotional, or physical abuse.

THE BOTTOM LINE

BPD is a multifaceted illness with many components that contribute to its formation. Studies present a variety of connections and possibilities. They implicate genes in impulsive aggression and mood instability, show abnormal neurotransmitter levels in BPD and abuse victims, and reveal certain brain regions to be either damaged or underdeveloped in BPD. Then there is the effect of poor parenting, disrupted attachment, sexual abuse and invalidation, and finally the effects of drug abuse and contemporary culture on the brain.

Thus BPD is not caused by a single factor. Rather the cumulative effects of the environment and genes acting upon the developing brain, its structures, and chemistry, come together to produce the clinical picture. The negative of all of this is that BPD develops over time and often takes years of treatment to heal. The positive is that there are multiple points at which to intervene, and these interventions will continue to improve over time.

CHAPTER SIX

The Research Behind BPD Adolescent Behavior and Thought Processes

RECENTLY RECEIVED THIS EMAIL from one of the patients who had been on our unit for a few weeks and was considering returning for longer treatment. The essence of her angst is clear.

"I want to tell you about my ex-boyfriend. I dunno, I call him like every week but he never answers. I guess it's really easy for me to call him because he doesn't answer. And I like giving to the relationship—it makes me feel good and it's easy 'cause all I have to do is make the call, you know? He has really lost it. I think I could have gotten really bad, Dr. A, but I have worked so hard on my own time. I have come to peace with myself, and if I hate myself in the moment, it's okay. A peace has come over me. And it's amazing. I like trying to find myself.

"My clothes had definitely gotten worse, but now they have all started to come more together. Basically I had the tight shirts and jeans I used to wear but I have some other now, more alternative, and some more loose stuff. I have tried to see the good in what seems to be bad to me. It's something like this: 'BLAM, whoa, there's a good in this!'

"I'm in Florida right now. I have done lots of relationship effectiveness with a lot of people. You would be proud. Things with my dad have been awesome. It's easy now to help the relationship grow. We're very much on our way.

"Okay and the bad thing in how I'm doing? Dr A, I think I'm a kleptomaniac. That's all I'm gonna say. And I know what you're gonna say. Anyways, I love it and I love free stuff but I know, I know, I know that I need to stop. But then, what will it be next?

"I still haven't really told [my ex-boyfriend] I love him and it's getting ridiculous. I know it would be good not to say anything because it makes things complicated but sometimes that's all I think and so I'm just silent. What do you think? Because the love is just really obvious on both our parts. He actually says that he hates me and I say I hate him back in love moments. Okay, I did tell him that I loved him when I was really upset and crying and he asked me why I felt so much. I told him it was because I loved him but he didn't say it back. I wasn't crushed—believe it or not— I was calm because I know he loves me. But what if he still doesn't? Maybe I will just say it casually—not when I'm emotional and all.

"Okay, enough of that. Also I had these high expectations of a Christmas present from him. I guess it's because I worked so hard on his (a gold pocket watch and chain) and it cost mega$$$ but he got me this blue necklace that I guess is kinda cool."

The girl is fifteen. Does she have BPD? In the email, the self-hatred, the interpersonal issues, the recklessness, shoplifting, the despair, the emotional dysregulation, the need for connection, and the searching for a defined self all seem clear. Is this simply normal adolescence? But what if this has persisted for more than a year, and her life is in a constant crisis— boyfriend to boyfriend, fight to fight, emotion to emotion?

How do we define her problem? What kind of help does she need? In an adult patient, her life might seem dysfunctional, but is it acceptable and normal for an adolescent to go through this?

There is very little specific research on adolescent borderline pathology and much more is needed. A lot of ideas in adolescent BPD are extrapolated from adult research. In this chapter we will look at significant adolescent BPD research. Because of the many changes in the concept of BPD in adolescents over the years, unless older ideas are still pertinent I will predominantly include research from 1995 onward.

ADOLESCENT BPD STUDIES

Clinicians often ask whether adolescents with BPD are any different from adults with BPD. There are some obvious differences. Many adolescents live with their parents, and the interpersonal conflicts lie there. For adults the interpersonal conflicts are often with intimate partners. Another difference is that because many adolescents don't drive or have much money, reckless driving episodes or wild spending sprees are less common than in adults.

In a 2002 study, Daniel Becker, M.D, and colleagues wanted to know whether BPD criteria could be applied to adolescents. They compared BPD symptoms in hospitalized adults to BPD symptoms in hospitalized adolescents and found that the BPD symptoms were very similar in both groups. The criterion that was best associated with BPD in the adolescents was abandonment fears. The least likely criteria to be associated with BPD was uncontrolled anger for the adolescents. The researchers concluded that in hospitalized patients, BPD and its symptoms appeared to be as frequent for adolescents as for adults.

RESEARCH ON COGNITIVE AND AFFECTIVE FEATURES OF BPD IN ADOLESCENTS

In a 1996 study, Aureen Pinto, Ph.D., and colleagues wanted to examine the mood symptoms and thinking in adolescents with BPD. They compared nineteen depressed female adolescents with BPD with twenty-one non-BPD depressed adolescents. They found that although both the BPD and non-BPD adolescents had levels of depression, anger, anxiety, hopelessness, self-hatred, and feeling as if they had no control, the adolescents with BPD had significantly poorer self-concept and emptiness than their non-BPD peers.

This finding is consistent with what we see on our unit. The depression in BPD adolescents is less about sleeping poorly or eating poorly than about feeling empty and self-loathing. And sadly, feeling empty and self-loathing often do not respond to anti-depressant medication.

RESEARCH ON CUTTING BEHAVIOR IN ADOLESCENTS WITH BPD

A mother in Texas sent this email:

"My thirteen-year-old daughter, I feel, is displaying signs of BPD. On one hand, I could easily dismiss her behavior as regular teenage behavior, on the other, what she is doing is causing her and us a lot of pain.

"Her relationships with her friends are so intense. She smothers them to the point that they hide from her; they now rarely initiate contact. She then becomes really upset because 'no one likes her.' If she makes a new friend, she insists that they instantly become her 'best friend' and insists they behave accordingly. Then, if they talk to other friends she is destroyed and feels incredibly betrayed.

"What I am most worried about is that whenever she gets upset about these friends, she cuts herself on her arms and legs. She is a beautiful girl, but now she has all these scars. She told us that she has been doing it for six months, but I only just found out when I walked into her room and she was doing it. I am very worried about her behavior with her friends but even more worried about her cutting."

Cutting is a very common symptoms in kids with emerging BPD. It can be very dramatic for parents, especially the first time that they see the scars and blood. Often this happens during times when the parent is already feeling a lot of fear, worry, anger, and agitation, which makes the whole experience understandably overwhelming. The "good" news is that cutting is almost never for the purpose of suicide, and as we have seen often is used to help the patient regulate or control her emotions.

In a 2006 study, Mary Zanarini, Ed.D., at McLean Hospital looked at when those BPD patients who self-injured or cut first did so. Of the 264 patients with BPD who self-injured, 86 patients reported first harming themselves at 12 years of age or younger. Eighty patients started self-mutilation as adolescents 13 to 17 years of age, and 98 patients started cutting as adults, 18 or older. Dr. Zanarini also found that patients with a childhood onset of self-injury reported more episodes of self-harm, a longer duration of self-harm, and a greater number of methods of self-harm than either those with an adolescent or adult onset to their self-mutilation. She concluded that a sizable minority of BPD patients first engage in self-harm as children, and that the course of this self-injury was particularly worrisome. These findings further underscore the need for early intervention in this group of patients.

Research on Sexual Abuse Among Adolescents with BPD

Many of the kids admitted to our unit with BPD or BPD traits have been sexually abused. This abuse comes in many different forms. Some patients describe less "invasive" forms of abuse where they were "fondled" by an older (usually) male perpetrator, and that this behavior left them feeling intense disgust and self-loathing. Others describe sexual abuse by a close relative that involved full penetration and terrifying fear and threat of harm if they ever disclosed the abuse.

What seems consistent with all the kids we see is that the more severe the abuse was, the more repeatedly it occurred, the closer the person was to the victim, and the more they were threatened to be "silent," the sicker they are. Some of the kids with profound abuse appear broken beyond any short-term hope and have little capacity to trust. Kids who experience this type of abuse most commonly suffer from PTSD, BPD, or both BPD and PTSD. Because so many kids with BPD have been abused, some parents suspect that their child might be keeping this a secret from them. In about 10 percent of adolescents with BPD admitted to our unit with no history of sexual abuse, such abuse will credibly be reported during their course of treatment.

Dr. Zanarini has studied the relationship between the severity of reported childhood sexual abuse, other forms of childhood abuse, childhood neglect, and the severity of BPD symptoms and overall impairment. In her group of 290 patients with BPD, she found that more than 50 percent of sexually abused patients with BPD reported being abused both in childhood and in adolescence, on at least a weekly basis, for a minimum of one year, by a parent or other person well known to the patient, and by two or more perpetrators. More than 50 percent also reported that their abuse involved at least one form of penetration and the use of force or violence. Consistent with what we see clinically, she has found that the worse the abuse, the worse the BPD symptoms and the worse the overall functioning.

The research shows that despite the fact the sexual abuse is neither necessary nor sufficient to cause BPD, it can certainly make the outcome of BPD much worse for BPD patients that have experienced such abuse.

RESEARCH ON CHILD MALTREATMENT, ATTENTION PROBLEMS, AND OTHER PRECURSORS TO BPD

Sexual abuse is a particularly destructive form of maltreatment; however, many adolescents with BPD report feeling neglected and emotionally abused by their caregivers. These too, can have a profound impact on developing personality.

In a 2005 study, Fred Rogosch, Ph.D., and colleagues wanted to look at the elements in children's lives that predisposed them to developing BPD later in life. In particular, they examined the effect of maltreatment such as physical and emotional abuse. They noted that maltreated children showed behavioral problems similar to kids diagnosed with BPD. These problems include increased suicidality, relationship problems, temperament, personality differences, and problems with self-image. Not surprisingly, they found that maltreated kids had many BPD symptoms, and that those who had attentional problems such as ADHD, were at high risk for developing BPD.

Another factor increasing the chance of BPD is family breakdown and parental criminality. The interplay of biology and environment is always present in BPD. Of particular tragedy is that research has shown that 10 percent of severely maltreated children as young as seven or eight have suicidal thoughts. To be tormented with such thoughts is one thing, but for an eight-year-old to be so plagued is almost unimaginable.

Research on the Progression of BPD in Adolescents

Many people have argued for years that symptoms of BPD in adolescents are simply extreme forms of normal adolescent behavior that will eventually disappear as the child ages. However, in an interesting study, researchers looked to see whether traits of personality disorders went away or persisted in adolescents. They initially assessed 101 fifteen- to eighteen-year-olds. Ninety-seven of those participants were re-interviewed, face-to-face, two years after their initial assessment. Of those who had a personality disorder diagnosis at first interview, 74 percent still had a personality disorder two years later. Even more striking was that in those study participants who had received inpatient care during the two-year period, 100 percent of those hospitalized still met criteria for a personality disorder. The conclusion is that a personality disorder in adolescence will generally persist into adulthood.

A 2001 study similarly found that borderline and other personality disorder symptoms in 407 adolescents remained across an eight-year interval from early adolescence to early adulthood.

Researchers in 2005 examined the continuity between emotional disorders (such as depression) and disruptive behavior disorders (such as ADHD) in adolescence and personality disorders in adulthood. They found that adolescents with disruptive behavior disorders were as likely to have personality disorders in adulthood as adolescents with emotional disorders. Of note was that adolescents with disruptive behaviors disorders, especially females, were significantly more likely to have BPD than adolescents with emotional disorders. Disruptive behavior disorders in adolescent males predicted antisocial personality disorder in men. (Antisocial personality disorder includes symptoms such as failure to conform to social norms with respect to lawful behaviors, deceit, or reckless disregard for the safety of others.)

RESEARCH ON CLINICAL FEATURES OF ADOLESCENTS WITH BPD WHO ATTEMPT SUICIDE

A 1981 study looked at the clinical characteristics of twenty-two teenagers with BPD who had attempted suicide. The essential pattern of BPD in these teenagers was a persistent instability in interpersonal relations, mood, behavior, and self-image. The most prominent characteristics associated with suicide attempts by these adolescents were a tendency to react severely to loss, poorly controlled anger, and self-defeating impulsivity. These findings in 1981 are consistent with what we see clinically today.

A 2006 study found that adolescent females with bulimia—an eating disorder characterized by binge eating and then induced vomiting or abusing laxatives—who made suicide attempts were more likely to suffer from depression and BPD than patients with bulimia who were not suicidal. The suicidal group was also more likely to have been exposed to significant physical and sexual violence in their childhood. As adults, they either lived alone or were more dissatisfied with their partnerships. They also had increased substance abuse, physical symptoms, and poor job performance, which often preceded their suicide attempts.

RESEARCH ON GENDER DIFFERENCES AND SUBTYPES IN ADOLESCENTS WITH BPD

Statistics show that women suffer from BPD at a rate of three to one over men. This ratio is consistent with what we see on our unit at McLean Hospital. In addition to the difference in numbers, there are some key differences between girls and boys who appear for treatment.

In a 1996 study, researchers wanted to look at the gender differences in personality disorders in adolescent psychiatric inpatients. They found that females were significantly more likely than males to meet the criteria for BPD and that narcissistic personality disorder was diagnosed only in males.

A 2005 study looked at the personality features of adolescent girls and boys with BPD. They found that the symptoms of BPD in adolescent girls were similar to those of adults. Adolescent boys meeting BPD criteria, however, were more aggressive, disruptive, and antisocial. This latter finding is important because some clinicians find these behaviors less "appealing" to treat than depression and self-loathing—thus making it more difficult to find good care for adolescent boys with BPD.

RESEARCH ON ADOLESCENT INPATIENTS WITH BPD COMPARED TO THEIR ADULT COUNTERPARTS

Adolescents who are hospitalized with BPD have similar symptoms to BPD adults who are hospitalized—though there are important differences.

A 2006 study found more current self-mutilation in adolescents but more alcohol abuse in adults. Researchers also found that the longer adolescents with BPD had been hospitalized, the more anti-psychotic medications they had been on. For adults, the longer they had been hospitalized, the more antidepressant and anti-anxiety medications they had been on.

Again we see that both groups are similar but the use of antipsychotic medications in adolescents concerns me given the potential side effects. The side effects of antipsychotic medication that are particularly bothersome are akathisia (which is characterized by restlessness and difficulty sitting still and an uncomfortable feeling of agitation) and tardive dyskinesia (which is a neurological syndrome in which the person has involuntary muscle movements, usually in the tongue, mouth, lips, trunk, or in the extremities, such as the hands or fingers).

However, one of the biggest concerns is that these medications can induce significant weight gain. This in turn may increase the risk of

Given the statistic that 10 percent of people with BPD commit suicide, the fear of a child killing himself or herself keeps many parents up at night. So what should parents do?

All adolescents with depression should be assessed immediately for suicidality. If parents are told that they can get an appointment in a month, they should consider an evaluation in an emergency room. Adolescents often are relieved that someone is worried, so although it may be a difficult topic to discuss, the discussion is essential.

Most adolescents feel that they cannot talk to their parents because their parents won't understand. Acknowledging that you might not understand is important but also that you will try your best to understand is critical.

The risk of suicidality is increased by many behaviors, and if these behaviors persist, the chance of suicidality increases. The following behaviors should make a parent or clinician worry, especially if the behaviors persist:

- Crying spells
- Discouragement
- Irritability

- A sense of emptiness and meaninglessness
- Negative expectations of self and the environment
- Low self-esteem
- Isolation
- A feeling of helplessness
- Markedly diminished interest or pleasure in most activities
- Significant weight and/or sleep changes
- Fatigue, loss of energy, or sluggishness
- Feelings of worthlessness
- Loss of concentration

It is also common for an adolescent with serious depression to complain of physical symptoms. Complaints such as abdominal pain, chest pain, and headaches could also be concerning.

Behavioral problems are also common for adolescents with serious depression. They include the following:

- Truancy
- Worsening academic performance
- Running away from home
- Defiance of authorities
- Self-destructive behavior
- Vandalism

- Alcohol and other drug abuse
- Sexual acting out
- Delinquency

Adolescents with behavior problems sometimes believe that they have disappointed their parents and family and consider suicide to be their only option.

Other than getting immediate help, parents or caretakers can reduce the risk of suicide by removing access to obviously lethal means. Lock up or remove firearms and medications from the house to make it less possible that a child will impulsively pull a trigger or down a bottle of pills.

Ideally, with proper therapy and treatment, suicide as an option for solving life's problems is taken off the table.

obesity, diabetes, and high cholesterol, and the Federal Drug Administration has told makers of the drugs to include these risks in product labels. Even if the other side effects take longer to develop or do not develop at all, weight gain in adolescent is troubling, especially as many struggle with body image issues.

RESEARCH ON NON-SUICIDAL SELF-INJURY AMONG ADOLESCENTS WITH BPD

A 2006 research study published in *Psychiatry Research* examined the diagnoses of adolescents who had non-suicidal self-injury (NSSI). NSSI is any intentional self-injurious behavior, which is not intended as a way to suicide, so cutting, for instance, would be NSSI.

Of the eighty-nine adolescents in the study who had engaged in NSSI in the previous year, seventy-eight met criteria for an Axis I diagnosis (such as major depression), including fifty-three who met criteria for substance abuse disorders. Sixty of the adolescents also met criteria for a personality disorder. Sixty-two adolescents reported at least one previous suicide attempt while forty-nine had made multiple attempts. Adolescents were more likely to make a suicide attempt if they had a long history of NSSI, if they used a greater number of methods (cutting, burning, branding, etc.), and if they felt little or no physical pain during NSSI.

The bottom line is that NSSI can occur with many psychiatric disorders. Even though it is in no way itself a suicidal behavior, NSSI is associated with a high risk of suicide attempts the longer it continues.

RESEARCH ON BPD MOTHERS AND THEIR BABIES

A 2003 study published in the *British Journal of Psychiatry* looked at mother-infant relations when the mothers had BPD. The researchers watched mothers with BPD interacting with their two-month-old infants. They found that the mothers with BPD were more intrusive with their children without being sensitive to their needs. When the mothers with BPD were asked to have expressionless faces, their infants spent more time than babies with mothers without BPD looking away and with dazed looks. This showed that even at this age the babies were having trouble regulating their stress!

Children of mothers who have BPD have higher levels of harm-avoiding behaviors (such as a fear to explore the world, high anxiety, or refusal to try something new) and tend to perceive their mothers as being overly protective. These children show more emotional and behavioral problems and feel they have low self-esteem. Because children of mothers with BPD are at greater risk of emotional and behavioral problems, early treatment of these children might prevent them from developing severe mental health issues in the future.

PSYCHOLOGICAL STUDIES

We have already reported on imaging studies that have found abnormalities in the frontal lobes and temporal lobes of patients with BPD. In 2004, Boston University researchers gave a series of neuropsychological tests to adolescents with BPD and found that the psychological tests confirmed the imaging studies in that these adolescents had deficits consistent with frontal lobe problems.

Of interest is that the researchers then gave the tests to university students who were not diagnosed with BPD and found that the university students who had poor frontal lobe testing patterns also had more features of BPD than those who tested normally.

Brain Imaging Studies

Even though a few studies have looked at the adult BPD brain, there have been very few in adolescents with BPD. Australian researchers conducted a brain scan study in adolescents with BPD. They found that as in adult studies, adolescents with BPD had less developed and smaller frontal lobes.

Another study—this time of adult women with BPD—showed that those with BPD had smaller hippocampi (the part of the brain that stores memory of persons, places, and things). The researchers felt that this could possibly explain the memory problems people with BPD can experience.

Of great importance is that the more severely these adult women with BPD had been abused in childhood, the smaller the hippocampus, and also the greater the memory loss. This shows once again that brain development and environment are intimately intertwined when it comes to BPD.

(One twenty-three-year-old patient with BPD who recognized that she had BPD symptoms when she was fourteen told me during an interview "I seem to have a lasting memory loss. It is as if there is only today, a today not connected to yesterday, no continuity, only glimpses of the past. I remember very little about myself as a child. I remember though that I had powerful emotions.")

Electroencephalography (EEG)

An EEG is a diagnostic test that measures the electrical activity of the brain using highly sensitive recording equipment attached to the scalp by fine electrodes. Researchers have looked at the EEGs of girls ages fourteen to nineteen and found that girls with BPD had less mature brains than those without it. Some people have argued that one of the reasons BPD seems to diminish over time is that is that the brain continues to mature and when the maturation process eventually catches up, patients experience fewer problems with executive functions like decision-making.

A FINAL WORD ON ADOLESCENT RESEARCH

Adolescent BPD studies are few, and certainly not enough to fill a book, but the number of studies is increasing as researchers recognize the importance of early life and the developmental factors involved in the formation of BPD.

In the next few years, we hope to develop a clear diagnostic questionnaire as a critical tool for identifying adolescents with BPD. In the future, however, genetics, body chemistry, and neuroimaging should be enough together with the child's history to be definitive about the diagnosis. But all of this is for little if it does not ultimately help guide treatment, and in this arena it looks as if we are finally making tremendous inroads, which we'll talk about later in this book.

CHAPTER SEVEN

What to Do When BPD Isn't Your Child's Only Psychiatric Disorder

C OMORBIDITIES ARE THE PSYCHIATRIC conditions that co-occur with BPD, and research has found that they are common in people with the disorder.

These conditions, which include mood disorders, substance abuse-related problems, eating disorders (notably bulimia), post-traumatic stress disorder (PTSD), anxiety, dissociative identity disorder, and attention deficit hyperactivity disorder (ADHD), can complicate both diagnosis and treatment. Depression is particularly common in patients with BPD.

It is not only depression, however, that complicates the course of BPD. On our unit, most of the kids with BPD who appear after multiple failed previous hospitalizations and treatments do not arrive with a BPD diagnosis. Most come in with a diagnosis of depression (because they have been suicidal in the past), bipolar disorder (because they have had episodes of rage and anger alternating with hopelessness), anxiety, ADHD (because they are impulsive), and substance abuse disorders.

Here is what the research shows regarding other co-occurring conditions. As a reminder, in an earlier chapter we noted that the *Diagnostic and Statistical Manual of Mental Disorders-IV* (*DSM-IV*) (the book used by clinicians to diagnose psychiatric illness) defined Axis I as "clinical disorders, including major mental disorders, as well as developmental and learning disorders." Axis II is reserved for the personality disorders, although in my opinion, if BPD is not a major mental health disorder, then I am not sure what is.

DISORDERS THAT CO-OCCUR WITH BPD

In a 2004 study, researchers looked at the co-occurrence of psychiatric disorders among patients with BPD older than sixteen. They interviewed the patients about their axis I disorders at two-year, four-year, and six-year follow-up periods, and found that patients with BPD experienced high rates of mood and anxiety disorders.

In patients whose BPD remitted over time (that is, former BPD patients who no longer had symptoms of BPD), they experienced a substantial decline in all axis I disorders, but those whose BPD symptoms did not improve over time reported ongoing symptoms of axis I disorders.

Importantly, the BPD symptoms of patients who did not abuse substances were far more likely to go into remission than patients who had substance abuse problems.

Patients with ongoing substance abuse problems were much less likely to get better than those who stopped using illegal substances or stopped drinking. This finding makes clinical sense because abusing alcohol and/or drugs can lead to worsening depression, increasing paranoia and impulsivity, worsening relationships, greater difficulty in retaining learning, less compliance with therapy, and potentially dangerous interactions with medications.

Given the finding of how much substance abuse affects the clinical outcomes in BPD, it makes sense to look at this co-occurring condition first.

Substance Abuse and BPD

One of the kids with BPD who had been with us for months had finally turned the corner, started doing well, got along with her parents, graduated from high school, and got a small job. Six months after her discharge her mother emailed me asking for help as the now eighteen-year-old had fallen back into a destructive pattern of marijuana abuse.

"Amy was largely absent most of the week, preferring to spend several nights with her friends. When she was here, she was civil, mostly distant, and nothing spontaneous. She initiated no conversations. It is what I would consider to be like living in a demilitarized zone. She is increasingly disheveled. I am quite concerned that the tide of depression is rising rapidly. Avoidance behavior has abounded this weekend. Finally we invited her to the dinner table tonight. She was reluctant to engage, many questions from us, monosyllabic grunts from Amy, and she seemed ready to snap at any moment.

"Unfortunate circumstances occurred in Amy's transportation world. The family car, which she has shared with us for the last few months, is now in the shop and will be for quite a while, due to major undercarriage damage, which occurred while she was driving it (although she can't seem to remember where, when, or how this occurred). No apologies, no remorse, no curiosity about how and when it's going to be fixed. I am wondering if she is even able, at this point, to think more than a day in advance. [This is] symptomatic of how she appears to be living most facets of her life.

"Anyway, at dinner, we told her that we absolutely want her at home along with specific praise for the progress she has made these last six months. All we wanted to know is what she is going to do after she finishes her job at the local bookstore. She only makes $8.50 an hour, yet she wants to move out and get a car. Stonewalled. None of our business, the usual. Her dad kept trying from a number of different tacks. We kept our cool, stayed in validation mode, but the longer this went on, the tougher it became for her.

"There exists such a wide semantic gap between us. Amy's version: We are kicking her out because she won't give up smoking dope. Our version: Amy is welcome to live here within the terms of the contract that we all agreed to. That includes no drugs. This is a marijuana-free household. Her choice."

Almost every adolescent we see at McLean Hospital has used drugs, and drug experimentation is certainly developmentally normal for adolescents. Among the adolescents with BPD, drug use ranges from the rare kid who has never used to those for whom drug use is potentially lethal. Most typically is the adolescent with BPD who uses recreational alcohol and marijuana. Parents often see how the drug use affects their child's ability to function, even if it is recreational. It affects relationships, academic performance, and work opportunities.

Adolescents who appear at our unit for substance abuse treatment are often addicted. BPD adolescents, too, become addicted but the meaning behind their drug use can differ from other teens in that it is a way to self-medicate, treat emptiness, induce numbing, and remove pain—rather than for the pure pleasure effects of the drugs.

Research shows that substance use disorders are common among patients with BPD. Studies put the number at anywhere from 14 to 56 percent in BPD patients. Given the finding that substance abuse disorders significantly affect the outcome of BPD, substance abuse treatment should be a main focus of treatment. Although treatment of substance abusing BPD patients has historically not been optimistic, a recent study showed that dialectical behavior therapy (DBT) was more effective for women with BPD and opioid dependence than a regular 12-step program.

The type of drug use has significant consequences on global functioning. For example, most non-substance-using BPD patients graduate from high school, whereas only half of stimulant abusers graduate. Prostitution and promiscuity is also correlated with substance abuse.

In a 2007 study, Eunice Chen, Ph.D., and colleagues looked at the rates of sexually transmitted diseases (STDs) in women with BPD and substance abuse problems. They found that women with BPD who abused substances appeared to be particularly at high risk for STDs, reporting significantly more STDs than women with BPD who did not abuse substances. Gonorrhea, trichomonas, and human papillomavirus were of significant concern in substance abusing patients with BPD. The risk was made even worse by poverty, prostitution in the past year, recent unprotected sex with two or more partners, and more than twenty lifetime partners.

A 2005 study by Dawn Thatcher, Ph.D., and colleagues looked at adolescent alcohol use and other adolescent characteristics as predictors of adult BPD symptoms. They found that in some adolescents who abused alcohol, the alcohol abuse made it easier for child physical and/or sexual abuse to occur and was associated with the development of adult BPD.

In a 2006 study, researchers compared adolescents with BPD who abuse alcohol with adolescents with BPD who didn't. The researchers found that those who abused alcohol were more impulsive than those who don't. Further, adolescents with BPD who also abused alcohol would go on to have more lifetime suicide attempts that were potentially more lethal than the adolescents with BPD who did not abuse alcohol.

Drug abuse is a horrible co-occurring condition to have with BPD. It can ruin relationships, academic success, physical health, mental health, and the eventual hope that BPD will go into remission. Because of this, substance abuse treatment should be prescribed along with other therapies in substance using BPD adolescents.

Major Depression and BPD

Depression, like substance abuse, is common in adolescents with BPD. Many clinicians like the simplicity of diagnosing depression because it is a psychiatric condition that is fairly easy to treat with medication and therapy, readily accepted by insurance companies when seeking reimbursement, easy to explain to parents and kids, and does not carry with it the stigma that the person is going to be difficult to treat.

Many clinicians will hide behind the diagnosis of depression to get approval for treatment of a suicidal adolescent with BPD. That's because saying that the person has BPD will often be met with the statement, "That's a chronic condition and we don't cover chronic conditions."

As depression does occur in adolescents with BPD, careful screening using established assessment techniques for depression is essential in establishing whether an adolescent has this co-occurring condition.

> *She still seems preoccupied. She is not as motivated about school as she was a few weeks ago, and she still has not written her psych paper. She hasn't done much with friends either. She's had more trouble sleeping at night. Sometimes she sleeps during the daytime.*
>
> —EMAIL FROM A MOTHER OF A FIFTEEN-YEAR-OLD WITH BPD, CO-OCCURING DEPRESSION, AND ONGOING SUICIDALITY

Following was the email from a mother of a fifteen-year-old with BPD, co-occurring depression, and ongoing suicidality. She had until recently been a straight A student and had realistic hopes of attending an Ivy League college. The email was prompted after yet another failed medication trial.

"She still seems preoccupied. She is not as motivated about school as she was a few weeks ago, and she still has not written her psych paper. She hasn't done much with friends either. She's had more trouble sleeping at night. Sometimes she sleeps during the daytime. The sleep issue appears to have worsened when Luvox [an antidepressant drug used to treat a number of conditions, including depression] was started—she thinks that the Luvox is sedating. She still looks depressed and is becoming less energetic."

This email is consistent with co-occurring depression. The teen has many classic symptoms of depression, including sleep problems, motivation problems, isolation, and loss of energy.

SUICIDE AND BPD

One of the major reasons the treatment of BPD is so critical is because of the high suicide rate. Although rates of suicide in BPD may finally be coming down as more comprehensive treatment approaches are provided, traditionally we know that about 90 percent of patients with BPD will make at least one suicide attempt and about 10 percent will succeed in killing themselves.

A 1997 study by Beth Brodsky, Ph.D., and colleagues found that impulsivity in patients with BPD is associated with a higher number of previous suicide attempts. They also found that a history of childhood abuse correlated significantly with number of lifetime suicide attempts. At McLean, we find that impulsivity tends to be high in the adolescents whom we treat, and many of them have histories of childhood abuse, which puts these kids at high risk for suicide, and again speaks to the need for early intervention, especially to address the symptom of impulsivity.

In a 2000 study, researchers found that co-occurring BPD and major depression increased the number and seriousness of suicide attempts, and that hopelessness and impulsive aggression increased the risk of suicidal behavior in both patients with BPD and in patients with major depression.

In a 2005 study, researchers found that the severity of BPD was associated with self-mutilating behaviors and that co-occurring depression and BPD had a more serious and impairing condition than co-occurring depression and other personality disorders.

In a 2007 study, researchers interviewed 188 people who had attempted suicide and had gone to their local emergency departments for help. The researchers found that people with BPD who attempted suicide had a greater severity of depression, hopelessness, suicidal thinking, and past suicide attempts, and had poorer social problem-solving skills than those without a BPD diagnosis. These findings again underscore the seriousness of BPD and that patients diagnosed with BPD will attempt suicide.

PTSD AND BPD

PTSD is a common but not universal co-occurring disorder among borderline patients. More than 55 percent of patients with BPD also meet criteria for PTSD. Although trauma can be due to a number of events, the kids we see who also have PTSD have most commonly experienced physical or sexual assault or abuse, family and domestic violence, or a life-threatening medical illness, or been involved in severe car accidents.

The symptoms of PTSD we commonly see in adolescents with BPD with a history of trauma include the following:

- Disturbing memories or flashbacks of the trauma
- Repeated nightmares, difficulty sleeping, or dreams of death
- Pessimism about their future lives
- Avoidance of doing anything, being somewhere, or with someone who will remind them of the trauma
- Fear of re-experiencing traumatic anxiety
- Emotional numbness, in which they seem to have no feelings
- Physical symptoms, such as stomachaches and headaches
- Feeling constantly on guard, nervous, and jumpy

The high degree of co-occurrence between BPD and PTSD is not unexpected, given that many studies have found that borderline patients often report traumatic childhood experiences. But what's also interesting is the finding that a substantial number of abused and traumatized BPD patients do *not* suffer from PTSD. This finding also puts into question older thinking that used to consider BPD as simply a chronic form of PTSD. Nevertheless, given the more than 50 percent co-occurrence, PTSD needs to be assessed for and treated when present.

DISSOCIATION AND HYPERAROUSAL

An important symptom in many patients with BPD, post-traumatic stress disorder (PTSD), and other disorders is dissociation. Dissociation is also found in people who have been abused or traumatized.

Dissociation is a psychological state in which certain thoughts, emotions, sensations, or memories are separated from the rest of a person's experience. During a dissociative episode, these thoughts, emotions, and memories are not associated with other current information as they normally would be.

Dissociation serves to create a temporary mental escape from the fear and pain of a traumatic recollection. At times, it may lead to a complete loss of memory of the traumatic event.

Researchers believe that dissociation occurs when the amygdala, a small, almond-shaped structure within the limbic system shuts down. The amygdala plays an important part in learning, social language, detecting fear, and emotional processing. When the amyg-dala shuts down, a person dissociates. By shutting down, the person can no longer effectively process emotions and so appears to have disconnected from them.

But at times, the exact opposite can occur—the amygdala works overtime. This is known as hyperarousal. When this happens, a person becomes emotionally moody or experiences rapid ups and downs. At this time, you might also see a startle response, or startle reflex. This is the response of the body to a sudden unexpected stimulus, such as a flash of light, a loud noise, or a quick movement. The reaction includes physical movement away from the stimulus, a tightening of the muscles of the arms and legs, skin changes, and blinking. It also includes blood pressure and heart rate increases and breathing changes.

Both dissociation and hyperarousal are common in people with BPD, and when a startle reflex is also present, it strongly indicates that the person has undergone trauma and is also suffering from PTSD.

Bipolar Disorder and BPD

The relationship between BPD and bipolar disorder, formerly called manic depression, has been examined ever since BPD was added to the *DSM-IV* in 1980.

Studies that used strict *DSM-IV* definitions of bipolar disorder have found that about 13 percent of patients with BPD also have bipolar disorder. Studies that used looser definitions—such as "mood swings"—or included patients who had family histories of bipolar disorder show that 80 percent of patients with BPD also have bipolar disorder. If all the studies that have looked at the co-occurrence of BPD and bipolar are averaged out, it seems about 40 percent of patients with BPD also have bipolar disorder.

It can be especially tricky to treat people with both BPD and bipolar disorder. This is because anti-depressants are frequently used in the treatment of BPD. If the person also has bipolar disorder, antidepressant treatment could potentially make the patient manic.

Some clinicians have asked whether BPD is a type of bipolar disorder. Studies show that typical bipolar medication treatments do not work for BPD patients, that even when bipolar symptoms are successfully treated in BPD patients, many of the BPD symptoms remain, and that patients with bipolar also have other types of personality disorders, not only BPD. These findings have led to the conclusion that BPD is its own entity and not a type of bipolar disorder.

ADHD and BPD

A 2002 study that looked at the relationship of childhood ADHD and BPD concluded that there was a strong association between the two conditions. The impulsive, erratic, intense temperament of ADHD children, and their low self-esteem, interpersonal problems, and moodiness are characteristics shared with BPD.

BPD CRITERIA AND AXIS I DISORDERS

In a 2006 study, researchers found that four adolescent BPD "symptom groups" were connected with Axis I disorders.

- Researchers linked the first group, which expressed suicidal threats or gestures and emptiness or boredom, with depression and alcohol use disorders.
- They associated the second group, which displayed affective instability, uncontrolled anger, and identity disturbances, with anxiety disorders and oppositional defiant disorder.
- They associated the third group, which experienced unstable relationships and abandonment fears, with anxiety disorders.
- They connected the fourth group, which showed impulsiveness and identity disturbances, with conduct and substance use disorders.

These associations are important as they clue the clinician to look for co-occurring disorders and can help focus treatment.

Consider this email from a mother in New Mexico who wondered about the similarities between the two conditions.

"My daughter, Krissy who is fifteen, began her troubling behavior when she was an infant. She is the youngest of four kids. She was the most colicky and fussy and yelled more than the others. The three others are doing well. Nothing ever changed in our family during her early life. My husband is still at his same job and until very recently we have been happily married for twenty-three years.

"When she was very young, Krissy would get so upset that she would hold her breath when she was crying. She would writhe her body, holding her breath, and her lips would turn blue. Eventually she would start to breathe again. It scared the heck out of me and I would hold her and try to soothe her but that did not seem to work when she was in that state.

"My neighbor is a psychologist and he said that even at eighteen months she was manipulating me for attention. He suggested I ignore her. I couldn't do that to a child so young. I ask myself if I did wrong in not listening to him. She was always needy and wanting my attention. She was very impulsive and I had her evaluated at age eight. The psychiatrist said she had ADHD and put her on Ritalin, which seemed to work for a few years, but she was always seeking thrills. We tried Adderall, Wellbutrin, Concerta, and Strattera. They all seemed to help with her school, but not with impulsivity and her being hyper. The doctors said that she would grow out of her ADHD and be like our other kids.

"Her early adolescence has been a nightmare for me. Here is where my husband and I started to argue after twenty-three years of an essentially conflict-free marriage! Krissy was extremely materialistic during this time. She would talk my husband into buying things she wanted. Of course, we didn't get these things for the other kids. They never complained! I overheard her telling her cousin how easily she could manipulate her dad.

"We were referred to a new psychiatrist because the so-called ADHD did not really get better, and he suggested she had BPD.

"I agree with the BPD diagnosis, but ADHD also seems accurate. Are they similar?"

The connection between ADHD and BPD can have several explanations. First, some researchers have considered that the two conditions are simply variations of one another. Second, ADHD in some children can be so disruptive that caregivers can sometimes resort to abusive or variable responses to this behavior. Children do not learn what responses to expect from their parents, or they learn that they will be punished for behavior that they cannot truly control. This caregiver behavior in turn results in an increased risk for BPD in the child. Third, both conditions may have some other common causative factor, for instance, both conditions have been shown to have significant deficits in the frontal lobe of the brain and executive function as well as impulse control.

An interesting point is that whereas BPD is more often diagnosed in females by a ratio of 3:1 over males, the opposite is true for ADHD. Joseph Biederman, M.D., professor of psychiatry at Massachusetts General Hospital, has said about ADHD in females: "In clinical life (kids who are seen in treatment), the ratio of males to females is 10 to 1. In real life, it's maybe 2 to 1." This means that we are missing the opportunity to treat too many girls with ADHD. One of the reasons some researchers have postulated why we are missing these girls is that boys with ADHD engage in more rule-breaking and behaviors more likely to get noticed by teachers and others than girls with the disorder do.

ADHD may be one of the pathways leading to BPD, particularly in girls, so clinicians need to keep in mind this possibility when assessing and treating ADHD patients, particularly if they are female.

EATING DISORDERS AND BPD

How often personality disorders occur among those with eating disorders is a matter of great debate. Some clinicians feel that many eating disordered patients have personality disorders, whereas many clinicians who treat the eating disordered population feel that when the eating disorder resolves so do any personality disorder features.

In 2005, Randy Sansone, M.D., and colleagues reviewed all of the studies on eating disorders and personality disorders. They found that BPD is the most common personality disorder in binge-eating/purging type anorexia nervosa and in bulimia nervosa, as well. Although I have not spent a lot of time working with eating disordered adolescents, I have consulted on these adolescents on occasion. I find that most of them do not have symptoms of personality disorders. Certainly if the patient with BPD features has been referred for an eating disorder, the eating disorder must be the focus of treatment, but as the patient improves, introducing a skills-based therapy such as dialectical behavior therapy (DBT) can help to provide a more comprehensive treatment.

CO-OCCURING CONDITIONS REQUIRE TREATMENT, TOO

BPD clearly co-occurs with other psychiatric conditions. This makes the treatment all the more difficult because it involves considering these other conditions in decision-making.

Are medications necessary if there is a mood disorder? Should certain drugs be used if there is substance abuse? Does the patient have medical complications of an eating disorder? What happens in family therapy if incest has led to PTSD? These are a few of the many possible questions that must be addressed if the adolescent with BPD is to be accurately diagnosed and treated.

CHAPTER EIGHT

The Challenge of Finding Treatment

TWO IMPORTANT QUESTIONS come up over and over again for parents desperate for help with their adolescents with BPD. The first is where and how to find appropriate treatment, especially when many clinics and therapists are not willing to consider treating such kids. The second is what parents should do when their children refuse to go to therapy or to get help.

This email from a parent in crisis speaks to both needs.

"We live in St. Louis, MO. Unfortunately lots of programs say they can help, but if the patient is suicidal or self-injurious, they say that they cannot help. But that is my fifteen-year-old daughter's actual problem, that she is suicidal, so these clinics cannot really help. My daughter says she doesn't need therapy or drugs to get better. She has no respect for our authority and will not conform to rules of the house. She says that she just doesn't want to live with us and proposes living with her friends. She is not really trying in school. She threatens us by bullying and screaming if we confront her on her lack of responsibility for her actions and shows no interest in doing her minimal chores. No consequence will make her do them either. We have tried it all.

"Because she is under eighteen, she hasn't been diagnosed per se, but her counselors and psychiatrist believe she has borderline personality disorder. Everything we have read about BPD describes her to a T. She also cuts herself, has low self-esteem, and is belligerent. Despite knowing that she has a mental illness, it makes it no easier to live with her. I worry about her younger brother and we try to do things outside the house so that he won't be exposed to the behavior. We don't trust her to be home alone, and so we have no down time.

"If patients under eighteen don't want to be treated, what are we parents supposed to do? Wait for her to kill us or someone else, or even just harm us? The system seems messed up. She talks about death a lot. If we send her to a wilderness program, her suicidal thoughts would make her ineligible, and she might even try it. BPDs have 10 percent suicidal success rate according to the National Institutes of Health. What are we to do?"

HOW TO FIND TREATMENT

A first step for families may be to go to their pediatricians. Pediatricians are often the first health-care professionals to see mental health problems. Generally when a pediatrician feels that he or she cannot deal with a problem, a child psychiatrist, child psychologist, or other therapist is called in. If parents think their children have BPD, asking their pediatricians for a referral to a child mental health expert is recommended.

Even within the child mental health field not many clinicians are comfortable either making the diagnosis of BPD or working with kids with the disorder. Clinicians who have expertise in dialectical behavior therapy (DBT), BPD, post-traumatic stress disorder (PTSD), and self-injury are generally more comfortable working with adolescents with BPD. It's true, however, that many parents are neither believed nor have medical resources in their geographical location to deal with such kids.

These families sometimes uproot their lives (by, for instance, moving across the country) to get help for their kids.

Consider this email, which speaks to the frustrations of parents seeking help for their children with BPD or suspected BPD.

"We are struggling with what to do with our sixteen-year-old. We think she has BPD, but we want to rule it in or rule it out if she has it. Our first thought was to get her into intensive therapy, so we went to our hospital for a consult. All they did was to pass her along to a doctor who administers her meds for ADD, who in turn passes us onto another list of therapists for her to see. We are so frustrated. All we want is to have her fully evaluated and get help for whatever is wrong with her. We don't feel that we have the expertise to help us."

In the resources section, I have included clinics and residential treatment facilities that work with kids with self-injury and BPD. Most of these clinics point out that they provide DBT for adolescents, which means that they have committed themselves to working with these high-risk kids. Unfortunately these resources are few and not very convenient geographically for everyone.

Hopefully, by the time this book is in print, more resources will be available, and an Internet search that includes words such as the adolescent's hometown, DBT, borderline, mental health, or self-injury, might provide resources not on my list.

If that still does not work, contact the National Alliance for the Mentally Ill (NAMI) at www.nami.org. Many towns have local offices of this national organization. NAMI is the largest consumer-driven mental health advocacy group in the nation, which in June 2006 moved to recognize BPD on its list of "priority populations," which means that NAMI recognizes that BPD is the serious condition that it is, and it has included BPD as a focus diagnosis. If even this does not help, strongly advocate that your local mental health clinic consider becoming familiar and comfortable with BPD by attending DBT training. This might not immediately help an adolescent in distress, but it may get the clinic to consider the possibility.

Sometimes, even if a local clinic does have clinicians who work with adolescents with BPD, outpatient services are not enough, and the child needs more intensive treatment. Some parents have resorted to paying for an expensive residential treatment center out of the adolescent's college money, arguing that the college money will be of little use if the teen kills himself. Some parents have made effective pleas to their state departments of mental health, social work, or youth services to have the state help foot the bill for the cost of care for this serious and chronic mental health issue. In one case a parent had successfully argued that because her child's mental health issue prevented her from completing her education that it was up to the school to find an appropriate setting in which to educate her child. School district officials, who in truth were terrified of this very self-destructive teen, agreed with the parent and funded a placement in a therapeutic school.

As a last note, many parents have found comfort and support in Internet chat rooms and bulletin boards such as the popular boards found at www.bpdcentral.com.

SEEKING STATE ASSISTANCE

In the first email in this chapter, the parents felt bullied and terrorized by their daughter. Those behaviors are not necessarily enough to have a child hospitalized, but if parents have lost much hope that they will be able to assert any authority at all over the adolescent, they should investigate whether their state has the capacity to step in or help.

For instance, Massachusetts has a Child in Need of Services (CHINS) petition in which the juvenile court tries to help parents and school officials deal with troubled youth. The person filing the CHINS petition must show the judge that the child regularly runs away from home, constantly disobeys the commands of a parent or legal guardian, misses school on a regular basis, or constantly fails to follow school rules.

A parent or guardian can file a CHINS petition on a child who is under seventeen, runs away, and/or does not or cannot follow the rules at home. A school district may file a CHINS petition on a child who is under sixteen, who is absent a lot or misbehaves at school. The police may file a CHINS petition on a child who is under seventeen and a runaway. Once the CHINS petition is issued, it is up to the judge, not the parent or the school, to decide when to dismiss the petition.

When a petition is filed, a judge decides whether there is merit to the case. If there is no merit, the case is dismissed. If the judge feels that there is enough concern, a probation officer is assigned to the case to decide what specific services a child needs (such as protective services, mental health services, social services, and so on). If the officer deems that the child is in danger and in need of protection, the child is referred to the department of social services, and if the allegations of abuse are verified, the child can be removed from the parent's home. If a child refuses to attend therapy, the court can mandate that the child go to therapy. If a child continues to refuse and remains at-risk, once again the department of social services is contacted to see whether an out-of-home placement is necessary.

Other states may have similar services and clearly such drastic measures are not always necessary, but when parents feel that without such help they might lose their child or be driven to measures that will put the child at risk, such intervention is worth considering.

GETTING AN ADOLESCENT TO AGREE TO TREATMENT

Finding treatment for an adolescent with BPD is one challenge. Parents face another challenge when they recognize that their adolescent might have BPD but the child refuses to get therapy.

FAMILY CONNECTIONS

The National Education Alliance for Borderline Personality Disorder (NEABPD) has developed an exciting initiative known as Family Connections.

Family Connections is a twelve-week series for family members with a relative who has BPD, or symptoms of the disorder. It provides education for the family on the latest understanding, research, and treatment of BPD. The idea is to provide the foundation for a better understanding of this complex disorder.

What is different in these groups is that they are led by trained family members (parents, spouses, children, and siblings) and have no formal "professional" presence. It is a skills training based on dialectical behavior therapy (DBT) in the context of a supportive group environment.

Unfortunately there are too few Family Connections groups, which are sited at present in the larger metropolitan areas, although more are forming monthly. See the resources section for more information.

The kids who are admitted to our unit are done so on a voluntary basis. It stands to reason that people who want therapy are more likely to get better than those who do not want therapy. Still, some teens who don't "really" want therapy accept is as a way to get their parents off their backs. Many of these kids end up feeling that their stay was actually worthwhile and not exactly what they thought it was going to be like. For example, the DBT we use on the unit can be full of irreverence and humor (together with the serious stuff). This type of approach often resonates with teens, as adolescence is a time of irreverence.

Many teens say to us, "I don't need to be here, but my parents are crazy." This may or may not be true, but treating the adolescent with BPD means treating the entire family. Even if the adolescent refuses treatment, it may be helpful for the parents to go into therapy. Often parents have been burned out by behavior that is seen as manipulative, by constant badgering by the teen, or by worry about the child's safety. Parents getting therapy might not necessarily get the adolescent into therapy, but it will help the parents deal with their own suffering. Sometimes, though, if the parent accepts therapy, the teen will follow.

WHEN A HOSPITAL STAY IS CRITICAL

Certainly if the adolescent has gotten to the point of severe self-injury or active suicidality, then there can be no compromise and a hospital admission might be indicated to assess lethality.

Many of the kids who come to McLean Hospital either have recently been suicidal, have made suicide attempts, or have ongoing suicide thoughts. Of teenagers who eventually attempt suicide, about 80 percent have shown up at doctors' offices at some point in the few months before making their attempts. They often complain of symptoms such as inability to sleep, exhaustion, or problems at school. These should be of concern to the pediatricians.

For parents, several warning signs indicate the possibility of suicide in adolescents. Unfortunately, unless an adolescent declares his or her intention, these signs are not specific enough. They neither tell us that an adolescent will attempt suicide, nor when. They are, however, signs that should alert parents as to the possibility of suicidal thinking

- Depression
- Statements that show a preoccupation with dying
- Drastic behavior changes
- Mood swings
- Lack of interest in future plans
- Making final plans
- Previous suicide attempts
- Sudden improvement after a period of depression
- Self-destructive behavior, including drug use and self-injury.

Anxiety, isolation, depression, drug abuse, delinquency, and family breakdown are also risk factors. Because no specific symptom will tell parents that their children will make an attempt, any of the above symptoms should be enough to seek expert help.

CHAPTER NINE

The New Way to Treat BPD

MAJOR RESEARCH TAKES PLACE around the world into illnesses that kill people. Yet, a surprisingly small amount of research focuses on BPD, an illness that kills a lot of people—by their own hands. BPD researcher psychiatrist John Oldham, M.D., points out that personality disorders are estimated to be present in more than 30 percent of individuals who die by suicide, 40 percent of individuals who make suicide attempts, and 50 percent of psychiatric outpatients in particular who die by suicide.

In clinical populations (that is people who seek out and are in treatment for their BPD), the rate of suicide of patients with BPD is estimated to be between 8 and 10 percent—a thousand times greater than that in the general population (where suicide occurs in 0.01 percent of the population). We know that up to 90 percent of patients with BPD make suicide attempts; so unsuccessful suicide attempts are obviously far more common than completed suicides in these patients.

As studies increasingly show that BPD is far more treatable than previously thought, keeping a patient alive to the point of recovery means getting them through suicidality. Treatment must initially gear itself at suicidality so that the prospect of a life of quality can be considered.

"Dialectical behavior therapy has not answered all my questions, but it has stopped me from killing myself. Now I can get on with the work of finding out what the hell is going on."

—JEN, A SIXTEEN-YEAR-OLD WITH BPD

This chapter will focus solely on dialectical behavior therapy (DBT), an effective and scientifically proven treatment for BPD. In particular, DBT is an effective treatment method for suicidal patients. The following chapter will focus on other treatments and medications.

DBT: A NEW THERAPY BRINGS NEW PROMISE

Marsha Linehan, Ph.D., director of the Behavioral Research and Therapy Clinics at the University of Washington in Seattle, developed DBT and described the research and treatment in her 1993 book *Skills Training Manual for Treating Borderline Personality Disorder*.

DBT is a form of behavioral therapy that focuses on teaching people skills that help them react more normally to overwhelming emotions. It significantly reduces suicidality and self-injurious behaviors. DBT therapists should have formal training in DBT. The therapy in adolescents consists of individual therapy, skills groups, and family groups, and it is further reviewed in this chapter.

Dr. Linehan's original work demonstrated the efficacy of DBT in reducing suicidal and self-injurious behaviors among women with BPD. Later, psychologist Alec Miller, Ph.D., and his colleagues modified DBT to address the needs of adolescents with multiple problems. Research has shown that use of this approach with adolescents reduces suicidal behavior, dropout from treatment, psychiatric hospitalization, substance abuse, anger, and interpersonal difficulties.

DBT is an acronym for dialectical behavior therapy. But what does that mean? The term "dialectical" is derived from classical philosophy. It refers to a form of argument in which an assertion is first made about a particular issue. This assertion is termed the "thesis." The opposing position is then stated, and this is known as the "antithesis." Finally a "synthesis" is sought between the two extremes, incorporating the valuable features of each position and resolving any contradictions between the two. It is not necessarily a compromise, however.

The therapy is behavioral as it focuses on present problematic behavior and the factors that control the behavior rather than focusing on the past, although it does not discount the past.

DBT offers great promise for adolescents with BPD. All the other treatments have less supporting data in adolescents and are reviewed in the following chapter.

DBT has revolutionized the treatment of BPD for three major reasons. The first is that scientific research has shown it to be effective in the treatment of BPD, something that few other treatment approaches can claim. The second is that, in part because of its effectiveness, it has increased the public awareness of BPD. Not only has DBT proven itself to be a good therapy for BPD, but it has given the therapists who treat patients with BPD a way to deal with their own potential burnout, which in turn allows the therapists to continue working with patients who have historically been seen as very difficult to treat.

DBT: THE NUTS AND BOLTS

DBT is based on a "biosocial" theory of BPD. The theory is that that the disorder is a consequence of an emotionally vulnerable individual growing up in an invalidating environment.

An emotionally vulnerable person in the biosocial theory is someone who reacts excessively to relatively low levels of stress and takes longer than

STUDIES SUPPORTING DBT TO TREAT BPD, SELF-INJURY, AND SUICIDALITY

A 2006 study from New Zealand described the outcome of ten BPD patients with the hope of implementing DBT into a standard New Zealand public mental health service.

In the small study, researchers found that DBT led to significant improvements in many measures of BPD functioning, including reductions in anxiety and depression. Further, the amount of time patients spent in the hospital dropped by more than 60 percent after treatment. Following this, Jan Brassington, Ph.D., and Roy Krawitz, M.D., who had authored the study, recommended that DBT should be offered more widely in New Zealand.

In another in 2006, German researchers noted that suicide ranked as the second leading cause of death in adolescents in their country. The risk factors for suicide in adolescents were identified as impulsive and self-injurious behavior, depression, and conduct disorder. The researchers wanted to test whether DBT was an effective method for treating suicidal teens.

The researchers found that by using a DBT treatment, self-injurious behavior declined significantly during treatment. Prior to entering the DBT treatment, eight of the twelve patients in the study had attempted suicide at least once. During treatment, there were no suicide attempts. The results were so promising that the researchers were planning to perform a much bigger study of DBT for adolescents in Germany.

In a 2006 Dutch study, Louisa Van den Bosch, Ph.D., and colleagues found significantly positive effects of twelve months of DBT on suicidal behavior and impulsivity in a group of female patients with DBT with and without substance abuse. Even after six months after the end of the DBT treatment, the patients continued to have lower levels of suicidal and impulsive behaviors and of alcohol use. This is great news because many patients using other forms of treatment for such conditions frequently go back to these behaviors when therapy ends.

normal to return to normal once the stress is removed. These people seem to feel things deeper and for longer than others. Their emotional vulnerability is thought to be a result combination of bio-physiological factors such as family genetics, intrauterine environment, temperament, and brain development.

An invalidating environment refers to a situation in which a person's experiences are disqualified or "invalidated" by the significant others in his or her life. The word environment in this context means the physical and interpersonal surroundings that can affect the mood and behaviors in any person.

More simply put, in an invalidating experience, a child has an experience or thought. The parent or caregiver indicates that this experience or thought is not accurate.

For example, seventeen-year-old Bruce is an emotionally intense adolescent who had his first admission to McLean's DBT residential unit after having been hospitalized for an overdose in an attempt to commit suicide. He completed the program and was discharged back home.

Nearly three months after discharge, Bruce's parents called looking for readmission to the unit because he was expressing intense thoughts of suicide. On admission, Bruce told the psychiatry resident that he could no longer live at home because he was fighting every day with his parents and they just did not understand him. During a meeting between Bruce, his parents, and the treatment team, Bruce wanted to talk about the fighting at home. He told us that fighting generally involved loud arguments, yelling, and the occasional throwing of "stuff," as well as a lot of anger.

Bruce's mother acknowledged the fighting—"that's why we are here"—but she repeatedly blamed it on Bruce's girlfriend, who was the "real problem." His mother's assertion that it was Bruce's girlfriend, and the problems that she was causing, invalidated his perspective. His perspective was that it was the fighting at home that had led to his suicidality, not his girlfriend. Bruce's history of emotional intensity together with his invalidating environment and the high level of chaos at home led to intolerable feelings that, in turn, led to his desire to commit suicide and increased risk of self-harm.

Even very well-intentioned parents can invalidate their children's experiences, so that statements such as "You're not ugly" or "You're not stupid" are invalidating to a child who sees him- or herself as ugly or stupid.

Obviously, situations such as incest or other forms of abuse are more clearly understood examples of invalidation. Patients with BPD frequently describe a history of childhood sexual abuse. This is regarded within the DBT model as a particularly extreme form of invalidation.

Another aspect of the invalidating environment is that it places a high value on children being self-motivated and able to control themselves. In this environment, the failure of children to control their behavior is blamed on the children. As the children are blamed for the behavior, they are seen as bad children, and their inability to control themselves is seen as a negative aspect of their character, rather than a failure of both the children and their caregivers to understand one another and recognize there is a collective problem.

Whether the invalidating environment is caused by well-intentioned support or destructive abuse, ongoing invalidation over time in an emotionally vulnerable individual is recognized by the biosocial theory as a powerful cocktail for the development of BPD.

When Parents Invalidate Their Children

When some parents first hear of the biosocial theory, they don't like the idea of seeing themselves as "invalidating," in other words, feeling blamed for the troubles of their children. It has helped some parents think about there being an emotional mismatch between them and their children and in the ways that they see the world. This explanation particularly resonates with adoptive parents.

Dr. Linehan describes the way that the child's emotional vulnerability interplays with the invalidating environment to create a borderline personality as follows: "Children won't have the opportunity to accurately label and understand their feelings nor learn to trust their own responses to events."

In such an environment, the children don't receive help to cope with situations that they find difficult or stressful, as many such problems are not acknowledged by their invalidating environment.

An extreme example of this is that of Jacqui, a very bright, attractive fifteen-year-old from California. She was referred to McLean for self-injury, self-loathing, and suicidality. Her mother, too, was attractive, enhanced by multiple plastic surgeries to remain in perfect proportion. The daughter, however, was far more concerned by her own mental health than the outward appearance of her body. But she struggled to please her mother who said that she wanted her daughter to be happy, and believed that if Jacqui "just lost a few pounds she would be happy."

Jacqui's mother had found her own happiness in her outward appearance (although Jacqui was not sure just how happy her mother was), and Jacqui was trying to find happiness in academic pursuits, which her mother felt was reasonable but that Jacqui would find true happiness if she focused more on her appearance than her learning. Jacqui's older sister saw life much more the way that their mother did. The problem is that Jacqui did not. The issue is far less about who is right or wrong than the recognition of the possibility of another perspective.

We had a family meeting to help Jacqui's mother recognize that her daughter experienced the world in a different way than she herself did. Her mother had a hard time accepting this—"She's a girl, isn't she?"

Jacqui said: "You see, I have been backed into a corner from which I can find no escape. Mom, you have literally told me you don't respect me, don't have to respect me, and will not respect me, yet I have to respect you. I do. I just think that right now I have bigger problems than my weight. Here I am in a hospital and because of that, you blame me for an inability to have a life. My dad has no idea what to do. He cries at night about me, and fights with you. Mentally, I am just above rock bottom, however, in the last few days the plunge has become a death spiral."

In response, her mother said, "I know that your body image issues play a huge role in your self-esteem and the possibility in your mind that as your parents we might not accept you if you do not appear healthy. Obviously your fear of abandonment is still a concern. Your grandparents are going to visit next week. I think that you are worried about how you will look to them."

As adolescents look to others for indications as to how they should feel or for help in solving their problems, they discover that they are expected to find the solutions themselves and control their behavior in a "socially acceptable" manner. Jacqui was expected to relieve her stress through losing weight and going to the gym. Instead she did so by slashing herself up.

Her behavior suddenly exploded and changed from blocking her emotions as she tried to get the approval of her mother to emotionally volatility as she tried to get her mother to acknowledge her feelings. Her mother responded erratically to her behavior, and Jacqui sometimes felt supported and at other times not. It was this inconsistency that created an enduring pattern of self-destructive behavior.

PHILOSOPHY OF DBT TREATMENT

The philosophy of DBT is thus: In any interaction between people—in particular, those in which they are at odds with—each person has a perspective, or thesis, to which there is an antithesis. The synthesis is the combination of the valuable features of each position.

This synthesis becomes the new thesis, and a new antithesis is formed and so on. Truth is seen as a process of synthesizing these positions over time. It is considered the middle way between positions but not just a compromise. It is an agreement on the valuable aspects of the position of each perspective.

BPD PATIENT CHARACTERISTICS AS TARGETS FOR DBT

Marsha Linehan, Ph.D., director of the Behavioral Research and Therapy Clinics at the University of Washington in Seattle, describes BPD patients as showing the following six typical patterns of behavior that the patient and therapist would target:

Emotional vulnerability. Patients with BPD are generally aware of their difficulty coping with stress. Yet they may blame other people for having unrealistic expectations and for making unreasonable demands. Patients with BPD would work on emotion regulation skills so they are better at regulating their emotions.

Self-invalidation. People with BPD invalidate their own responses and have unrealistic goals and expectations. This is a characteristic learned from their invalidating environment. To make matters worse, they then feel ashamed and angry with themselves when they experience difficulty or fail to achieve their goals. Here the goal would be to teach the person to self-validate or to recognize that their perspective can be as valid as anybody else's.

Unrelenting crises. People with BPD tend to exhibit a pattern of unrelenting crises, where one crisis follows another, often before the previous one has been resolved. Patients learn to use realistic judgment in evaluating whether a specific situation requires a response that takes it to a crisis level.

Inhibited grieving. Because of their difficulty with emotion regulation, people with BPD are unable to face negative feelings, particularly feelings associated with loss or grief. Patients learn to label feeling states and experience their emotions without labeling them as good or bad.

Active passivity. Patients with BPD can be *active* in finding other people who will solve their problems for them, but they are *passive* in solving their own problems. The goal here is to teach patients to become active in solving their own problems.

Apparent competence. BPD patients have learned to give the impression of being competent in response to an invalidating

continued on the next page

environment. In some situations, they may indeed be competent, but their skills do not generalize across different situations and are dependent on the patients' moods at the moment. For this behavior the target would be for the adolescent with BPD to be able to be competent in a way that is *not* dependent on their moods.

These patterns of behavior can lead to powerful and frequently painful emotions. Sometimes, a pattern of self-mutilation tends to develop as a means of coping with these emotions. At times the feelings are so painful and persistent that suicide is seen as the only solution to the misery.

This email from the mother of fourteen-year-old Sally shows this process in action. Sally was cutting herself and had tremendous black-and-white, all-or-nothing thinking. Her mother had wanted to know what was "wrong" with her daughter. Instead we looked at their relationship with the goal of understanding the perspective of each in the relationship.

Her mother wrote: "After years of anger at my daughter, I see how I withdrew from her when my husband left us. Therapy is changing this. I'm not my dependable, flawed self. I'm still taking care of everyone's nuts and bolts needs, but I am trying to alter some long-standing patterns, forcing a little distance between us, and I think this is what Sally feels in subtle ways. The intensity of our relationship is exhausting, especially now that this therapy shines a beacon on my bad behavior.

"Sally, too, is changing as she sees me change. She and I have had some real moments of lighthearted affection in the past weeks (and it's interesting how easy it is to forgive your own child). This is wonderful and new and often initiated by Sally—who does rise above her preoccupation and pain as she learns to trust that I am making an effort. I look at my behavior for her, and she trusts me for me. We both take risks, but ultimately we have this beautiful new relationship. I'm proud of her and I'm sorry I'm not more reaffirming, and Sally wonders why I'm not, I'm sure."

COMPONENTS OF DBT TREATMENT

The dialectical approach to understanding people and the treatment of human problems is not dogmatic, but instead open and purposefully transactional between therapist and patient.

The most basic or fundamental of the principles in DBT is the need for change on the one hand and the need for acceptance on the other. In other words to accept that things are the way they are because of all that has happened to a person and yet that there is also a need to change in order to be better able to cope with life. DBT has specific techniques of validation designed to counter the self-invalidation of the patient.

The success of treatment depends on the quality of the relationship between the patient and therapist. The emphasis is on this being a real human interaction.

For a complete and comprehensive look at DBT for adolescents, the book *Dialectical Behavior Therapy with Suicidal Adolescents* by Alec Miller, Ph.D., and Marsha Linehan, Ph.D., is essential reading, but for the purpose of this chapter I'll give a simple overview of the skills that form the basis of DBT therapy.

The following are the components of a DBT treatment:

Weekly Individual Psychotherapy

Each week, the patient meets one on one with her therapist to look at issues that have come up during the week following what's called a treatment target hierarchy. Treatment hierarchy means dealing with the most concerning behaviors first and then moving on to less concerning behaviors. So, self-injurious and suicidal behaviors would take first priority. Once these have been addressed, therapy would deal with therapy-interfering behaviors (such as missing or coming late to sessions, phoning at unreasonable hours, and not returning phone calls). Once these have been addressed, therapy would deal with quality of life issues (such as depression, substance abuse, and chronic truancy), and finally working toward improving the quality of one's life.

Group Skills Training

Each week, the patient meets with a group of other people with BPD and a therapist for group skills training. This is absolutely essential for adolescents.

Some parents have told me that their children want nothing to do with treatment, and when we meet the kids, the parents are right that the teens have no commitment to change. Often is takes the fear of losing something important that helps the person accept the need for treatment. The fear of loss can be the fear of dying, losing a relationship, or losing a family and living the rest of life moving from one crisis to the next. We have had no success trying to force therapy on children who absolutely do not want therapy, however, our experience is that once children experience being in group skills training, an environment where many of the other kids have had similar experiences, they readily engage in therapy.

In group skills training, adolescents learn to use specific skills that are broken down into the following four components:

Mindfulness. The essential part of all skills taught in skills group training is the core mindfulness skills. Mindfulness skills are the vehicles for balancing "emotion mind," which is the mental state controlled primarily by the current emotional state, and "reasonable mind," which is the mental state brought about by excessive rationality and logic, to achieve a "wise mind," which is the synthesis of emotion and reasonable minds.

Interpersonal effectiveness. Interpersonal skills training includes teaching patients with BPD effective strategies for getting what they need, learning to say no effectively, and coping with interpersonal conflict. The skills taught are intended to maximize the chances that a person's goals in a specific situation will be met, while damaging neither the relationship nor the patient's self-respect.

Distress tolerance. DBT emphasizes and recognizes that patients with BPD experience profound pain but that it is necessary to learn to bear this pain skillfully. Distress tolerance skills build on mindfulness skills in the sense that patients learn to accept, in a nonjudgmental fashion, both who they are and the current situation. Distress tolerance skills are concerned with tolerating and surviving crises and with accepting life as it is in the moment.

Emotion regulation. Adolescents with BPD are frequently emotionally intense and labile. They can be angry, intensely frustrated, depressed, or anxious. The DBT skills for emotion regulation teach how to manage emotions rather than being managed by them, to reduce vulnerability to negative emotions, and to build positive emotional experiences.

Phone Consultation

This as-needed consultation allows for the patient to contact his therapist, who is also sometimes known as a skills coach, during "real-life" moments when "real-life" problems appear, and the adolescent needs help in remembering and applying his newly learned skills. Telephone contact with the primary therapist between sessions is important for coaching the patient in using his DBT skills during crisis situations. Patients are offered skills coaching when they are not certain which skill to use or exactly how to apply the skill in a particular situation.

DBT patients are typically encouraged to call before suicidal crises, or at least before they harm themselves. As the therapist—and patient—aim for adaptive (healthy) behavior, telephone contact must occur prior to self-injury or other suicidal behavior. If the patient has already injured himself, a "twenty-four-hour rule" states that he cannot have supportive phone contact with the therapist for twenty-four hours after self-injury, except for basic medical management (such as telling the person to go to an emergency room or to cover the injuries with a clean bandage). This rule provides reinforcement for adaptive coping and negative consequences for maladaptive behavior.

Phone calls are also sometimes used to resolve misunderstandings and conflicts that arise during therapy sessions, instead of waiting until the next session to deal with the emotions.

Generally the therapist is available to take the patient's calls around the clock, but in a team practice there might be an on-call schedule. Patients would know the skills coach if it was not their primary therapist.

When the concept of phone consultation was initially proposed, many clinicians felt that they would be inundated with phone calls, but generally speaking this is not the case and at McLean Hospital, we have not found that patients have abused the system. In one case, for instance, a patient told me that she *wanted* to page me but did not *need* to page me but that she just wanted to talk at 2 in the morning. She decided instead to leave me a message on my voicemail.

Therapist Support

Therapists who treat patients with BPD attend weekly therapist consultation team meetings with other DBT-trained colleagues. The purpose of these meetings is to support the therapist and prevent the burnout that is so frequently found in therapists who treat people with BPD.

Here is one key point about DBT therapists: The therapist must accept the following assumptions about the patient and that these assumptions will establish his or her attitude to the treatment. Patients generally want to change and sometimes, in spite of appearances, are trying their best at any particular time.

DBT FOR THE FAMILY

We have looked at the use of DBT for an individual patient, but BPD affects not only the individual but also the family and friends who love them. Family interventions in DBT support both the adolescent patient and target the improvement of family relationships.

Individual DBT addresses the problems of the individual's emotional vulnerability, which we defined earlier as a high sensitivity (a quick reaction to a stimulus), high reactivity (a more intense reaction to a stimulus), and a slow return to baseline mood state.

But in adolescents especially, it is critical to tackle the invalidating environment as well. That's why the family should participate in treatment for the best possible prognosis. Often, and despite the best of intentions, families have reinforced maladaptive behaviors in the patient, for instance, only acknowledging the patient when she is cutting herself. DBT for the family hopes to teach the family to reinforce an adolescent's effective functioning in a consistent manner, which can, in turn, be a potent change intervention. Further, DBT teaches the adolescent to reinforce effective parental interactions.

One important way in which the whole family can be involved is during the intake process. This is the point at which the patient and her family first appear for treatment. The clinical team meets with and coordinates the family's ongoing participation in the treatment program.

An interesting aspect of doing an intake interview with parents is that when we describe the behaviors that define BPD, parents will recognize some of the very same difficulties they share with the adolescent. At times parents acknowledge that they have some of the borderline traits.

Another important way in which the whole family can be involved in treatment is by attending family group therapy sessions. The group therapy sessions require a strong commitment from the family members. The two types of family group therapy sessions are as follows:

Parents' DBT support group. These group therapy sessions support the parents of adolescents in DBT treatment and provide parents with an overview of the principles of DBT treatment. This group is only for parents and a DBT therapist; it does not include other family members or the patient.

The purpose of this group is to extend and sustain the DBT treatment structures into the home lives of adolescents and their families and clarify how family members can participate in and reinforce the treatment process. Parents are encouraged to communicate with each other and share successes, frustrations, and the challenges of helping their children modify problematic or dangerous behaviors.

Most parents' DBT support groups in the outpatient setting generally meet for an hour and a half each week for six months with a group of six to nine couples.

Multi-family DBT group. This group is similar to the parents' DBT support group except that it includes other family members and the adolescent with BPD. The group also shares in all aspects of treatment and research and is run in participation with a DBT clinician. One particularly appealing aspect of this group is that newer group members are able to witness more "advanced" families communicate, problem-solve, and demonstrate skill application.

Most multi-family groups for outpatients meet for an hour and a half each week for six months with a group of six to nine families.

The sessions are generally divided into two parts. DBT skills are usually taught in the first half, with a particular emphasis on family relationships. The second half of every meeting is a multiple family skills application group. In a consultative manner, participants bring up a family issue on which they would like to focus, and group members apply DBT skills to the problem.

In addition to these group sessions, whenever possible, parents should participate in scheduled treatment reviews with the clinical team. It is essential that the parents know what the adolescent with BPD is being taught so they can implement the strategies.

BRAIN CHANGES AND DBT

In a 2006 study, Knut Schnell, M.D., and Sabine Herpertz, M.D., stated that emotional dysregulation was the hallmark of BPD and the main target for DBT. They wanted to see whether improved emotional regulation following DBT led to changes in the brain.

The researchers applied five MRI scans each to six female patients with BPD while the patients attended a twelve-week inpatient treatment program. Then the researchers compared the results to the MRIs of six female patients without BPD. They found that patients who got better on DBT showed less activity in the parts of their brains that are associated with high levels of arousal (such as the amygdala and hippocampus).

So this study appears to show that patients with BPD who use DBT have brain changes leading to less activity in the part of their brains that overreact to stress. This implies that the problem-solving parts of their brains would show more activity.

In conclusion, DBT provides the best hope at this time for the treatment of adolescents with BPD, especially when provided by a skilled, compassionate and flexible treatment team.

RESEARCH ON ADOLESCENT DBT

Most of the research on DBT has been conducted in adults, however, a 2004 study looked at the outcome of the first twenty youths who had lived in the Grove Street DBT residential treatment program in Westborough, Massachusetts. This highly structured residential program serves adolescents referred by the Massachusetts Department of Mental Health.

The data was on fourteen girls and six boys whose average age was 16.6 years. The average length of stay in the residence was ten months. The researchers reported that twelve of the twenty youths completed the program. Of those twelve, eight were living in the community six months after discharge, three were in a group residence, and one was hospitalized. Half of the twenty residents had a history of

numerous hospitalizations, and in the six months before program entry, four of the adolescents had spent a total of 690 days in the hospital. Six months after discharge, only two had been hospitalized, for a total of 183 days.

Nine of the twenty youths had a history of self-injury in the six months before entering the residential program. No incidents were reported in the six months after discharge.

The researchers recognized that adolescents who were admitted to the program often performed poorly in programs that are not equipped to make a commitment to adolescents who were too threatening or self-injurious. The researchers concluded that the DBT system of care understood that provocative behaviors needed to, and could be, modified.

CHAPTER TEN

Other Psychotherapies that May Help Teens with BPD

N OT ALL ADOLESCENTS WILL commit to dialectical behavior therapy (DBT) as a primary psychotherapy, and not all clinics or individual practices offer it. So this chapter will examine other types of psychotherapy for BPD.

Helping adolescents with BPD make therapeutic changes is difficult for at least two reasons. The first reason is that they often feel that getting them to change their motivation or learn new behavioral skills is invalidating and that the therapist is missing the problem. This is because as a rule adolescents with BPD generally feel misunderstood and generally don't have the experience of adults trying to understand them. Until the diagnosis of BPD is clear, clinicians might think that the person is simply depressed if the adolescent is thinking of suicide, or has ADHD if the adolescent is impulsive, or is "acting up" if the adolescent is in conflict with their parents. In these situations patients have told me that they feel like "Okay, here we go again. Nothing is ever going to change."

This belief can precipitate behavior ranging from withdrawal, noncompliance, and early dropout from treatment to anger, aggression, and self-injury.

The second reason is that ignoring the need for the patient to change and not working hard at encouraging such change can have serious consequences. Neglecting the need for change can lead to clinicians missing ongoing despair and hopelessness, and worse, suicidality.

THE DIFFICULTY IN TREATING BPD

People who work with adolescents with BPD face many challenges. These challenges are even more difficult when a therapist works alone in private practice, with no peer support or supervision. The following are a few of the challenges therapist face:

- Probably the most frightening behaviors, especially for the new therapist, are the self-destruction and suicidal tendencies, both of which are common in BPD. Many of these behaviors are often not intended as suicidal gestures, but more as a relief from the terrible psychic pain that an adolescent is feeling. In my experience, suicide attempts in adolescents tend to be below lethality and take place where they are likely to be found. Many of the adolescents I work with have reported their suicide attempts to friends via phone calls, instant messages, or text-messages. Despite this, every attempt must be taken seriously, and any attempt can prove fatal.
- Another issue is that of abandonment. Often when adolescents feel understood by their therapists, they cannot tolerate the fear that the therapist will leave them. The adolescents can become suicidal when the therapist goes on vacation, for example. This fear often puts tremendous stress on therapists—sometimes intolerable stress. Sometimes they end up referring the patients to someone else, in effect abandoning the adolescents and making their worst fears come true.
- As adolescents get closer to the therapist and begin to open up and reveal themselves, they can become desperate for the closeness, cling to the therapist, and make great demands on the therapists' time.

On the other hand, the adolescents' experience of closeness has frequently not been a fulfilling one because of previous abandonment or abuse. This fear of closeness and the threat of abandonment can then cause adolescents to start distancing themselves from the therapist as the closeness begins to feel intolerable. Therapists often find it overwhelming to deal with the clinging as they try to help the desperate needy child and the distancing behavior, which can include tantrums, hostility, and terrible devaluation of the therapist.

- Another difficult issue is that the depression that comes with BPD does not respond all that readily to medication. The depression of adolescents with BPD appears to be more "existential" in nature. Adolescents with BPD tend to struggle with questions about the meaning of life, but when they find no meaning, they become despondent and hopeless. The depression of adolescents with BPD is not a classical depression characterized by sleep and appetite and energy disturbances, although a more classical depression can co-occur.

Therapists have to be able to tolerate the profound depression that the adolescents feel—sometimes for many years—while continuing the therapeutic work with them.

TREATMENTS OTHER THAN DBT

Defining both treatment and recovery are important. Recently a colleague who has recovered from BPD and is a tremendous advocate for not only BPD but also peer-to-peer support sent me this email:

"Call me a dreamer, but I envision the day when people who have been treated for BPD can be involved in defining whether a treatment is effective or not. A clinician's definition of my 'remission' is not necessarily a life worth living."

How true! Just because a person with BPD no longer cuts and rages does not mean that he is "cured." The issues of wholeness, completeness, and hope are essential components of health, and this is not less true in BPD.

Researchers are testing to see whether some of the new treatment approaches work better than existing standards of care. For instance, they compare new treatments (such as DBT) to treatment as usual (TAU).

TAU is whatever form of treatment would happen under normal conditions in a typical practice or clinic. New forms of treatment for BPD include:

The STEPPS Program

STEPPS stands for Systems Training for Emotional Predictability and Problem Solving. It is a cognitive-behavioral, skills training approach, where BPD is characterized as a disorder of emotion and behavior regulation.

STEPPS was created in the Netherlands in 1998 and rapidly gained use as a treatment for BPD there. Researchers in a 2006 report stated that the reasons for its rapid dissemination included its user-friendly manual, twenty-week duration, ability to maintain the patient's current treatment team, and the ease of therapist training. It soon became modified for use in other settings, such as programs for adolescents.

"If any therapy is going to claim it brings about 'recovery,' it would be helpful to have the BPD community, including those with the disorder and their families, articulate the standards. If we had agreed-upon standards of recovery, treatment outcomes and goals of treatment would be more concrete. The consumer recovery movement has designed assessment tools to measure levels of hope, resilience, and community integration . . . I find these aspects of recovery to be just as important as developing behavioral control."

—Kiera Van Gelder

Nancy Blum, M.S.W; Don St. John, P.A.; Bruce Pfohl, M.D.; and Don Bartels, M.A., at the University of Iowa Hospitals and Clinics adapted and revised the STEPPS program from its original incantation. The goal is to provide the person with BPD, closely allied friends, family members, and the treating clinicians with a common language to communicate clearly about the disorder and the skills used to manage it. Clients learn specific emotion and behavior management skills. Key professionals, friends, and family members whom clients identify as part of their "reinforcement team" learn to reinforce and support the newly learned skills.

The basics of the STEPPS program include two phases—a twenty-week basic skills group, and a one-year, twice-monthly advanced group program.

COGNITIVE-BEHAVIOR THERAPY

Also known as cognitive-behavioral therapy or CBT, this approach is a form of psychotherapy that emphasizes the role of thinking in how we feel and what we do. It is aimed at pointing out and recognizing unhelpful or destructive patterns of thinking and reacting and then helping the patient to change or replace these patterns with more practical or useful responses. CBT is considered to be the "fastest" of the psychotherapies, with therapists often recommending an average of sixteen total sessions per psychotherapy. CBT therapists often point to the fact that psychoanalysis, which is another form of psychotherapy, can take years.

Here's an example of how CBT works. Sheila is an eighteen-year-old who feels depressed and abandoned because her drug-abusing boyfriend left her. A CBT therapist would recognize the triggering event to be that Sheila's boyfriend left her, that this caused her to believe that she is not worth loving, which in turn led to her to be depressed.

The therapy would aim to identify irrational beliefs, and the therapist would work with Sheila in challenging the negative thoughts on the basis of evidence from Sheila's experience by reframing it, meaning to re-interpret it in a more realistic light. This helps Sheila to develop more rational beliefs and healthy coping strategies.

From the example above, a CBT therapist would help Sheila realize that there is no evidence that she must have this boyfriend to be loveable. It would be important to recognize that she desires a boyfriend but that not having one at the present time does not make her worthless.

If Sheila realizes that her boyfriend leaving her is disappointing, but not catastrophic, and that it means that she and her boyfriend failed as a couple but that she is not a failure as a person, she will feel sad or disappointed, but not depressed. The sadness and disappointment are likely healthy negative emotions that may lead Sheila to consider her choice in boyfriends the next time.

PSYCHODYNAMIC THERAPY

Psychodynamic therapy is a general term for therapies that try to get patients to bring their "true feelings" to the surface. It uses the basic assumption that everyone has an unconscious mind and that feelings, memories, and associations held in the unconscious mind are often too painful to explore and so psychological defenses are formed to protect the person against having to deal with the pain. An example of a defense would be denial, which is when a person refuses to acknowledge what is readily apparent to others. The classic example is an alcoholic who denies that he is dependent on the use of alcohol.

If these defenses overwhelm the person, psychological problems such as depression can occur. Psychodynamic therapists delve into a person's past, searching for the pain from the past to unlock it and allow it to be expressed in a safe environment.

One issue that many non-psychodynamic therapists have had with this approach is that it might take years of intense therapy to find such pain, which means that patients will be "stuck" in therapy until they can work it out.

Because the idea of this kind of therapy is so theoretical, it is difficult to research psychodynamic therapies. Also it is not clear that all psychodynamic therapists practice the therapy in the same way, which makes it further difficult to gauge.

Nevertheless, there is increasing research into the effectiveness of psychodynamic therapies, much of it done by professors Peter Fonagy, M.D., and Anthony Bateman, Ph.D. Dr. Bateman recommended modifying psychodynamic therapy for it to be successful. He feels that it is less important to find the ways in which patients defend against painful feelings and more important to use a treatment approach that is collaborative, structured, and organized, which he says "takes into account the behavioral and emotional crises that are inevitable during treatment of BPD."

A dynamic therapy approach to BPD can be useful. Many adolescents with BPD are hungry for a deeper understanding of their troubles and relationships, and they engage readily in dynamic therapy. Further, once the adolescents have the skills to better regulate their emotions and reactions, they appear better able to look at the nature of their past relationships. Dynamic therapy is also useful for those adolescents who refuse to do DBT and will engage only in what they call "talk therapy."

Family Therapy

Family therapy is the treatment of more than one member of a family in the same therapy session. It has been a critical component of adolescent therapy for many years. The core theory is that the behavior of individuals is influenced and maintained by the way other family members interact with them.

Family therapy has two main goals: It should both educate the family on BPD and treat the family. Both of these goals in turn help the adolescent feel understood. Education, communication, reinforcing adaptive behavior, and collaborative problem solving should be at the core of the family therapy.

When we at McLean Hospital begin to explore the features of BPD in family therapy, a parent sometimes identifies with the BPD symptoms and looks for therapy for himself or herself. This in turn has motivated some teens to continue in therapy as they see their parents getting help, and for those parents who get help it has led to improvements in themselves and better relationships with their families.

During family therapy, the therapist should be aware of the non-verbal communication between the patient and parents. The therapist should point these out during the session to make the family aware of any maladaptive interactions.

A particular type of family therapy is parent skills training groups, which aim to provide support and education for families who often struggle with their children's extreme behaviors. Such groups can also target the sometimes dysfunctional environment to which the adolescent plans to return as well as teach the family members how to model and reinforce adaptive behaviors.

Interpersonal Psychotherapy

Interpersonal psychotherapy (IPT) is a short-term, highly structured type of psychotherapy that focuses on one area of interpersonal problems. It can be used when a major problem is poor interpersonal relationships, in terms of both number and quality of the relationships. It generally lasts for twelve to sixteen weeks.

In IPT, the patient and therapist generally focus on both existing relationships as well as the relationship with the therapist. Together they try to identify common maladaptive patterns to relationships. In using the therapeutic relationship, the therapist aims to identify problematic interactions and patterns of behavior that occur during the therapy, with the idea that this understanding will serve as a template for further relationships.

Because IPT helps to build social skills, some clinicians believe that it can benefit patients with BPD whose major problem is interpersonal deficits.

Supportive Psychotherapy

Supportive psychotherapy is the most widely practiced form of individual psychotherapy today. It emphasizes the strength of the therapeutic relationship, environmental interventions, education, advice and suggestions, encouragement and praise, limit-setting and prohibitions, undermining maladaptive defenses while strengthening adaptive defenses, and strengths and talents.

A therapist using supportive therapy uses active listening and helps the patient to see alternatives to her hopelessness. The therapist helps the patient move toward creating a meaningful set of plans and goals. Because of this, patients need a sense that the supportive psychotherapist can cope with the despair and hold on to hope for the patient's recovery. The belief is that as patients establish trust in their therapists, they learn to generalize that experience to significant others in their lives. The goal is that they eventually learn healthy self-advocacy to get their needs met rather than what is often seen as "manipulative" behavior.

Robert Friedel, M.D., author of *Borderline Personality Disorder Demystified*, is a strong advocate of this approach, but as with any form of therapy, supervision is essential, especially for the inexperienced therapist.

Other therapists think of supportive psychotherapy as simply "being nice." In treating adolescents with BPD, simply "being nice" can quickly backfire, as splitting, idealization, and devaluation—not to mention aggressive anger, acting out, and psychotic symptoms—can soon leave clinicians regretting having a single "nice" bone in their bodies.

Cognitive-Analytic Therapy

This therapy uses a collaborative approach between the patient and therapist to identify self-states, which are the different ways that person behaves under different circumstances. Generally, we all have self-states that we pull together into one sense of who we are. People with BPD, however, cannot easily do this. Adolescents with BPD often describe being very different (or having different personas) with different people or in different situations.

Cognitive-analytic therapy (CAT) believes that inadequate parenting leads to an inability to integrate these self-states, leading to rapid shifts between these states and further leads to overall instability of behavior in interpersonal situations.

CAT supposes that a person's difficulty is because they have developed patterns of unchanging and unhealthy behaviors, and at that at times this is simply because the person has had few options in the choices they could make or could have made. This is best illustrated in the following case example.

Kathy was an eighteen-year-old with BPD who spent her entire life in state custody and for the past six years, in a residential home. Kathy came to McLean with a worry about compulsive promiscuity and also complained that she was intensely lonely. She had few friends. CAT would recognize that the interpersonal behavioral patterns that had served Kathy well in the residential home, where staff and other kids often came and went, favored both rapid and relatively non-discriminating attachment and equally rapid detachment. In that situation, Kathy was actively discouraged from making close friendships with members of staff. Now in a "normal" life, she continued to use the pattern of quick and shallow attachments and detachment. This approach, which had served Kathy well in the residence, now led to her forming superficial relationships with similarly uncaring others and feeling lonely as a result. The CAT therapist would work with Kathy to recognize her maladaptive patterns and to change these patterns by, for instance, practicing change in therapy.

Schema Therapy

Schema therapy is a relatively new treatment for BPD developed by Jeffrey Young, Ph.D., a faculty member at Columbia University. Dr. Young defines schemas as "broad pervasive themes regarding oneself and one's relationship with others, developed during childhood and elaborated throughout one's lifetime, and dysfunctional to a significant degree." In other words, these are self-defeating life patterns.

Schema theory believes that early patterns have their origins in negative childhood experiences and are particularly resistant to change. For instance a patient whose parents were cold and distant might have a pattern of getting involved in intimate relationships that don't meet her needs. Then when her needs aren't met, she becomes angry. In part this anger is justified, but in another part it is an overreaction and a response to her experience from childhood of never having had her needs met. Schema therapy consists initially of identifying and recognizing the early patterns of behavior, which the therapist and patient then discuss. These patterns are then altered using cognitive reconstruction, behavioral and experiential techniques, and discussion of issues that arise in the therapist-patient relationship.

Schema therapists view patients with BPD compassionately and as needy. The therapist serves as the "good parent" to the patient's vulnerable side. Through the therapist's "limited reparenting," patients with BPD develop a strong, healthy side to calm, soothe, and care for their emotionally intense, labile temperament.

In a 2006 study, half of the patients with BPD using schema therapy showed so few symptoms that they were evaluated as recovered after three years of treatment.

Electroconvulsive Therapy

Electroconvulsive therapy, also known as electroshock or ECT, is a type of therapy involving the induction of an artificial seizure in a patient by passing electricity through a patient's brain, and it is commonly used in depression and other mood disorders. ECT is sometimes used as a treatment for people with BPD who also have depression, although research has shown that it is not very effective.

In a 2004 study, researchers noted that 30 to 80 percent of patients with major depression would be diagnosed with a co-occurring personality disorder during their lifetimes and that as many as 50 percent of patients with BPD will experience major depression at some point. Further, the researchers noted that depressed patients with personality disorders often fail to respond to common medications for depression and that they suffer frequent relapses back into depression.

Electroconvulsive therapy (ECT) is often considered as a treatment option in patients for whom different antidepressants have failed to lift the depression. In the 2004 study, the researchers found that people with depression who had BPD did not respond as well to ECT as depressed people without BPD and further, the worse the BPD, the less likely the patients were to improve. As is true of many treatments for depression, having a co-occurring BPD makes the treatment of the depression far more difficult. Therefore although ECT *is* used in these cases, a dramatic improvement should not be expected.

Partial Hospitalization

This is when the patient continues to live at home, but goes to the treatment center three to seven days a week and usually lasts from one to three weeks.

In a 1999 study, Peter Fonagy, M.D., and Anthony Bateman, Ph.D., studied the effect of a partial hospital group that offered psychoanalytic therapy compared to a standard psychiatric care group (which is a group of patients receiving whatever type of therapy they were receiving in their partial hospitalization) in patients with BPD. Treatment was up to eighteen months. The researchers measured the frequency of suicide attempts and acts of self-harm, the number and duration of inpatient admissions, the use of psychiatric medication, and self-reported depression, anxiety, distress, interpersonal function, and social adjustment.

The researchers found that patients who were partially hospitalized showed better outcomes on all measures, including an improvement in depressive symptoms, a decrease in suicidal and self-mutilation, reduced inpatient days, and better social and interpersonal function. These improvements began at six months and continued until the end of treatment at eighteen months. In contrast, the standard psychiatric care group showed limited change or deterioration over the same period.

The researchers concluded that psychoanalytically oriented partial hospitalization is superior to standard psychiatric care for patients with BPD.

Residential Treatment

Some adolescents with BPD need a structured out-of-home placement for their behavioral or emotional problems. Residential treatment facilities provide twenty-four-hour care with counseling, therapy, and trained staff (which can include psychiatrists, psychologists, nurses, social workers, and mental health counselors). Adolescents are usually placed in residential treatment only after their families have unsuccessfully tried other ways to help the child. If residential treatment is required for an extended period of time (four months or more), it is known as a long-term residential setting. If the length of time is shorter than that, it is known as a short-term or acute residential setting. As with most therapies, residential treatment works best when the family is involved through family counseling.

The acute, short-term (that is four to eight weeks) residential treatment unit at McLean Hospital has been working with borderline adolescents for many years, and sometimes refers adolescents to long-term residential settings if it becomes evident that the adolescent requires extended therapy.

The different treatment methods include a DBT-based classroom run by a DBT trained tutor, DBT therapists and groups, psychopharmacology with a view to addressing comorbidities, group therapy, family therapy, milieu (which is the residential or non-clinical part of the day where kids interact in much more developmentally natural ways), and dynamic therapy.

McLean Hospital has a dedicated adolescent DBT unit for adolescents with BPD and adolescents who need a skills-based therapy to deal with emotional and behavioral dysregulation.

There are many benefits to residential treatment. For one, a highly trained and experienced staff is less likely to be vulnerable to splitting (where a staff person is seen as all-good or all-bad) and boundary violations (where a staff person crosses the bounds of the patient-therapist relationship).

While our unit at McLean Hospital treats patients for four to eight weeks, an increasing number of longer-term residential centers in the United States work with kids with BPD for a year or more. You'll find a partial list of them in the resources section, beginning on page 232.

Hospitalization

While admitting people with BPD to the hospital is of course an option, long-term inpatient treatment is not generally available. In fact clinicians agree that hospitalization for BPD should be minimized.

Canadian psychiatrist Joel Paris, M.D., has been consistent and clear in pointing out that hospitalizations are not generally necessary—or even useful—for the majority of patients with BPD.

In a 2004 article that examined the value of hospitalization for chronically suicidal patients with BPD, Dr. Paris recognized that although one in ten of those patients might eventually complete suicide, the outcome of suicide is not readily predictable. He noted that hospitalization is of unproven value for suicide prevention and that it can often produce negative effects such as a child learning that all she has to say is that she is suicidal and wants to get out of their house in order to avoid the repercussions of some consequence for inappropriate behavior. Another consequence is that adolescents sometimes learn more about self-destructive behavior from other self-destructive kids *in* the hospital than out of it! Dr. Paris further argued that studies show day treatment to be more effective than hospital admission, and that chronic suicidality could best be managed in an outpatient setting.

In a 1998 paper, Gunnar Kullgren, M.D., compared fifteen patients with BPD who had committed suicide while under inpatient care or within a month after discharge with a group of thirteen inpatients with BPD who did not kill themselves. Suicides occurred in all ages, from twenty to forty-nine years. The ages, sexes, Axis I disorders, and BPD symptoms were similar between the two groups. The patients who committed suicide had been hospitalized more often and had made more suicide attempts in their lifetime. Male patients who killed themselves showed more extensive suicidal behavior at admission than the patients who did not kill themselves. Earlier suicide attempts during inpatient treatment were identified only among the patients who committed suicide. An imminent mandatory discharge preceded the inpatient suicides in five patients.

Clearly, hospitalization does not prevent suicide in all patients with BPD. If a patient with BPD and strong suicidality is to be discharged, a careful assessment of all the biosocial factors in the person's life needs be taken into account prior to discharge.

Even though hospitalization might not prevent suicide, hospitalization must be considered when a patient's suicidal thinking becomes a suicidal plan with intent to carry out the plan or when there has been significant self-injurious behavior requiring medical attention (such as laceration of tendons, deep cutting with blood loss, or a combination of self-injurious behavior and overdosing with an intent to suicide). This is especially true when patients with BPD have a clear episode of major depression or worsening substance abuse.

Marsha Linehan, Ph.D., once quipped that the best hospital for a borderline patient was a "dirty, dark place with hard beds and bad food where no one will ever talk to them or ever visit!" From a behavioral perspective we should avoid reinforcing hospitalization, as many patients with BPD can be highly charming and become staff favorites. Some patients with BPD learn to get hospitalized to have the staff give them the attention they so desperately crave.

CHAPTER ELEVEN

Does Medication Help Adolescents with BPD?

I N A WORLD OFTEN MARKED BY a quest to have our needs instantly gratified, it is ironic that there is no simple answer or quick fix to BPD. Though medications are frequently prescribed for BPD, none of them cures this disorder.

Many parents have noted that medications have only marginally helped their children. The following email could represent the frustrations and feelings of many parents of adolescents with BPD.

"My daughter is a fourteen-and-a-half-year-old freshman at a local public high school here in Connecticut, but she is currently an inpatient in the adolescent psych unit under the direction of a child and adolescent psychiatrist. This is her eighth hospitalization, and for over three years she has been treated for depression, bipolar, anxiety, ADHD, you name it. Since her first hospitalization she has been treated with Depakote, Lexapro, Seroquel, Prozac, Zoloft, Abilify, Clonidine, Ritalin, Benadryl, Trazadone, and others I can't remember. She is on five different drugs at the moment. Now she is diagnosed with bipolar II with borderline personality.

"I'm feeling after three years of medications that little progress has been made.

"Her psychiatrist has struggled with her diagnosis. I think that he has shifted to the borderline diagnosis because none of the meds seem to help and she seems to meet the profile.

"Her uncle had bipolar disorder, but he has done well on lithium for many years. I myself was hospitalized for depression ten years ago and after a year on medications I was taken off and am doing well except for the troubles with my daughter.

"Basically my question is: Are there other medications we can use?"

The answer is that medication can only be a part of a more comprehensive solution for adolescents with BPD.

WHY PRESCRIBE?

Clinicians prescribe medications for BPD for several reasons. The first is that BPD has mood symptoms and impulsivity that sometimes respond to medication. One important principle in the treatment of BPD is to slow the person down enough to allow him or her to use newly acquired problem-solving skills. If medication can reduce impulsivity, it might be useful.

The second reason why clinicians prescribe medications for BPD is that BPD frequently co-occurs with other disorders—such as anxiety, depression, and bipolar disorder—which can respond to medication.

In an attempt to more specifically address the role of medication in BPD, the American Psychiatric Association (APA) issued a *Practice Guideline for the Treatment of Patients with Borderline Personality Disorder* in 2001. It recognized that psychotherapy is the primary form of treatment for BPD, but it also recommended the use of medication to target specific symptoms. The APA states:

"Pharmacotherapy [medication] is used to treat state symptoms during periods of acute decompensation [i.e., unstable behavior] as well as trait vulnerabilities. Symptoms exhibited by patients with borderline personality disorder often fall within three behavioral dimensions—affective dysregulation [i.e., mood symptoms], impulsive-behavioral dyscontrol [i.e., impulsivity], and cognitive-perceptual difficulties [i.e., paranoia]—for which specific [medical] treatment strategies can be used."

For mood-related symptoms and impulsivity, the APA suggested antidepressants, anti-anxiety drugs, mood stabilizers, and, as a last resort, electroconvulsive therapy (ECT). For paranoia, hallucinations, and dissociations, the APA recommended low doses of antipsychotic drugs.

However, the APA made these recommendations with adults with BPD in mind. When it comes to children and adolescents, the use of psychiatric medications has become increasingly scrutinized and debated. Controversy has arisen over the rampant use of stimulants to treat attention deficit hyperactivity disorder (ADHD), the suicidality caused by certain antidepressants, and the use of unapproved medications for certain psychiatric conditions. Further, concern has focused on the effect that high doses—and frequently, multiple medications—have on the developing adolescent brain.

Many adolescents arrive at McLean already using, and having been tried on, multiple medications. We often see little positive effects to all the medication, but many of the side effects, such as weight gain and sedation. It is, however, sometimes true that the medications simply need to be adjusted to optimize treatment. The lowest dose possible that treats the symptoms is ideal.

Patients may need to be weaned off one medication before starting others, depending on the medication. The symptoms of too-rapid withdrawal from psychiatric drugs can include extreme nausea, anxiety, insomnia, restlessness, muscular reactions, and even odd behavior.

In the case of minor tranquilizers and sedatives, the reactions to sudden withdrawal can be life threatening, such as the sudden onset of seizures. Sudden discontinuation of a selective serotonin reuptake inhibitor, such as Prozac, can lead to severe flu like symptoms, such as headache, diarrhea, nausea, vomiting, chills, dizziness, and fatigue. There may be insomnia. Agitation, impaired concentration, vivid dreams, depersonalization, irritability, and suicidal thoughts sometimes occur. These symptoms last anywhere from one to seven weeks and vary in intensity. Patients and families should consult a physician before making the decision to come off any prescribed medication.

MEDICATIONS USED TO TREAT BPD

No medication has received approval from the Federal Drug Administration for the treatment of adolescent BPD. In this section we will discuss medications that have been studied in treating BPD, although these studies have solely focused on adults with BPD.

ANTIPSYCHOTIC MEDICATIONS

Several antipsychotic medications (which are also called neuroleptic medications) have been used to treat BPD. These drugs were originally developed to treat schizophrenia.

Olanzapine (Zyprexa). This atypical antipsychotic was approved by the Food and Drug Administration (FDA) for the treatment of schizophrenia, acute mania in bipolar disorder, agitation associated with schizophrenia and bipolar disorder, and as maintenance treatment of bipolar disorder and psychotic depression.

Research has shown that olanzapine can reduce anxiety, paranoia, anger/hostility, and interpersonal sensitivity, in BPD. (Interpersonal sensitivity is the accuracy and appropriateness of perceptions, judgments, and responses that we have with respect to one another. People with

GETTING YOUR ADOLESCENT TO TAKE MEDICATION

It's important to take medication consistently and properly. Yet it can be difficult to convince adolescents to take medication. There are six main reasons why: anger, side effects, impulsivity, rule-breaking behavior, negative attitudes toward treatment, and substance abuse.

Compliance tends to be greater when parents and adolescents agree on four things: the purpose of the medication, who is responsible for medication administration, their understanding of medication instructions, and the effectiveness of the medication. Better compliance occurs with adolescent understanding of their psychiatric illness.

An open, honest, and thorough level of communication with adolescents and their families is essential.

An interesting component to compliance that I have seen in the past few years is that both parents and adolescents have tremendous access to information because of the Internet. Some websites discuss each and every possible side effect, even if these issues are not generally seen in clinical practice. Parents and adolescents should ask if they are concerned about a specific issue; the prescribing clinician must be aware of the possibility of "too much knowledge" being a deterrent to compliance.

BPD are sometimes too interpersonally sensitive, and they over-judge situations, such as feeling that no one loves them or that people are talking about them.)

However, one concern about the use of olanzapine, especially in adolescents, is the tremendous amount of weight gain it can cause, even more than other atypical antipsychotic medications. Adolescents with BPD frequently have poor self-images, and little could make it worse other than weight gain. This is why I have not prescribed olanzapine for adolescents in BPD.

Quetiapine (Seroquel), another atypical antipsychotic medication, has received FDA approval for the treatment of schizophrenia, acute mania in bipolar disorder, and depressive episodes associated with bipolar disorder.

Although it hasn't been approved by the FDA for this use, doctors prescribe quetiapine to treat other disorders, such as post-traumatic stress disorder (PTSD), alcoholism, obsessive-compulsive disorder (OCD), and anxiety disorders, and as a sedative for sleep difficulties. (When doctors prescribe a medication for a condition other than one for which it has been approved by the FDA, it's called an off-label use. This practice is common not only in psychiatry but across medicine.)

Research has shown that quetiapine is effective in patients with BPD for treating low mood, anxiety, and aggression. I have found quetiapine to be effective in reducing anxiety in adolescents with BPD. Anxiety frequently plagues adolescents, but anti-anxiety medications—such as the benzodiazepines clonazepam (Klonopin) and lorazepam (Ativan)—have their own problems. These medications are potentially addictive, and drug addictions can be a problem for adolescents with BPD.

Aripiprazole (Abilify). This is another atypical antipsychotic medication the FDA approved to treat schizophrenia and acute manic and mixed episodes associated with bipolar disorder. Studies have shown that aripiprazole reduces depression and anger in patients with BPD.

Risperidone (Risperdal). This atypical antipsychotic medication is most often used to treat schizophrenia and other psychotic states, but it is also prescribed for acute manic episodes of bipolar disorder. Most recently, the FDA approved it for the treatment of irritability associated with autistic disorder, including symptoms of aggression toward others, deliberate self-injuriousness, temper tantrums, and quickly changing moods in children and adolescents ages five to sixteen.

Research in BPD has found that at an average dose of between 3 and 4 milligrams of risperidone per day, there is a significant reduction in aggression and an overall reduction in depressive symptoms.

As all medications, antipsychotics come with side effects. The FDA requires the manufacturers of all atypical antipsychotics to include a warning about the risk of increased blood sugar and diabetes with these drugs.

In addition, increased fat levels in the blood may also be an issue with this medication. Some atypical antipsychotics cause tremendous weight gain.

This is particularly worrisome because two of these side effects (impaired glucose metabolism and obesity), combined with high triglycerides make up what is known as the "metabolic syndrome," a condition which may increase the risk of cardiovascular disease. Data suggests that olanzapine may be more likely to cause adverse metabolic effects than some of the other atypical antipsychotic medications.

ANTIDEPRESSANT MEDICATIONS

Media coverage in the past few years has focused on the use of antidepressants in children. Here is a typical warning the FDA has asked manufacturers of antidepressant medication to include in their prescribing information:

"Antidepressant medications are used to treat a variety of conditions, including depression and other mental/mood disorders. These medications can help prevent suicidal thoughts/attempts and provide other important benefits. However, studies have shown that a small number of people (especially children/teenagers) who take antidepressants for any condition may experience worsening depression, other mental/mood symptoms, or suicidal thoughts/attempts. Therefore, it is very important to talk with the doctor about the risks and benefits of antidepressant medication (especially for children/teenagers), even if treatment is not for a mental/mood condition."

Trials of one type of antidepressants in particular—the selective serotonin reuptake inhibitors (SSRIs), such as Prozac—and other antidepressant medications in children and adolescents with major depressive disorder, OCD, and other psychiatric disorders show that the average risk of suicidal thinking was 4 percent, which was twice as much suicidal thinking as occurred in people who took a placebo (sugar pill) in the studies. No suicides occurred in these trials.

The FDA required that the following black-box warning be included for all types of antidepressants.

"Antidepressants increase the risk of suicidal thinking and behavior (suicidality) in children and adolescents with MDD [major depressive disorder, which is another term for major depression] and other psychiatric disorders. Anyone considering the use of an antidepressant in a child or adolescent for any clinical use must balance the risk of increased suicidality with the clinical need. Patients who are started on therapy should be observed closely for clinical worsening, suicidality, or unusual changes in behavior. Families and caregivers should be advised to closely observe the patient and to communicate with the prescriber."

The FDA requires manufacturers to include a statement with the medication regarding whether the particular drug is approved for any pediatric indication(s) and, if so, which one(s).

I have found increasing suicidal ideation with the use of antidepressants, however, I have also found that starting these medications at much lower doses than suggested by the manufacturer appears to lead to less rapid changes in brain chemistry, which may lessen the irritability and suicidality. It is true that starting at a lower dose may mean that it takes longer for the treatment to take effect, but this is certainly better than the intolerability of suicidal thoughts.

Selective Serotonin Reuptake Inhibitors. Because of the potentially lethal side effects of older classes of antidepressants, researchers continued to look for drugs that maintained the benefits but shed the more troublesome side effects. The SSRIs were developed and are now the most commonly prescribed class of antidepressants. They work by blocking the reuptake of serotonin from the synapse back into the nerve, thereby increasing the serotonin that is available in the synapse.

The SSRIs include fluoxetine (Prozac), sertraline (Zoloft), paroxetine (Paxil), fluvoxamine (Luvox), citalopram (Celexa), and escitalopram (Lexapro).

Two of these SSRIs in particular have research support for being prescribed for BPD: fluoxetine and fluvoxamine.

Fluoxetine is an antidepressant drug used in the treatment of depression, body dysmorphic disorder, obsessive-compulsive disorder, bulimia nervosa, premenstrual dysphoric disorder, and panic disorder. Compared to other SSRIs, fluoxetine has a strong energizing effect, which sometimes leads the adolescents we treat to complain of feeling more irritable. Fluoxetine has been shown to reduce the chronic dysphoria (depression) and impulsive aggression common among borderline patients.

Fluvoxamine is an SSRI used to treat OCD by decreasing persistent and unwanted thoughts (obsessions) and urges to perform repeated tasks (compulsions such as hand-washing, counting, and checking) that interfere with daily living. Although not approved for depression or bulimia, it is sometimes used for both of these conditions. Research has shown a long-lasting reduction in rapid mood shifts, but not in impulsivity or aggression when compared to a placebo (sugar pill). In an earlier chapter we looked at the hypothalamic pituitary adrenal (HPA) axis, which is the group of nerves and hormones that deal with human stress and is very active in people who have been abused or experienced trauma. Research has shown that fluvoxamine reduces the over activity of the HPA axis in BPD patients with a history of sustained childhood abuse.

Tricyclic antidepressants. Tricyclic antidepressants are drugs that work by preventing the re-uptake or re-packaging of the neurotransmitters norepinephrine, dopamine, or serotonin by nerve cells. The neurotransmitter theory of depression is that these "chemicals" are low in the brain. Generally after a neurotransmitter has been released by a nerve cell, it is either broken down or taken back into the nerve cell. The purpose of taking the neurotransmitter back into the cell is so that it can be re-packaged and then used again. This process is known as re-uptake. By preventing or blocking the re-uptake, more of the chemical is available in the brain, and thus available to counter depression caused by low levels of the chemical.

The tricyclic antidepressants include amitriptyline, nortriptyline, desipramine, and imipramine. (I haven't included brand names for these drugs because many of them are old and no longer branded.)

Although this class of medications works very well for depression, it is seldom used today as a first choice because of potential side effects. These drugs can cause bladder problems, constipation, dry mouth, sexual problems, blurred vision, dizziness, drowsiness, and unwanted weight changes. Far more serious, they can cause the heart to have abnormal beats and rhythms. When taken in an overdose or a suicide attempt, they can quickly lead to death from cardiac arrest.

Imipramine is an old antidepressant that has also been used to treat attention deficit disorder (ADD) and bedwetting in children. Due to its side effects, it is rarely used in child psychiatry today.

However, imipramine has been studied in children with BPD. In a 1981 study, the authors looked at three case histories of children with BPD. Each child had failed to benefit from intensive hospital treatment until imipramine was added to the treatment. On the medication, there was substantial improvement in peer interactions, treatment compliance, and bizarre behaviors.

MOOD STABILIZING/ANTI-SEIZURE DRUGS

This type of drug has been approved to even out moods and decrease seizures in conditions such as epilepsy. However, sometimes doctors prescribe them for BPD.

Divalproex or divalproex sodium (Depakote) has been approved to treat manic episodes associated with bipolar disorder. A manic episode is a distinct period of abnormally and persistently elevated, expansive, or irritable mood, with symptoms such as talking too fast, motor hyperactivity, reduced need for sleep, racing thoughts, and poor judgment. This medication also treats epilepsy and migraines.

A 2002 study found that divalproex sodium was a safe and effective agent in the treatment of women with BPD and comorbid bipolar II disorder, significantly decreasing irritability and anger, the tempestuousness of relationships, and impulsive aggressiveness.

Common side effects of this drug are tiredness, dizziness, upset stomach, vomiting, tremors, hair loss, and changes in behavior, such as irritability. Weight gain affects 30 to 50 percent of people who take Depakote. Exercise and a reduced-calorie diet can help, but nevertheless weight gain is a problem.

Most of the aforementioned side effects are "nuisance" side effects and disappear after stopping the medication or as the adolescent gets used to the medication. However, there are rare side effects that require medical attention, such as weakness, sluggishness, swelling of the face, loss of appetite, vomiting, and yellowish eyes or skin, which may indicate a serious liver problem. Other serious concerns are pain in the abdomen, upset stomach, vomiting, or loss of appetite, which may indicate a serious pancreas problem. Finally, easy bruising, nosebleed, and other abnormal bleeding can occur, which may indicate a serious blood system problem.

Topiramate (Topamax) is an anti-seizure drug that is only approved for the treatment of seizures or epilepsy. In psychiatry, it has been used—though not approved—for rapid cycling, (which is a form of bipolar with rapid mood changes when a person has four or more episodes of mania and or depression per year) mixed bipolar states, and PTSD. It has also been successfully used to decrease binge eating and overeating caused by other psychiatric medications. Unlike other mood-stabilizers, topiramate does not appear to cause weight gain, and in fact it may actually cause weight loss.

The major side effects of topiramate are psychomotor slowing, memory problems (which are of special concern with adolescents in school and are particularly common when a high starting dose is used or the medication dose is increased suddenly), fatigue, confusion, sleepiness, and kidney stones, which affect only about 1 percent of people who take the drug.

Topiramate has been shown to be safe and effective in the treatment of anger in women with BPD, and it may also cause significantly greater weight loss in patients with BPD compared with a placebo. Again, this is important to consider as many of the medications used in psychiatry cause significant weight gain.

Lamotrigine (Lamictal) is an anticonvulsant that the FDA approved in 2003 to treat bipolar disorder. Psychiatry is now increasingly using it because of its relatively benign side effects. It has also been used in certain people with major depression and PTSD, although it is not approved for these conditions.

About one in ten people taking lamotrigine develops a mild rash (like a sunburn) and about one in a thousand develop a severe rash (like a bad case of poison ivy) that requires treatment. The more severe the rash, the less likely it is that a patient will be able to continue the medication. In any case, all rashes should receive immediate medical attention. A few deaths have occurred in people who have developed a severe, lamotrigine-induced rash known as the Stevens-Johnson syndrome.

In clinical practice, and as with the use of many drugs in adolescent psychiatry, side effects are dose-dependent. For lamotrigine, the rash is more likely to develop when the initial dose is high or started too rapidly or when someone is also taking divalproex.

Other side effects tend to be nuisance in nature, however, patients should be aware of the following rare side effects: agitation, anxiety, irritability, difficulty in concentrating, confusion, depression, and emotional instability.

Research has shown that both BPD and bipolar symptoms improved in bipolar patients with BPD taking lamotrigine.

Oxcarbazepine (Trileptal) is an anticonvulsant and mood-stabilizing drug, used primarily in the treatment of epilepsy and bipolar disorder. Side effects can include fatigue, nausea, vomiting, headache, dizziness, drowsiness, and blurred or double vision. It can cause hyponatremia (low blood sodium), so blood sodium levels should be tested if the patient complains of severe fatigue. A 2006 study by Silvio Bellino, M.D., and colleagues from the University of Turin in Italy found oxcarbazepine to be effective and well tolerated in their study of seventeen patients with BPD.

BENZODIAZEPINE AND OTHER ANTI-ANXIETY DRUGS

There are different categories of drugs that treat anxiety. Some of the aforementioned antipsychotic drugs, such as quetiapine, markedly reduce anxiety, although given the potential side effects of the anti-psychotics, psychiatrists would generally not prescribe these medications if anxiety is the only symptom.

Other drugs, however, are specifically prescribed for anxiety. In clinical practice with BPD adolescents, the benzodiazepines (or "benzos" as the kids like to call them) and Clonidine are the most commonly prescribed medications to treat anxiety. It has been my clinical experience that the benzodiazepine class of drugs is not predictably effective in adolescents with BPD because "benzos" are easily addictive and can cause disinhibition or a feeling of intoxication in people who take them. Many adolescents with BPD already struggle with addiction or disinhibited behavior so it makes little sense to compound the problem. However, they are worth considering when the chance of addiction is low or when nothing else has worked.

Benzodiazepine Medications: Commonly known "benzos" are diazepam (Valium), lorazepam (Ativan), and clonazepam (Klonopin). They are used primarily in people with anxiety, but also for sleep problems, seizure prevention, and in cases of alcohol withdrawal. They are all potentially addictive.

Clonidine (Catapres) This medication is not a benzodiazepine, and is better known for its use in treating high blood pressure. However, it is frequently used in psychiatry because it appears to block the effects of adrenaline, which can lead to anxiety, so although not approved by the FDA for these purposes, it has also been used to relieve anxiety, alleviate sleeping difficulties, aid in alcohol withdrawal, and help smoking cessation and other conditions. Common side effects can include chest pain, low blood pressure, weakness, and sedation. Research has shown that clonidine significantly reduces the aversive inner tension (which is a very unpleasant mood or inner, emotional state), dissociative symptoms, urge to commit self-injurious behavior, and suicidal ideations commonly found in BPD. The strongest effects are seen between thirty and sixty minutes after taking the drug.

NATURAL REMEDIES USED TO TREAT BPD

Many people remember a time when mothers and grandmothers made children swallow spoonfuls of fish oil every day. They claimed that it was good for everything that ailed or could possibly ail the young ones. It looks like research is proving that this old wisdom is true. The big issue is the intake of what are known as the essential fatty acids (EFAs).

Fatty acids are components of fats. Essential fatty acids (EFAs) are so called because the body cannot produce them, yet they are essential to life. Because they cannot be produced by the body, they must be included in our diet. Two fatty acids vital to our survival are EPA (eicosapentaenoic acid) and DHA (docosahexaenoic acid). Some researchers consider EPA to be the single most vital nutrient in the functioning of the brain and nerve stimulation. DHA is thought to constitute a major building block of the brain, forming about 8 percent of the brain by weight.

An important fact is that EFAs make up 45 percent of the fatty acids in the membranes of the nerve cells in our brains and are critical to nerve cell function. EFAs make cell membranes more fluid, and omega-3 fatty acids in particular improve communication between the brain cells.

Many studies support the intake of omega-3 fatty acids for good health, most significantly mental well-being and cardiac health.

Sadly, as a nation we have reduced our consumption of fish (the best source of EFAs) and markedly increased the amount of refined foods in our diets. Because of all of this, it is estimated that the amount of omega-3 fatty acids in our diet has reduced somewhere between 50 and 80 percent.

Here is just some of the research on the importance of EFAs. One study found that fifty-three children with attention deficit hyperactivity disorder (ADHD) had significantly lower blood levels of EFAs, compared with forty-three children who were not diagnosed with ADHD.

Depression has been directly related to fish consumption. A 2001 study reported a strong relationship of fish consumption with lower rates of depression in countries such as Japan, Korea, and Taiwan.

A 2004 study looked at the relation of dietary intake of EFAs with hostility in young people. Researchers found that consumption of any fish rich in EFAs, compared to no consumption, was associated with lower odds of hostility in young people.

Between these three studies, we have evidence that low EFAs are associated with depression, anger, and impulsivity, which are three major symptoms of BPD.

In 2003, Mary Zanarini, Ed.D., at McLean Hospital and colleagues conducted an eight-week study of twenty female patients with BPD who were given omega-3 fatty acids and compared their results to ten women with BPD who were given a placebo. They found that omega-3 fatty acids were superior to a placebo in diminishing aggression as well as the severity of depressive symptoms in BPD. The researchers concluded that omega-3 fatty acids are a potentially useful form of medication therapy in BPD.

On a personal note, as many studies appear to show that our diets have plenty of vitamins, I am not a big advocate of multivitamins or other supplements. However, it is absolutely clear that we have significantly decreased the amount of omega-3 fatty acids in our diets. Because of this, it is the one supplement that I encouraged my own kids to take. We make fish oil as part of our morning breakfast ritual.

TREATMENT OF BPD CO-OCCURRING WITH ANOTHER PSYCHIATRIC ILLNESS

It's important to remember that having BPD co-occur with any other condition forces the clinician to consider that an already challenging treatment is going to require even more thought and energy. For an example, consider BPD co-occurring with bipolar disorder.

In a 2005 study, researchers noted that patients who suffered from both BPD and bipolar I disorder posed unique treatment challenges. They found that patients who had both disorders took more than twice as long for their symptoms to stabilize than those with bipolar disorder alone.

The bipolar-BPD group received significantly more atypical mood-stabilizing medications per year than the bipolar-only group. The rate of patients dropping out of therapy was also higher in the BPD-bipolar group.

CONCLUSION ON MEDICATION

Medication is a useful part of the treatment of targeted symptoms of BPD such as anxiety, impulsivity, and paranoia. It is also important in the treatment of co-occuring conditions. However, medication neither cures BPD nor effectively treats BPD in the absence of appropriate psychotherapy.

CHAPTER TWELVE

Understanding BPD Through Stories from Patients, Parents, and Health Care Professionals

ONE OF THE MOST SOBERING STATISTICS on BPD is that it kills 10 percent of its victims. If we are to have any hope of changing this statistic, it is essential that we recognize how profoundly painful the emotional turmoil of BPD can be.

BPD can ravage a person's self-esteem. After a difficult phone call with her mother that made her feel worthless and alone, a seventeen-year-old girl told me:

"I've never had lower self-esteem in my entire life. In my entire life! Do you know how low my self-esteem has been during the course of my life? It's been low. It's been so low that I've made myself throw up for hours just because I had a bagel. And it's lower now. I feel like shit."

It is a feeling like this, compounded by aloneness and hopelessness over many years, that makes patients with BPD seriously contemplate suicide. Even if we cannot contemplate such utter self-loathing, accepting that people who suffer from BPD experience self-hatred and worse is important if we are to understand this condition.

It is vitally important to recognize that BPD occurs, and has its roots, in childhood and adolescence. The scientific data to date supports this, the clinical work validates it, but more compelling, the personal stories demand it. Without an accurate diagnosis, patients are often destined for lives of misery as they struggle to be understood and at times are treated with therapies that are not effective.

THE VOICES OF PATIENTS

The following words by eighteen-year-old Lauren—who felt that her experience of living with BPD might best explain the suffering, hoping, and coping with the condition—are compelling:

"What do you do when your feelings are so overwhelming that it's uncomfortable to just sit with yourself? You squirm around in your chair, or your bed, or the couch trying to get rid of this thing that's causing so much discomfort but you can't because it's inside of you. And you just want it out.

"You're smothered in these absolutely horrible feelings and you can't breathe and there's just no way to get away from it. You know that feelings can't kill you, but you're sure this is the one exception. Nothing can even distract you from these feelings because they're so prominent. They've taken over everything. You try to walk around and hope that maybe these feelings will disappear on their own. But the more you try to ignore them, the worse they get.

> *"You know that feelings can't kill you, but you're sure this is the one exception."*
>
> —LAUREN, EIGHTEEN, ON HAVING BPD

They're determined to make you miserable. You just want to shake yourself, or bang your head against a wall. Tear up a pillow or smash a mirror. All because you're so angry with yourself for letting these feelings consume you like they have.

"And then you want to self-destruct somehow—cause pain in some other place so you can get away from the pain that's gnawing at your insides. Focus on something else. Pain that is self-inflicted and controlled is tolerable. Pain that you can't stop or get rid of is even more reason to be mad at yourself.

"Why can't I control my feelings? Why can't I stop this? Why can't I just be numb? Why can't I get away from the awfulness that is following me?

"The magnitude of these feelings increases by the second. You think you've had all you can take, and then the feelings consume you even more. You try to act normal because you don't want to give in to these feelings. Don't want to let them win. But in reality, they've already won. They've taken over every aspect of your life.

"So tell me. What do you do with these horrific feelings that are buried so deep within you that you wouldn't even know where to start looking to dig them out? They're like cancer—they just spread and spread and spread.

"What do you do?

"Anger and sweetness can be turned on and off like the flick of a switch, and all the emotions in between can take over in one second, and wash away in the next. Self-hatred and self-loathing run far deeper than anybody can imagine, to the point of being able to *physically* feel them. BPD is a disorder that's hard to escape from, hard to change, and even harder to live with.

"I battle myself every day to maintain some sort of control over these symptoms. There are days when I feel like I've gotten a grip on myself and that I've finally begun to overcome my battle. Other days, I feel like I *am* my disorder, and it's all I ever will be: a shell of person, who is halfway between being alive and being dead.

"I describe myself as having two conflicting personalities—one being the 'good' me, the other being the 'bad' me. They are continuously at war with each other, each begging to have a permanent place in the spotlight.

"The 'good' me is the healthy me. I'm confidant, energetic, sweet, witty, and open. I'm in control, I want to get better, and I'm motivated to accomplish life's daily tasks. The 'bad' me comes out when I feel vulnerable, attacked, or abandoned. I'm absolutely horrific to be around when I'm in this state because I say terrible things to the person my anger is directed toward. My all-or-nothing thinking takes over, and nobody can say anything to retrieve me from the funk I fall into. I'm always completely aware that I'm doing it, and don't *want* to be doing it. Yet I feel powerless to stop it. Once the anger washes over me, I'm a completely different, awful person. I'm someone I don't know, and someone I don't want to be.

"When the anger subsides and I have time to reflect on my actions, the guilt comes in full force. Why did I get so mad in the first place? Why couldn't I stop myself? How could I say that? I bet that person hates me. I hate me. I should just die. No matter how guilty I feel afterwards, it'll happen again, and eventually the relationship will end. I lashed out because I felt abandoned, and I got abandoned in the process. And then the self-hatred intensifies.

"Every emotion and every feeling that I feel is intense. I don't feel sad, I feel painfully miserable. The misery seems to filter through my veins, cycling through my body with the blood, hardly ever being released. I don't get mad, I get furious. My rage always feels justified, never inappropriate. And all the guilt funnels into self-hatred. I suppose this goes hand-in-hand with the all-or-nothing thinking that is so classic of BPD. If I feel, I feel as strongly as possible. Otherwise, I don't feel at all. This has always been the case for me, and only recently did I find out that most people with BPD share in this. I don't think anybody could ever fully register the magnitude and intensity in which we feel.

"The self-hatred, guilt, and intensity of my emotions take their toll. I crave for a way to end the pain, to somehow let that filtering misery out of my veins. Cutting almost always provides that relief. When I hate myself, I want to self-destruct in any way imaginable. I want to inflict physical pain on my body to match the emotional turmoil going on inside me. I want to punish myself for being such a dreadful person.

As soon as the razor crosses over my skin, I feel the release of all the pent-up anger, hatred, and sorrow that the skin seems to be holding in. The deeper the cut, the more satisfaction I find. I want the ugliness that's on the inside to be seen on the outside. The benefits are always temporary, and shame sets in rather quickly. Yet in the midst of such misery, even a second of relief is worth it.

"I wouldn't necessarily say that I feel sorry for myself, but I do feel a great deal of sadness for the person I've become. I know who I am underneath this mess, and I know the potential I have to do great things in life. The real me shines through every once and awhile, and that is the person I know I want to revive. I'm sad for the way I treat the people I love and care about. I absolutely despise BPD, and I hate that I've let it consume me the way that it has. At times, I don't feel like I have enough fight or drive to overcome my disease, especially when I feel it has overcome me. I've been suicidal more days than not, and prior to my last bout of treatment, had no idea how I was still alive.

"I've found that hope is one of the hardest things to maintain with BPD. It can be lost so easily in the poor prognosis, horrible stigma, and self-loathing. Hope is lost in the guilt, the despair, the pain, the loneliness and the constant fight. At my worst, I lost all hope, and was living to die. I was stashing pills and alcohol, waiting for the exact right moment when I could take them all and leave everything behind.

"But my hope was restored due to the extraordinary care I received at McLean Hospital. Hope came to me through sharing a room with two other amazing girls also diagnosed with BPD, and through feeling less alone because of it. It came from dialectical behavior therapy and a magnificent support team. It especially came to me through a wonderful doctor, who had the patience to deal with me at the toughest times and saw me at my worst, yet still continued to tell me I could beat this. The support given to me brought back the will to conquer my illness. I was continuously told I could do it. That recovery was indeed possible. That I wasn't a lost case. I was an empty person when I walked in the doors of that hospital, and a whole one when I walked back out.

"There isn't a day that goes by when I'm unaware of my disorder. It's always on my mind, and I continuously question the validity of my feelings and actions. I struggle to tell the difference between borderline thoughts and normal ones, and I'm nowhere near perfecting this art. I constantly worry that I'm going to lash out at someone, or get angry for something ridiculous. I fear the loss of my relationships with others due to the horrible track record I have so far. And my black-and-white thinking is far more frequent than I even realize. I still struggle with suicidal thoughts and urges to hurt myself, and sometimes I'm positive I won't be victorious in the war with myself.

"I've realized the battle with BPD will never really end, but I've also realized that help is available, and I don't have to feel the wretched misery that comes along with the disease. I have hopes and dreams, and the strength to go on. I do know that some day, somehow, I will be okay."

One of the major problems I hear about from many of the adolescents with BPD we work with is their difficulty in romantic (and other) relationships. There is often a tremendous fear that the other person will discover just how "bad" or "awful" they are. Another fear is that they will "poison" the other person with their "badness." But even after years of therapy and increasing confidence, and even when the BPD symptoms are no longer present, the fear that their past will be discovered can make many shy away from intimate relationships.

Eric, twenty, now living a life worth living, but with a past full of self-doubt, self-injury, and substance abuse, put it this way:

"It is difficult for me to initiate talking to a girl, especially if I am interested in her because I fear that she will ask me about my past. I don't want my past to taint her view of me now, or for her to think that I am crazy. Eventually, I have to become more comfortable talking about myself to new people, but I think that the kind of relationship that would work for me is someone who is more understanding, and more focused on the present."

THE VOICE OF A PARENT

In as much as adolescents with BPD suffer with their condition, parents, too, suffer profoundly. Parents often have to deal with the rage of adolescents with BPD, the guilt of feeling they might have done something to cause the problem, the accusations of bad parenting by other members of the family, the feeling that they have not given their other children enough attention, and the stigma of having children who are "known" as having troubles.

The mother of a seventeen-year-old with BPD shared the following thoughts:

"There were signs, but we didn't see them. As people who approach life with confident optimism, we embarked on the adventure of creating a family with naïve, enthusiastic energy.

"Nature versus nurture? As adoptive parents we were convinced that the loving environment we'd create for our first child would guide his development and form a personality as open and gregarious as ours.

"Mother nature is a powerful force. She equipped Sean with a temperament that rebuffed our relentlessly misguided efforts to shape our son in our image. Convinced that he would eventually emerge from his wary, reluctant ways, we unwittingly practiced invalidation early and often. Failing to appreciate how fragile his makeup truly was, we forged ahead, exposing him to new experiences without realizing the layers of trauma they provoked.

"When Sean was three, a neighbor trained in early childhood education asked with concern if we had noticed that he was unusually solemn and guarded. 'He's just shy,' we replied. A dozen years later, a forensic psychologist described hypervigilence.

"When he was four, we took him to the performance of his favorite musician, a performer of silly animal-themed songs. As children around him enthusiastically clapped, sang, and laughed, Sean sat through the show without expression. After the concert we gently sought to understand what about the experience had so frightened him. On the contrary, he described the afternoon as the best ever. Our inability to read any emotion in his flat affect continued for years.

"When he was ten, Sean's pitching helped his Little League team make the playoffs. During the final game the opposing coach bellowed jeers and catcalls at every throw. The crowd watched the league's leading pitcher wither under the assault. The game was lost on walks. Sean left the field in stoic silence. Our attempts to encourage him to express his feelings, to process the defeat, met with resolute resistance. He never picked up a baseball glove again. A pattern of dissociating when faced with traumas large and small was emerging.

"When he was in middle school Sean took up lacrosse. Wielding the stick with ferocious intensity, he left his understated personality on the sidelines. He played attack with a vigor that caused spectators to gasp. Deep-seated anger had found an outlet. We were perplexed that even though he wore heavily padded gloves during these contests, his knuckles were constantly bloodied and scabbed. Eventually we discovered that he was punching holes in the walls of his room to further express anger and pain.

"Our charming, handsome, artistic, athletic son became an unrecognizable stranger. Attempts to reach him were met with silence or explosive anger. Therapists were unable to develop any kind of relationship with him."

—THE MOTHER OF A SEVENTEEN-YEAR-OLD WITH BPD

"When he was fourteen, his first girlfriend chose his best friend as her graduation dance date. Unbeknownst to us, he began chugging a couple of beers on the way to school to dull the pain of seeing the newly formed couple together. A pattern of self-soothing through substance abuse had begun.

"When he was a freshman in high school, he quarterbacked the junior varsity football team. A series of concussions undermined his short-term memory, but he never revealed that he was suddenly unable to retain geometry formulae, history dates, or Spanish verb forms. A month after telling us that he looked forward to making the honor roll at his new school he was failing every class and sitting on the bench at every practice and game. He withdrew to the point that the school psychologist mused that Sean lacked a core identity.

"Neuropsychological testing indicated mild ADHD. First Adderall and then Concerta became part of Sean's daily regimen. As his school performance continued to fail to meet expectations, he self-medicated with dextromethorphan and marijuana. Eventually he dabbled in cocaine and mushrooms. His depression deepened to the point that he wouldn't leave his bed. At the beginning of the spring term he was sent home from boarding school on a medical leave. Chronic feelings of emptiness pervaded his being.

"Former teachers who loved and supported our winsome, mysterious son answered the call when we sought tutors to help him complete the school year. Unable to generalize the success that their cheerleading helped him achieve, Sean sought solace in liquor, secretly drinking himself to sleep every night.

"Engagement in family life declined into total avoidance. Our charming, handsome, artistic, athletic son became an unrecognizable stranger. Attempts to reach him were met with silence or explosive anger. Therapists were unable to develop any kind of relationship with him.

"As a new school year approached, we sought the advice of educational consultants, realizing that Sean was unable to successfully navigate public high school. The plan for a comprehensive intervention was laid; therapeutic boarding school was the next stop on his journey. His perception of abandonment manifested itself in extraordinary cutting behaviors. He was placed on twenty-four-hour watch, accompanied everywhere to ensure his safety. When it became clear that he was finding ways to self-injure while alone in the toilet stall, the school declared him too risky a resident. The first of eight psychiatric hospitalizations, ranging from three days to three months, ensued.

"So there you have it. This piece is a series of examples demonstrating the underlying borderline clues, some of which began to manifest themselves earlier than adolescence: fear of abandonment, chronic feeling of emptiness, dissociation, anger, and impulsivity in the form of substance abuse. There were early signals of the disorder unobserved/ignored, thereby unwittingly deepening the sense of invalidation. We continue to look for answers to the source of his suffering. Are they unresolved loss issues stemming from his adoption? Was it due to a lack of resilience to sustain the dislocation of our multiple geographical moves? We have not ruled out sexual abuse at the hands of a day care provider or camp counselor. Was there neurological damage from his football concussions? Finally, the BPD diagnosis makes sense of the symptomatology. Once that is understood, a case can be made for the efficacy of a commitment to DBT, family therapy, a structured environment, the Family CONNECTIONS model*, and hope."

Such thought and careful consideration to trying to answer the BPD puzzle takes time and reflection, and it is such unwavering

> *"[A] major challenge is sitting calmly with the patient's anger, particularly when the anger is directed at you, which it often is as the borderline patient is exquisitely sensitive and can react to minor or perceived slights."*
>
> —JENNIFER MEHRTENS, CASE MANAGER, MCLEAN HOSPITAL, BELMONT, MASSACHUSETTS

---

* The Family CONNECTIONS model is a twelve-week series developed by Perry Hoffman, Ph.D., and Alan Fruzzetti, Ph.D., at the National Education Alliance for BPD for family members with a relative who has BPD or symptoms of the disorder. The course provides education on BPD, research on BPD, and skills training based on dialectical behavior therapy in the context of a supportive group environment.

dedication to understand and hope that gives kids with BPD and their families a chance, and makes working with such families a blessing.

THE VOICES OF MENTAL HEALTH COUNSELORS

Mental health staff have historically been pessimistic about and often unsympathetic toward clients diagnosed with BPD. Research shows that by the time patients with BPD reach adult mental health services their behaviors are often difficult to manage and sadly, they often suffer significant re-victimization by these health services.

By the time the adolescents with BPD are admitted to our unit, many of them have had multiple hospitalizations or been institutionalized in some setting. Early identification and intervention for children and adolescents who exhibit BPD symptoms is essential if we want to significantly change these "difficult behaviors" later on in life.

Nursing and residential staff often spend many more hours than clinicians do with residential or hospitalized patients. Paul Jay is a senior social worker who has worked with adolescents for many years and been director of the residential unit at McLean Hospital for more than seven years. He oversees and supervises the mental health staff on the unit. Paul has often pointed out that the residential staff or mental health counselors spend more time with the patients than the clinicians do, and as such have a more comprehensive and authentic perspective on the day-to-day interactions that our kids have with their parents and peers. His staff provides invaluable daily feedback to the clinicians. These are his thoughts.

"Not until recently have clinicians begun talking about adolescents having a diagnosis of borderline personality disorder. Twenty years ago only irreverent clinicians behind closed doors would whisper their contempt for the *Diagnostic and Statistical Manual* for not considering the idea of adolescents having BPD. The rule was that adolescent development in the realm of social, emotional, and cognitive functioning was too immature and unformed to support the diagnosis of BPD. Instead, adolescents were diagnosed with bipolar disorder, ADHD, oppositional defiant disorder, PTSD, and mood disorders.

"Medication was used readily to control adolescent behavior. The problem was that in too many cases the medication did not work. Symptoms were muted, but only delayed until the age of consent to treatment was reached and medication was no longer a parental prerogative. By that time too many adolescents had grown weary of the required and enforced counseling sessions, which seemed to focus on changing behavior because of guilt and shame. Their failure in therapy to conform to the behavioral expectations of the therapist, parents, and others in authority further degraded their sense of competence and self-esteem. Yes, many felt guilt and shame for the way they behaved, but few could translate those feelings into why they behaved the way they did. They felt hopeless and helpless.

"I remember attending a clinical conference in the late 1970s on the diagnosis and treatment of personality disorders. The instructor saved the discussion on BPD until the very end. As with celebrity, there was excitement and anticipation in the audience as the topic neared. When the instructor finally mentioned BPD, there was a collective buzz. We all knew that we were about to discuss the Cadillac of all the personality disorders and the bane of every clinician. The instructor labeled it as such. After going through the diagnostic criteria for BPD, the instructor said, in effect, that there was little understanding as to how BPD developed and even less understanding as to how to treat it. The instructor continued to say that the weekly crises, poor application of learning, and low motivation for change in people with BPD burned out clinicians. Further, people with BPD were manipulative, attention seeking, chronically suicidal, and treatment rejecting. He ended by saying that those who did in fact choose to work with BPD clients needed to limit their sessions to a maximum of five for their own well-being. It's a wonder how we all survived!

"Today there is growing support for the idea that the clusters of symptoms associated with BPD is seen in adolescents. The talk among clinicians now is, while still hesitant, that adolescents have 'features' and 'emerging' characteristics of BPD. This is progress mostly because the advances in the clinical understanding and treatment of adult BPD can now be applied to adolescents. In adults, the stigma associated with BPD has been reduced by recognition that the stereotype is not true. Adults are not manipulative, but rather attempting in their behavior to lessen the overwhelming feelings of inadequacy and pain. Adults with BPD act in maladaptive ways to relieve pain, suffering, and emptiness when no other way seems possible.

"Studies have found that the development of adult BPD has its roots in the biological predisposition to stimulus overload in transaction with an invalidating environment created over time. This is the bio-social theory of dialectical behavioral therapy. It stands to reason that the development of BPD, if this theory is correct, certainly begins in adolescence if not before.

"Children with a biological predisposition to emotional stimuli, living in an environment of perceived invalidation, begin to develop symptoms of BPD that will mature over time if not addressed. In particular, many adolescents perceive improvement of unendurable emotional pain as a consequence that reinforces dysfunctional behavior. They tell their therapists, for example, that cutting is to relieve pain and that it makes them feel better. The cutting behavior regulates dysregulated emotions or is a consequence of failed emotional regulation. The road for adolescents who develop such a strategy is clearly destined for a life of pain and sorrow leading into adulthood."

THE RESIDENTIAL ENVIRONMENT

"Adolescents are admitted to McLean because they are temporarily no longer able to live at home. They have often become self-destructive or suicidal. The hallmark for treating adolescents with BPD is an environment that is safe, structured, and consistent. In the acute residential treatment (ART) at McLean, our staff is trained in DBT and the bio-social theory. Our staff applies the behavioral, cognitive, and learning principles that continue to prove effective in working with adolescents who present with BPD symptoms. Understanding the bio-social theory of BPD helps staff provide firm, but caring and nurturing intervention with residents that promotes motivation for change while helping them accept who they are.

"Without such training, staff can rapidly burn out in dealing with what appears to be manipulative behavior. Also BPD adolescents can at times see people as either all-good or all-bad, and staff can often feel targeted and personalize the attacks. A strong and supportive consultation team is an essential asset for the residential team working with this population group.

"For the adolescents, change capability is developed through the areas of skills training in the areas of mindfulness, interpersonal effectiveness, emotional regulation, self-soothing, and contingency planning. Once the skills are learned, staff also apply the behavioral interventions of rewards and punishment to modify persistently disordered behavior.

"During the residential component of the day (after the 'clinical' and school day parts are over) the kids return to a less scripted environment where they interact with each other and participate in cooking, journaling, watching TV, and other activities of daily living. These interactions can at times lead to the problematic behaviors that had the adolescent admitted in the first place as they argue over cliques being formed, etc.

"Residents are then required to analyze problematic behavior through the completion of a chain analysis, which is a detailed look at the antecedents (what happened before) and the consequences (what happened after) the behavior. The chain analysis helps the staff and adolescents understand what skills are needed to stop the problem behavior and what reinforcers contribute to the motivation to continue the behavior.

"Work of this nature must be done in an environment that validates the emotional pain experienced by residents and provides the safety necessary to explore reasons to change. Adolescents in the ART find plenty of reassurance from peers with similar problems and patterns of behavior [and learn] they are not alone in their feelings and that help is possible. Many find relief in just learning that others experience similar emotional discomfort and have relied on similar maladaptive means to feel better. In particular, adolescents with a trauma history, especially sexual abuse, benefit from finally being able to express their sense of self-loathing and despair to a peer group that can relate to many of their feelings. They often feel as if a burden has been lifted and that they are allowed to move on in their lives to a healthier sense of well-being.

"One major difficulty in treating adolescents with BPD on a residential unit is the generalizing of learning back to the home environment. Often, adolescents perceive their home environment to be invalidating and unsupportive. Patterns of destructive interactions have developed over time and become intractable.

"Adolescents feel that the balance of power in their family is heavily shifted toward the parents and that, regardless of how much they change, things simply will not improve. It is not uncommon to hear adolescents say during their course of treatment, 'I think that my parents should be admitted here.'

"It is imperative that parents learn to understand and make changes along with their adolescents in treatment. Staff know the skills that each adolescent is working on, which allows them to reinforce these skills and encourage parents to continue this work [when their adolescents return home].

"While working with adolescents with BPD symptoms can be difficult, it is also tremendously rewarding in many ways. Witnessing these adolescents learn and develop new ways to navigate the world and overcome hopelessness and despair is impressive and inspiring. Adolescents finding hope where there previously was none create an appreciation for

ATTITUDES OF CLINICIANS TOWARD BPD

The author of a 2000 study reported the impact of being a community mental health center case manager for someone with BPD. The case managers spent more time with BPD patients than with other patients, monitoring their own thoughts and feelings, expressing concerns about the potential for patient suicide, and setting boundaries with the BPD patients.

In a 2006 study, the authors noted that caring for patients with a diagnosis of BPD was a problem area for mental health professionals and that a diagnosis of BPD at times influenced the level and quality of interaction that staff had with patients with patients. The authors stated that it is inherent to psychiatric nursing that nurses be able to establish rapport, develop trust, and demonstrate empathy with psychiatric patients.

In their study, they found that a proportion of psychiatric nurses experienced negative emotional reactions and attitudes toward people with BPD. Further, the majority of nurses perceived people with BPD as manipulative and almost one-third of nurses reported that patients with BPD made them angry. Further, more than one-third felt that they did not know how to care for people with BPD.

What we see is that as a general rule, counselors, nurses, case managers, and clinicians of all types find it difficult to work with patients with BPD. This compounds an already bad situation for patients with BPD. They suffer with their pain and then feel uncared for. Education is an important part of addressing this issue, as is providing clinicians who work with this population group with skills to treat patients with BPD and a support team to help deal with the potential burnout.

life that is untarnished by years of suffering. Watching while parents of adolescents come to realize that their children can be better, and seeing their sense of relief, is gratifying. Hearing the adolescent and parents communicate with each other without contempt is its own reward, and knowing that you have helped someone to live a life worth living is what all clinicians strive to accomplish."

THE VOICE OF A CASE MANAGER

Jennifer Mehrtens is a case manager on the adolescent treatment unit at McLean Hospital. She is extensively trained in DBT and has worked with clients with BPD across a wide range of settings—not only on our unit but with prison populations and in outpatient clinics as well.

Here she talks about the challenges of working with adolescents with BPD, their families, and the healthcare system.

"The greatest struggle is a patient's pattern of idealizing (you are wonderful!) and devaluing (you are terrible and you aren't helping!) of the therapist. The task is to maintain a balance so as to not reinforce this pattern while acknowledging the equally unhelpful nature of trying to be the all-good therapist (constantly trying to rescue the patient) or all-bad therapist (constantly trying to get rid of the patient).

"Another major challenge is sitting calmly with the patient's anger, particularly when the anger is directed at you, which it often is as the borderline patient is exquisitely sensitive and can react to minor or perceived slights. Staying calm and not defensive is an important skill to develop.

"Adolescents are rarely in treatment alone. You work with a system that can often be as reactive and chaotic as the individual. There are frequently multiple competing agendas, such as insurance companies feeling that they will no longer cover patients' treatment, supervisors feeling that you are trying too hard or not hard enough, parents who are frantic for a faster cure, schools that are not convinced by reassurance that a kid is safe, colleagues who see that treatment should go one way or another, and then ultimately self-doubt that maybe you can't help. Maintaining a clear focus on your role, treatment plan, and formulation can be a major challenge as the pressure to respond to the intense desperation in the system increases.

"Finally, the risk of a negative outcome with the borderline adolescent is higher then with any other group. It is a challenge to resist acting out of fear and also responding appropriately when the patient is at acute risk. Finding a way to manage your own anxiety in response to the patient's desperate emotions and behavior is critical, and perhaps only possible in the presence of a very supportive team of colleagues."

BPD AND CONTEMPORARY CULTURE

In the earlier reflection by Lauren, her writing showed a profound ability to express a very personal pain. The clarity of her writing leaves little doubt as to her enduring distress, sprinkled with hints of hope. Not all adolescents with BPD are as articulate, even if their pain is as disabling. Others feel that poetry, music lyrics, and movies capture their experience.

Adolescents often point out *Girl, Interrupted*, the autobiographical account of author Susanna Kaysen's two-year treatment for BPD took place at McLean Hospital. In the movie of the same title, Kaysen (portrayed by Winona Ryder) was admitted to McLean after an impulsive suicide attempt in which she downed fifty aspirin with a bottle of vodka. Given her suicide attempts, moodiness, and history of promiscuity, she was diagnosed with BPD. Needless to say *Girl, Interrupted* (both book and movie) is a favorite on our unit.

Many psychiatric units have posters on their walls with lists of famous people who have suffered form mental illnesses. The kids know that Abraham Lincoln suffered from depression, that Virginia Woolf had mood swings and committed suicide, and that Vincent van Gogh had bipolar disorder and cut off his ear. Some adolescents want to know if anyone famous has suffered from BPD, especially given that 2 percent of the population has the condition.

Perhaps the most famous person to have suffered from BPD may have been the late Princess Diana. Although many authors have made the claim, in her excellent and meticulously researched book *Diana in Search of Herself: Portrait of a Troubled Princess*, author Sally Bedell Smith writes:

"While one cannot say with certainty that Diana had a borderline personality disorder, the evidence is compelling. The most important factor setting the borderline personality apart from those with other disorders is early parental loss—in Diana's case the departure of her mother and the emotional withdrawal of her father for several years following the Spencer divorce."

Here is an excerpt from a November 1995 interview that the BBC conducted with Princess Diana. Note the classic BPD themes in her answers.

Q: Were you overwhelmed by the pressure from people initially?

A: Yes, I was very daunted because as far as I was concerned I was a fat, chubby, twenty-year-old, twenty-one-year-old, and I couldn't understand the level of interest.

Q: What effect did the depression have on your marriage?

A: Well, it gave everybody a wonderful new label—Diana's unstable and Diana's mentally unbalanced. And unfortunately that seems to have stuck on and off over the years.

Q: According to press reports, it was suggested that it was around this time things became so difficult that you actually tried to injure yourself.

A: Mmm. When no one listens to you or you feel no one's listening to you, all sorts of things start to happen.

For instance you have so much pain inside yourself that you try and hurt yourself on the outside because you want help, but it's the wrong help you're asking for. People see it as crying wolf or attention-seeking, and they think because you're in the media all the time you've got enough attention . . .

But I was actually crying out because I wanted to get better in order to go forward and continue my duty and my role as wife, mother, Princess of Wales.

So yes, I did inflict upon myself. I didn't like myself, I was ashamed because I couldn't cope with the pressures.

Q: What did you actually do?

A: Well, I just hurt my arms and my legs; and I work in environments now where I see women doing similar things and I'm able to understand completely where they're coming from.

Q: The depression was resolved, as you say, but it was subsequently reported that you suffered bulimia. Is that true?

A: Yes, I did. I had bulimia for a number of years. And that's like a secret disease.

You inflict it upon yourself because your self-esteem is at a low ebb, and you don't think you're worthy or valuable. You fill your stomach up four or five times a day—some do it more—and it gives you a feeling of comfort.

It's like having a pair of arms around you, but it's temporarily, temporary. Then you're disgusted at the bloatedness of your stomach, and then you bring it all up again.

And it's a repetitive pattern, which is very destructive to yourself.

Q: Did you seek help from any other members of the Royal Family?

A: No. You, you have to know that when you have bulimia you're very ashamed of yourself and you hate yourself, so—and people think you're wasting food—so you don't discuss it with people.

And the thing about bulimia is your weight always stays the same, whereas with anorexia you visibly shrink. So you can pretend the whole way through. There's no proof.

As is true of many patients with BPD, both the early loss of an important attachment figure and the effects of Diana's parents' divorce were traumatic and in her case led to lifelong problems, including abandonment fears, anxiety, mood swings, bulimia, self-mutilation, lying, and medication abuse. Diana was prescribed Prozac and psychotherapy, but none of it seemed to help, and during an official visit to a women's mental health clinic she said that the women "were unlikely to find much help from some psychotherapist."

Although Princess Diana was thought to have BPD, some well-known media figures not diagnosed with BPD have shared their own histories of despair and self-injury in media interviews. A seventeen-year-old patient showed me the following piece on musician Courtney Love from his favorite magazine *Spin*. She had been asked about Kurt Cobain's overdoses and she said the following:

"Some people OD. I've never OD'ed, ever. I've gotten really f***ing blasto, but instead of OD'ing, I chatter and start talking too much, screaming and running around naked and getting hysterical, cutting my arms, you know, crazy shit. Breaking windows. But I never have fallen on the floor blue."

Fiona Apple, a singer and songwriter, has been very open about being raped when she was twelve. She described the consequences of this horrific trauma in a *Rolling Stone* magazine interview.

"I definitely had an eating disorder. What was really frustrating for me was that everyone though I was anorexic, and I wasn't. I was really depressed and self-loathing. For me, it wasn't about being thin; it was about getting rid of the bait attached to my body. A lot of it came from the self-loathing that came from being raped at the point of developing my voluptuousness. I just thought that if you had a body and if you had anything on you that would be grabbed, it would be grabbed. So I did purposely get rid of it."

Soon she started to self-injure and would bite her lip until it bled. She continues in the interview:

"I have a little bit of a problem with that. It's a common thing. It just makes you feel. And it'll be bleeding, and I can't stop, because it almost feels so good when I bite my lip. I'm just saying, 'This happened to me, this happened to a lot of people.' Why should I hide sh*t? Why does that give people a bad opinion of me? It's a reality. A lot of people do it. Courtney Love pulled me aside at a party and showed me her marks."

BPD in adolescence presents as an emotional roller coaster, with numbing, loneliness, hopelessness, self-injury, suicidality, drug use, and promiscuity. Many of the songs that these adolescents listen to, the artists they identify with, and the celebrities they attempt to emulate personify many of the symptoms of BPD. It is important that parents recognize the darker side of adolescent culture as they attempt to understand their adolescents with BPD.

CHAPTER THIRTEEN

BPD and Adoption

I WROTE THIS CHAPTER AFTER long consideration. This is because I strongly believe in adoption and all the promise and hope it has given to countless children and families.

However, research shows that adopted children are more likely than biological children to have special health care needs, moderate or severe health problems, learning disabilities, developmental delays, and other mental health difficulties.

On the adolescent treatment unit at McLean Hospital, a significant percentage of adolescents diagnosed with BPD were adopted. Although the data on this are scant, one anecdotal report of a family support group for parents with adolescents with BPD showed that 40 percent of the adolescents had been adopted. Parents often ask whether the adoption had anything to do with their child having BPD.

"I have a seventeen-year-old daughter with BPD, and I need more information regarding adoption and borderline personality disorder," one parent recently asked me. "I have read that there is a larger than normal percentage of adopted people with attention deficit disorder, learning disabilities, depression and other psychological problems. My questions are:

Are adopted kids more prone to BPD? Is there any research? Can reuniting my daughter with her birth mother change the course of her BPD?"

I am not aware of any comprehensive studies. My hope is that the new dialectical behavior treatment (DBT) unit at McLean Hospital will shed some light on the matter.

Certainly the question of reunification has not been answered, and I am not sure that it is a good idea for adolescents with BPD to meet their biological parents if they have had no contact, but I have no data that supports this idea. Although there are many reasons why children are available for adoption, some of those reasons arise from issues in the biological parents. Some kids are taken away from their parents by courts and state agencies because of the chaotic and abusive nature of their households, which are factors associated with the development of BPD. Sometimes parents with their own psychiatric problems recognize that they cannot parent a child, and a genetic predisposition to emotional problems may have been passed on to their children. These are simply some of my thoughts and have no scientific proof on which to base them. Future research is essential.

Despite all of this we generally have little data about an adopted child's biological home or background, and so we may need to infer information. Also, as there is no going back, it is important to deal with what is rather than what might have been. Why? In part, because research has shown that attempted suicide is twice as common among adolescents who live with adoptive parents than among adolescents who live with biological parents.

Further, adopted adolescents are more than twice as likely as their non-adopted counterparts to receive mental health services. Although these findings don't exactly tell us why this is true, it should alert parents and clinicians to the possibility of the need for earlier mental health assessment in adopted children who begin to have behavioral problems.

FAMILY CONNECTIONS

One thing that appears to diminish the risk of suicidal behavior in adopted adolescents is "family connectedness." Family connectedness is a combination of family engagement in shared interests, curiosity about each other's lives, and a non-judgmental approach when considering each other's perspectives.

The types of fears that adopted adolescents with BPD have expressed in therapy have included a sense that they were taken away from their biological parents because they were bad people and that because of this that they can never measure up. Others have said that they felt that they were simply being "given" to someone else. A most haunting fear that some kids express is the concern that how could they possibly trust that anyone could love them if their own biological mother (or father) could not love them.

Although there is no guarantee that adoptive parents can prevent these fears in their adopted children, focusing on the connection is essential. Parents have shared a variety of strategies for connecting, including establishing family rituals that bond and celebrate the family and involving the child in establishing such rituals. One family said that they had a karaoke night once a month. The father admitted that he was a terrible singer while his adopted daughter had a wonderful voice. His willingness to initially feel humiliated allowed for great mirth within the family, and later his own ability to laugh at himself and tolerate distress improved!

Another family went on a camping trip twice a year armed with cameras to try and capture each other on film doing "interesting" things like wallowing in mud, or building a bonfire. Other families have said that connecting their own past (like a dad fishing with his dad) with their present (dad now fishing with his adopted son) helped to maintain a sense of family history.

Sometimes though, despite trying these bonding activities, adopted kids feel an ongoing disconnect. It is essential to recognize this and to consider that the child might simply not see interactions and events the way that parents see them. Becoming curious and listening non-judgmentally is critical in both developing a deeper understanding of the child and establishing that despite seeing things differently, children can trust that their parent will listen. This process can at times take months and years, even in a safe and nurturing environment.

Further, when parents see the rumblings of difficult behavior in their adopted children, they need to have a clear idea how they will respond to difficult issues. Waiting to respond only when a situation has erupted is too late and can lead to unhealthy and poorly thought out responses. Parents should recognize and avoid habitually showing irritation and annoyance in response to misbehavior, as this often leads to an escalation of the problem behavior by the adolescent. In some adopted children and adolescents, behavior is a direct consequence of pre-adoption trauma, and anger and frustration by the adoptive parent can simply reinforce a pattern of familiar consequences for the child. Responding with empathy to the anger or sadness the child is expressing can be profoundly validating and healing.

A mother who was looking for treatment for her sixteen-year-old daughter with BPD, whom she had adopted at fourteen months from Columbia, told me the following:

"While it is difficult to discern what is what, I could in one sense say that I noticed things the minute I met Julia at ten months old. She was very distressed when the adoption worker left us together and just seemed anxious to me, but she was an adorable child. At that time I spent one week with her because that was all the Columbian adoption authorities would allow until the paperwork was complete. I then had to leave her in Colombia, return home, and did not see her again for four months, when, again, more behaviors appeared that I now realize were probably significant.

"Her behavior during her initial introduction to her sister, Jamie, who we had also adopted, was very interesting to me. It took place at fourteen months on the kitchen floor, and Julia's reaction was strikingly similar to the 'goodbye' behavior when the two parted last September, at fourteen years, as Julia was off to the residential program. At fourteen months old, she appeared distant and not interested in Jamie (they were born eight days apart). At fourteen-years-old, she was far more concerned with her fingernails and new hairdo than the enormity of the moment. In both cases, Jamie looking for connection, meaning, etc., in the moment was figuratively slapped in the face and visibly hurt. What was a temperamental difference between the girls versus the early symptoms of a disorder is impossible to say.

"Anyway, she is at a therapeutic residential school now and she called me last night. For the first time in sixteen years (!) she asked me about some scarring on her back and shoulders. It has taken her all this time to be ready for that question. I had been ready for years, but it was still difficult. I explained that it had occurred in Colombia sometime between my first visit and when I eventually picked her up at fourteen months and that beyond that, I had no explanation, she went very 'dark' and into what her new therapist describes as 'full borderline behavior.' I think that I mentioned that she was adorable, that's what got me hooked, but when I saw the scars, I had to get her out of the country. The authorities told me that she had fallen, but it looks as if someone had taken a stick to her, at least that's what our pediatrician says."

"Full borderline behavior" was hopeless emptiness, which alternated with reactive rage and then rapidly back to isolation and finally behaving as if nothing had happened. What the therapist was describing was what Julia's mother had struggled with for years before finding help.

POSSIBLE RISK FACTORS FOR BPD IN ADOPTED CHILDREN

Why should an adopted child be at greater risk for developing BPD? For one thing, if the biological family's mental health history is not known it is possible that a child inherited genes for psychiatric illness.

Also, it is possible that if the child has a markedly different temperament than his or her parents that an environment for being misunderstood and ultimately "invalidated" has been created. A common experience on our unit is that of the emotionally intense or dysregulated kid and the reserved parents with far less emotional range. If temperament is genetically determined (as it appears to be), then it is possible that the child inherited an emotionally intense nature which, when exposed to a less reactive or uncertain response from its adopted parents, would make attachment, and therefore the capacity to form a stable image of the self, more difficult. (See the description of this as described by Peter Fonagy, Ph.D., on pp. 93–96.)

Another question that arises is whether adopted children sense the initial rejection by their biological parents as abandonment and therefore has to answer the question, "If my own parents abandoned me, why won't everyone else?" If this fear is present, it clearly contributes to the fear of abandonment in patients with BPD. The loss of the birth parents as a result of adoption sets the stage for the feelings of loss and abandonment that some adopted adolescents experience. Another element that can compound such feelings of rejection and abandonment are other losses, such the loss through separation of a brother or sister, grandparents, and others in the extended family because of the adoption. In many of the adolescents we see, there is also a loss of cultural connection or language, especially when the kids are adopted from abroad.

It is obviously impossible to know whether these children would have developed BPD had they remained with their birth parents or been adopted by temperamentally closer parents. However, a case could be made for considering temperament in the adoption match.

Another important issue to consider is that often, adopted people begin to have questions about identities during adolescence. The task of identity development during adolescence is often more difficult for the adopted teenager because of the additional adoption issues. Adopted adolescents' identity development includes questions about their biological families and what became of them, why they were placed for adoption, whether they resemble their birth parents, and where the adolescents "belong" in terms of education, social class, and culture.

In one case, for instance, a wealthy WASP family had adopted a young girl from the Philippines. They recognized that their daughter began to have problems when she turned fourteen. What they missed, however, was that the family had hired a cleaning crew that would come twice a week to the house, and that the crew consisted of young women from the Philippines. The girl told us that she recognized that (in her words) "these cleaning people" looked more like her and acted more like how she felt, than her adopted family. Also she suddenly felt very uncomfortable with her wealth in the context of the relative poverty of the cleaning crew. Her sense of who she was became confused and precipitated a crisis that led to cutting behaviors and suicidal thinking. It took months of therapy and the family recognizing the need for their daughter to have a connection with her strong sense of culture, for her to get better.

SIBLING COMPETITION

Another complicated issue that appears in adolescents with BPD is that of the relationship with the biological children of the adoptive parents.

Carlos was referred to us from New Mexico. He had become increasingly depressed over many years and no amount of therapy or medication seemed to change the course of the depression. His parents told us that Carlos had been adopted soon after birth, given up by his teenage mother who was the daughter of a seasonal agricultural worker from Mexico. The parents considered themselves particularly blessed as the mother had experienced fertility problems and was unable to have children of her own, and Carlos was the wonder child.

As is sometimes the case, a few years after the adoption, the mother became pregnant. The pregnancy was complicated, which required her to spend less time with Carlos. Her son was born four weeks premature, causing her to spend much of the next four months with him, in and out of the hospital.

Carlos became sullen and distant, although did not otherwise appear to have behavioral problems. He never truly bonded with his younger brother. He was not mean, but not close, and his mother acknowledged that she spent a lot of time with her biological child as he had been sickly.

Carlos' withdrawal became a depression and his parents started to look for therapy soon after his eleventh birthday. Eventually Carlos started cutting himself, and he appeared at our unit with multiple scars all over his body. After months of therapy, he was able to talk about his sense that his mother loved his brother more than she loved him, and that he had been angry that his brother had ever been born, but that because his brother had been sick, he couldn't express his anger.

The theme appears again and again of whether a child feels that he or she can be loved enough—in Carlos' case, that his first mother had given him up, that his adoptive mother had bought a substitute child, but that now that she had her own, he once again had been abandoned.

For highly sensitive children, these early attachments and problems in the attachment can have profound and enduring consequences in the ongoing development of the child

WELL-INTENTIONED LOVE

The following thoughts are worth repeating from an earlier chapter. They accurately capture the experience of parents raising their adoptive children with BPD, and they will also resonate as true with parents raising their biological children with BPD.

"There were signs, but we didn't see them. As people who approach life with confident optimism, we embarked on the adventure of creating a family with naïve, enthusiastic energy. Nature vs. nurture? As adoptive parents we were convinced that the loving environment we'd create for our first child would guide his development and form a personality as open and gregarious as ours.

"Mother Nature is a powerful force. She equipped Sean with a temperament that rebuffed our relentlessly misguided efforts to shape our son in our image. Convinced that he would eventually emerge from his wary, reluctant ways, we unwittingly practiced invalidation early and often. Failing to appreciate how fragile his makeup truly was, we forged ahead, exposing him to new experiences without realizing the layers of trauma they provoked."

A capacity for insight such as this, which acknowledges that a child's experience may have been different from what the parents perceived, goes a long way toward reversing the effects of any invalidation. With such acknowledgement, therapists need to work with parents and adolescents in a non-blaming, non-judgmental approach that recognizes that things are the way they are, and the focus is on a future worth living for the entire family. This is true whether the child is adopted or not.

CHAPTER FOURTEEN

The Future of Today's BPD Teens

W HEN I ASK SENIOR CLINICIANS about what happened to patients with BPD in their day, many acknowledge that a patient having a BPD diagnosis meant the patient was destined to a life of misery and disdain. Staff believed they were terrible patients because they caused all kinds of troubles. The great news on the outcome of people with BPD, however, is that most of them get better with treatment. This new perspective is supported by research.

YESTERDAY

The early studies of BPD outcomes were not optimistic at all. BPD was more than a diagnosis; it was a label that, once earned, was not removed.

When I first became interested in BPD in the early 1990s, I read the scant literature available at the time, and I found one study particularly interesting. It was the first study that held some promise of change in BPD. Thomas McGlashan, M.D., reported on the outcome of patients with BPD who had spent years in a long-term psychiatric facility. He noted that generally the patients manifested poor work and social functioning through their twenties and early thirties and that functioning improved and stabilized during their forties. He also noted that a subgroup of patients deteriorated during their late forties and early fifties, usually in response to a divorce, death of a spouse, or breakup of a significant relationship.

These findings were important because they were the first to show some improvement in functioning or that patients could get better. I remember thinking, "Okay, if people can hang on for another fifteen to twenty years, they can get better!"

Dr. McGlashan found the older a person was, the less likely he or she was to continue to suffer from BPD. It was as if the rage of BPD simply burned itself out. The thinking was that if patients who suffered from BPD could be kept alive long enough, things would get better.

TODAY

The following quote is from a therapy session with a seventeen-year-old patient.

"You may not be 100 percent sure of anything, but I sure as hell am. This may be the only thing I'm sure of. I am genuinely convinced that I do not belong in this world. Some people have bad days. I've had a bad life. I don't think anything surprises me anymore. I used to be surprised that, after thinking I had rock bottom, I found an even lower place. But I know now that things will get worse and worse. I honestly don't think most people could spend a day inside my head without wanting to jump out a window themselves."

How could I possibly tell this young woman that all she had to do was stay alive for the next fifteen or twenty years and then she would be better, unless she got divorced, had a break-up, or experienced the death of a spouse? With the offer of such unrelenting misery, who wouldn't consider suicide as a possible solution?

Today, however, there is tremendous hope. In 2005, the McLean Hospital Study of Adult Development found that with new treatments, nearly 75 percent of patients have no active symptoms after six years and after this period of time only 6 percent will relapse back into BPD. This study, which I will describe more completely later in this chapter, was on outcomes in adults with BPD. Our thinking is that if we can get to the BPD symptoms earlier in the course of the disorder, we might shorten this time period even more.

TOMORROW

The McLean Hospital Study of Adult Development in 2005 reported on the course and outcomes of BPD. Researchers led by Mary Zanarini, Ed.D., one of the world's foremost researchers in BPD, found the following five significant results after years of studying these patients.

- They found that the absence of active BPD symptoms after six years of treatment was much more common than had previously been thought. For many years, clinicians thought that this group of patients was a lost cause. However, the McLean study showed that 74 percent of patients were without active symptoms after six years.
- These remissions were generally stable, and the recurrence of BPD once in remission was rare, only about 6 percent. What this means is that once a person gets better, the chance of the symptoms returning is low, which is great news.
- Completed suicides were far rarer than anticipated—about 4 percent as compared to the 10 percent in previous outcome studies. Despite this finding, because it is only one study, until more studies are completed, most researchers and clinicians still quote the 10 percent figure. Nevertheless any study showing a reduction in suicide is great news.

- A "complex" model of BPD best describes the condition. In this model, some symptoms—suicidality, self-injury, and impulsivity—improve relatively quickly. These symptoms are often the immediate reason for needing costly forms of treatment, such as psychiatric hospitalizations. The symptoms that are closely associated with ongoing psychosocial impairment—such as chronic feelings of intense anger, emptiness, and profound abandonment concerns—are much more difficult to treat.

- People with BPD overall continuously improved their life functioning over time. The study groups felt that people with BPD were somewhat belatedly achieving the developmental milestones of young adulthood. This is significant because we found that some imaging and electroencephalogram (EEG) studies have suggested that brains of people with BPD appear to mature more slowly than those without BPD pathology.

The researchers' final and heartening conclusion was that all these findings, taken together, suggest that the prognosis for BPD is better than previously recognized.

Despite this optimism, it is worth repeating what Kiera van Gelder, a leader in the BPD peer-to-peer recovery movement, in which former patient help current patients, has had to say about measures of recovery.

"Call me a dreamer, but I envision the day when people who have been treated for BPD can be involved in defining whether a treatment is effective or not. A clinician's definition of my 'remission' is not necessarily a life worth living."

With this in mind, let us look at what other outcome studies say about BPD.

BPD AND POST-TRAUMATIC STRESS DISORDER (PTSD)

A 2006 study noted that there was limited research on the impact of PTSD co-occurring in people with BPD. Researchers found that patients with PTSD and BPD reported significantly higher levels of general distress, physical illness, anxiety, and depression than those with BPD alone. People who suffer with both BPD and PTSD are likely to require more intensive clinical services to reduce distress and improve their functioning. Perhaps not surprisingly, it is our clinical experience that BPD patients who suffer not only from PTSD but any other psychiatric condition such as bipolar disorder or substance abuse tend to be significantly more impaired than those who do not have co-occurring conditions.

TREATMENT OUTCOMES IN ADOLESCENTS

As noted earlier in the book, a 2006 study from Germany found that suicide ranked as the second leading cause of death in adolescents in that country. Study researchers further noted that impulsivity, self-injurious behavior, depression, and conduct disorder put these adolescents at high risk for suicide and suicidal behavior (which incidentally, though not unexpectedly, are similar to the risk factors for adolescent suicide in the United States).

Because dialectical behavior therapy (DBT) directly addresses suicidality, the researchers wanted to test whether DBT for adolescents was an effective method of treatment for these patients. In their study they studied adolescents who had made repeated suicide attempts and found that during treatment there were no suicide attempts. They found these results so promising in adolescents that they were planning to perform a wide-scale study in Germany. This type of study is beginning to change the perspectives and attitudes of clinicians working with highly suicidal adolescents.

AN OUTCOME STUDY FROM JAPAN

The hope of treatment is highlighted in the fact that researchers are beginning to study the outcome of BPD everywhere from Germany to Australia, from Canada to Japan. Although there are some (at times significant) societal differences between these cultures, the outcomes of BPD are fairly similar.

In a 2006 study, Japanese researchers reviewed the records of seventy-two patients with BPD who had received treatment at a university hospital between 1973 and 1989. Five of the seventy-two had committed suicide. This is similar to the findings of American and Canadian BPD researchers. A significant difference from American studies was that Japanese patients with BPD were more likely to live with their families than American patients with BPD. The Japanese researchers also found that over-involvement in family relationships and the number of hospitalizations predicted poor outcomes. This latter finding is interesting as many families are "accused" of not being involved enough, especially in BPD.

In overinvolved families, the members become too involved and sometimes are overprotective of their loved ones with BPD. As a result, the overprotected family member with BPD remains dependent and fails to grow and develop. Overinvolvement can create conflict and resentment among family members who try to break out of the dependency role.

THE BOTTOM LINE ON OUTCOMES

Little research exists on adolescent BPD outcomes. In my clinical experience (and the experience of senior colleagues with whom I work), there are no adults with BPD who did not have symptoms in adolescence, so not treating adolescents with BPD symptoms risks a bleak future.

I was asked recently: "What if you are wrong and you are teaching skills to people who don't have BPD?" I don't personally have a problem with this for two reasons: First, adolescents are referred for some problematic behavior generally related to self-injury or suicidal thoughts. These symptoms deserve treatment. Second, the skills we teach are applicable to many aspects of life, including conflict resolution, test-taking anxiety, stage fright, interpersonal disputes, and many other situations.

Parents sometimes quip that they don't know if their children learned anything, but they sure learned skills that help them in their everyday lives. A skills-based treatment has, in my opinion, little downside.

Anecdotally, we hear back from parents of adolescents who have completed an intensive dialectical behavior therapy treatment on the residential unit that the majority of them are doing well. We will soon undertake more formal research to have a better sense of the actual outcomes.

One such anecdote comes from the parent of a sixteen-year-old female with BPD discharged a few months earlier from McLean Hospital. She had been admitted after a serious suicide attempt, and her family was in a state of crisis.

"Apart from a few minor blips, Lindsey is doing very well, and we're all making strides together and apart. I'm learning to take it day-to-day, and we're both learning to enforce the positive and draw lines in the sand with the negative. We're all learning from each other, and it's all good."

1938   American psychoanalyst Adolph Stern refers to the borderline between neuroses and psychoses and referred to these patients as being in the "border line group." His clinical description of the condition includes many of the symptoms that are included in the *Diagnostic and Statistical Manual of Mental Disorders-IV* (*DSM-IV*) today.

1941   Psychiatrist Gregory Zilboorg describes a disorder that he considered to be a mild version of schizophrenia; patients with this disorder had disturbances of reality testing, associative thinking, shallowness of affect, and pervasive anger.

1942   Psychoanalyst Helene Deutsch describes a group of patients who lack a consistent sense of identity and lacked a source of inner direction. She creates the term "as-if" personalities because the patients completely identified with those upon whom they were dependent.

1949   Psychiatrists Paul Hoch and Phillip Polatin create the term "pseudoneurotic schizophrenia" to describe a condition characterized by pan-anxiety, pan-neurosis, and chaotic sexuality, but which was not a thought disorder.

1952   In the original *DSM*, published in 1952, many patients with borderline syndrome would have been given the diagnosis of emotionally unstable personality. The *DSM-II*, published in 1968, had no diagnostic criteria that adequately described borderline personality. In the *DSM-III*, BPD became a diagnosis based on the description of observable clinical characteristics. This description was carried over to *DSM-III-R* in 1987 and the *DSM-IV* in 1994.

1953   Psychiatrist Gustav Bychowsky also describes a group of patients who appear to be neither neurotic nor psychotic, but whose psychopathology lay on a level between the two. He uses the term "latent psychotic."

1959   Psychiatrist Melitta Schmideberg first describes borderline disorder as a disorder of character and describes a group of borderlines as being "stable in their instability."

1967   Psychiatrist Otto Kernberg, M.D., conceptualizes borderline personality disorder as a diagnosis in a group of patients who show particular primitive defenses.

1968   Psychiatrist Roy Grinker makes the first efforts to describe borderline personality through systematic empirical investigation. He names the condition "borderline syndrome."

1975   Psychiatrist John Gunderson and psychologist Margaret Singer publish the historically important article, "Defining Borderline Patients: An Overview."

1993   Behavioral psychologist Marsha Linehan, Ph.D., writes her seminal work, *Cognitive-Behavioral Treatment of Borderline Personality Disorder.*

THE TIMELINE AS IT PERTAINS TO ADOLESCENT BPD

1949   Margaret Mahler, M.D., described a group of children who were neither psychotic nor neurotic. They displayed "low frustration tolerance, poor emotional differentiation from their mothers, and [were] beset by a series of neurotic-like defenses."

1963   Mary Engel, Ph.D., publishes *Psychological Testing of Borderline Children.*

1965   Psychoanalysts Sara Kut Rosenfeld and Marjorie Sprince formulate the borderline concept more clearly. They outline four central themes: 1. Bisexual conflict is present but not central. 2. Faulty ego apparatuses evident early in life. 3. Anxiety characterized by feelings of disintegration. 4. Precarious maintenance of object cathexis and easy slippage of such cathexes into identifications.

1969   Anna Freud proposes that borderline children suffer from massive developmental arrests, an inability to be comforted by others, poor reality-testing and synthetic functions, and inadequately developed defense mechanisms.

1972   Psychiatrist James Masterson challenges the view that BPD does not occur in adolescents. His book, *Treatment of The Borderline Adolescent: A Developmental Approach*, is published.

1974   Psychologist Fred Pine presents the most comprehensive description of childhood BPD at a meeting at Tufts University.

1978   Paulina Kernberg authors the article, "The Diagnosis of Borderline Conditions in Adolescence."

1979   Professor of social work Morton Chethik authors the chapter, "The Borderline Child" in the *Basic Handbook of Child Psychiatry*, stating that "these children suffer from severe developmental failure or disturbed ego function and object relationships."

1982   Psychologist Fred Pine develops a working classification of borderline syndromes in children.

1983   The most comprehensive academic text to date, *The Borderline Child: Approaches to Etiology, Diagnosis, and Treatment*, edited by Kenneth Robson, is published. All the leading thinkers on borderline pathology in children contribute to the book. In the book Robson acknowledges the "inherent instability of the diagnostic process in childhood."

1984   Jerald Simon, M.D., describes a perspective that adolescents with BPD have disturbed object relations and describes a therapeutic approach that includes a day treatment program. Individual therapy is considered from a developmental object-relations viewpoint.

1986   Psychiatrists Deborah Greenman and John Gunderson and psychologist Peter Salzman publish a retrospective study of eighty-six children ages six to twelve who had been hospitalized for psychiatric reasons that adult criteria for borderline personality disorder could identify a group of children with many of the features attributed in the literature to the borderline child.

1990   Psychiatrist Theodore Petti authors *Borderline Disorders of Childhood: An Overview.* He concludes his overview by stating that "sub-classification of borderline disorders should result in more cost-effective diagnosis and treatment."

1991   Judith Block, Ph.D., and colleagues produce research that concludes that the diagnosis of BPD can be appropriate in adolescent girls. They note that adolescent girls with BPD are indistinguishable from adult patients in terms of the early history, current behaviors, and coexisting axis I disorders.

2001   Thomas Crawford, Ph.D., at Columbia University showed that symptoms of "dramatic-erratic" personality disorders, including BPD, persisted in a group of adolescents across an eight-year interval from early adolescence to early adulthood.

2004   Researchers at the University of Melbourne in Australia produce data showing that out of 101 adolescents between ages fifteen and eighteen with an original diagnosis of BPD, 74 percent still met criteria for BPD two years later, concluding that the diagnosis is justified and implies the need for early intervention in this age group.

This list of resources for parents of an adolescent with BPD or an adolescent looking for answers is far from exhaustive. It is based on resources that parents have found useful or programs that have collaborated with our program at McLean Hospital in the treatment of self-injurious, emotionally dysregulated adolescents. Over time this list should grow, and I encourage parents to use these resources and the Internet to keep current.

ONLINE RESOURCES

National Education Alliance for Borderline Personality Disorder
www.borderlinepersonalitydisorder.com

The mission of the National Education Alliance for Borderline Personality Disorder is to raise public awareness, provide education, promote research on borderline personality disorder, and enhance the quality of life of those affected by this serious mental illness.

BPD Central
www.bpdcentral.com

BPD Central is a list of resources for people who care about someone with borderline personality disorder. It is one of the oldest and largest sites about BPD on the Web.

Borderline Personality Today
www.borderlinepersonalitytoday.com

The aim of this site is "to provide the latest information about mental health disorders to mental health clinicians as well as consumers and families who are now beginning to demand better treatment."

BPD World

www.bpdworld.org

According to this site, "BPD World is here for one and all, our information focuses on borderline personality disorder, but we have a lot of information available to all, including depression, self-harm, anxiety, and much more."

Borderline Personality Disorder Resource Center

www.bpdresourcecenter.org

The Borderline Personality Disorder Resource Center at New York-Presbyterian Hospital-Weill Cornell Medical College has been set up specifically to help those impacted by the disorder find the most current and accurate information on the nature of BPD, and on sources of available treatment.

Borderline Personality Disorder Research Foundation

www.borderlineresearch.org

The Borderline Personality Disorder Research Foundation is a non-profit organization that supports international research on the underlying causes, characteristics, and treatment of borderline personality disorder.

National Alliance on Mental Illness (NAMI)

www.nami.org

NAMI is the nation's largest grassroots mental health organization dedicated to improving the lives of persons living with serious mental illness and their families. Founded in 1979, NAMI has become the nation's voice on mental illness, a national organization including NAMI organizations in every state and in more than 1,100 local communities across the country who join together to meet the NAMI mission through advocacy, research, support, and education.

Treatment and Research Advancements National Association for Personality Disorder

www.tara4bpd.org

TARA's mission is to foster education and research in the field of personality disorder, specifically but not exclusively borderline personality disorder; to support research into the causes, psychobiology, and treatment of personality disorders; to support and encourage educational programs and endeavors targeting mental health professionals, consumers of mental health services, families and/or the community at large in order to reduce stigma and increase awareness of personality disorder; to disseminate available information on etiology and treatment; and to advocate for accomplishments of these goals.

Dialectical Behavioral Therapy Self Help
www.dbtselfhelp.com

This website is a service for people who are seeking information about dialectal behavior therapy (DBT). This is a great website for people who want a comprehensive, yet easy-to-read understanding of DBT.

OUTPATIENT CLINICS THAT TREAT BPD

Although many clinics offer psychiatric services to adolescents, not all have a long and expert history of treating adolescent BPD. The clinics I mention here are not an exhaustive resource, but they have been recommended by parents or other clinicians.

Not all the resources have a full outline of their adolescent programs, but I have included those that do describe such services. My hope is that by the time this book is published many more such resources will be available. I encourage you to use this list as well as the Internet.

California

Vista Del Mar Self-Injury Outpatient Program
www.vistadelmar.org/frameindex.html

The Self-Injury Outpatient Program provides an opportunity to develop alternatives to self-injury, leading to more satisfying and intimate relationships.

South County Psychotherapy
www.southcountypsychotherapy.com/self_injurious_behavior.htm

According to their website, "At South County Psychotherapy, our psychotherapists utilize effective, no-nonsense therapy. This treatment is designed to cut to the heart of your problem, implement individualized treatment strategies to aid you in resolving your problem, and assist you in self-understanding so that you can avoid or manage future pitfalls. Effective, no-nonsense therapy is an innovative therapeutic approach which enables you to: (1) identify your negative thoughts and feelings, (2) determine where the negative thoughts and feelings come from, (3) and learn how to resolve them."

Marin County Center for Innovative DBT
www.innovativedbt.com/currentevents.htm

This center's comprehensive DBT programs for adolescents include individual DBT psychotherapy, weekly DBT skills training classes, phone skills coaching, and a consultation team.

San Francisco DBT Center
www.sfdbt.com

Offers DBT for adolescents.

Connecticut

Center for Dialectical and Cognitive Behavioral Therapies
(CDCBT) www.cdcbt.com/problemsadolescents.html

CDCBT offers DBT for adolescents in a program that focuses on helping teenagers and their families. Adolescents are required to attend a sixteen- to eighteen-week program that combines individual psychotherapy and group skills training.

The Dialectical and Cognitive Behavior Therapy Center
www.behaviortherapyct.com

Offers adolescent DBT.

Georgia

Atlanta Dialectical Behavior Therapy Clinic
www.atlantadbt.com/faq.htm

Offers adolescent DBT.

Ridgeview Institute
www.ridgeviewinstitute.com/pat_serv_youth_services.htm

Offers adolescent DBT.

Indiana

Park Center Adolescent Day Treatment Program
www.parkcenter.org/Child%20and%20Adult%20Services.htm

Offers an intensive day treatment program for adolescents coping with emotional regulation, interpersonal problems, family stress, and instability. It is aimed at treating adolescents who have particular difficulty managing their strong emotions and as a result engage in self-destructive behaviors. This half-day structured program allows for half-day school attendance as tolerated, and it is designed as a step-down from hospitalization or as hospitalization prevention. Youth are instructed in DBT skills, by trained DBT therapists, to learn emotional regulation, interpersonal effectiveness, stress tolerance, and crises planning.

Kansas

Bert Nash Community Mental Health Center
www.bertnash.org/services/index.html#child

At this center, DBT groups meet weekly for sixteen weeks. To participate in the DBT group, clients ages thirteen to eighteen must attend individual therapy with a DBT therapist. In addition, to attend the client must be accompanied by a legal guardian, parent, or foster parent with the expectation that both the youth and parent will learn the skills together.

Maryland

Rathbone and Associates
www.rathboneandassociates.net

Offers a weekly DBT skills group.

Massachusetts

Two Brattle Center
www.twobrattle.com

This center offers several options for the treatment of adolescents: an intensive adolescent DBT day treatment program, an adolescent after-school program, a parent DBT support group, and an adolescent DBT skills group.

The Bridge of Central Massachusetts
www.thebridgecm.org/programs.htm

This agency serves children and adolescents with serious emotional, behavioral, and family problems, in a variety of programs with a strong DBT component.

Michigan

InterAct of Michigan Center for DBT Services

www.interactmich.org/dbt.html

According to their website, "DBT-trained clinicians provide weekly individual therapy and group or family skills training to help adults and adolescents who want to end the cycle of hurting themselves."

Ionia County Community Mental Health

www.ioniacmhs.org/Supp-Treat%20Groups.htm

Offers adolescent skills training and DBT groups for thirteen to seventeen year olds.

Grand Rapids Fountain Hill Center

www.fountainhillcenter.com/gails_specs/BPD.htm

Offers DBT for adolescents with BPD.

Minnesota

Willow Counseling Services

www.willowcounselingservices.com

Offers DBT skills training groups.

Eagan Counseling

www.woodburycounseling.com/adolescent_DBT.htm

An adolescent DBT meets weekly. Group size is limited to ten.

Nystrom & Associates

www.nystromcounseling.com/group.html

Offers adolescent DBT groups.

New Hampshire

The Youth & Family Services of Community Partners

www.dssc9.org/youth_and_family.htm

Offers DBT groups for adolescents.

New Mexico

Albuquerque Collaborative Therapeutics
www.abq-act.com

Offers weekly adolescent DBT skills group and an eight-week parent group. Parental participation in skills training is required for teens to participate in the DBT adolescent program.

Santa Fe Dialectical Behavior Therapy
www.dbtsantafe.net/whatisdbt.html

Offers DBT services for adolescents.

New York

Cognitive & Behavioral Consultants
www.cognitivebehavioralconsultants.com

Offer DBT and CBT for BPD and other diagnoses. Psychologist Alec Miller is a founder of this clinic and is recognized for his work in adolescent depression, suicidology, self-injury, and BPD, and he was instrumental in adapting DBT for adolescents.

Madison County Mental Health Department
www.madisoncounty.org/MH/mhd.htm

The adolescent DBT group is an introductory ten-week supportive skills training group for adolescents ages fourteen to seventeen who have problems coping with emotions or engage in impulsive and/or self-destructive behaviors. The group focuses on improving skills to cope with stress, emotions, and interpersonal conflict. New referrals will be admitted at the beginning of each new module (approximately every five weeks).

Oregon

Portland DBT Program
www.portlanddbt.com/pages/info_descriptions.html#Anchor-Teen-47857

The teen program is a modified version of the adult program and targets improved self-awareness and acceptance, distress tolerance, emotion regulation, communication, and problem-solving skills. Program services include weekly individual therapy, a sixteen-week skills training group, a concurrent parent group, and as-needed telephone consultation. DBT-informed family therapy is provided as appropriate. Teen programs are available for age groups eleven to fourteen years and fifteen to seventeen years.

Texas

Karyn Hall, Ph.D.

www.karynhallphd.com/group.htm

This practice offers full-service DBT.

Virginia

Poehailos, Dupont & Associates

www.pdakids.com

This practice offers a specialty treatment program, designed for adults with BPD and adolescents with a history of parasuicidal, self-injurious behavior in an outpatient setting. It includes a combination of individual psychotherapy, DBT, pharmacotherapy, family therapy, and vocational rehabilitation counseling.

Washington

Rebecca Schneir, LMFT

www.rebeccaschneir.com/dbt.php

This outpatient clinic is just one of many clinicians who provide DBT for adolescents and their families in Seattle, the birthplace of DBT.

Youth and Family DBT of Seattle

www.youthandfamilydbt.com

This center offers a DBT family skills group for adolescents and their parents. The primary goal of the group is to eliminate suicidal and self-harm behavior by increasing family interactions, which promote validation, interpersonal effectiveness, and emotion regulation.

SHORT-TERM RESIDENTIAL PROGRAMS

Massachusetts

McLean Hospital: Dialectical Behavior Therapy Program for Young Women

www.mclean.harvard.edu/patient/child/atp.php

The DBT treatment components include individual DBT therapy, group skills-based therapy, individual skills coaching, and family therapy, with an emphasis on parental skills development. Additional treatment components of the program consist of case management, psychopharmacology evaluation, and treatment along with milieu therapy and recreational therapies.

Texas

Menninger Clinic Adolescent Treatment Program
www.menningerclinic.com/p-adolescent/index.htm

This program serves adolescents ages twelve to seventeen who are experiencing family, school, and social difficulties due to moderate to severe behavior issues (such as school behavior problems, oppositional/defiant behavior, poor impulse control, and self-harm), psychiatric disorders (such as major mood disorders, psychotic problems, developing personality disorders, and anxiety disorder), substance abuse, and more than one diagnosis (such as chemical dependency accompanied by depression).

Vermont

Brattleboro Retreat's Adolescent Residential Program
www.retreathealthcare.org/children/residential.html

The Brattleboro Retreat's Adolescent Residential Program offers an age-appropriate approach, which nurtures compassion and care, balanced with a strong emphasis on self-discipline, personal accountability, and social responsibility. The adolescent residential program provides treatment for adolescents ages thirteen to eighteen in a dormitory style setting with both an all-girls and a coed floor.

LONG-TERM RESIDENTIAL AND RESIDENTIAL SCHOOL PROGRAMS
California
Summitview Residential Treatment and Nonpublic School Services
www.summitviewtreatment.org/index.html

Summitview treats girls ages ten to seventeen who have been educationally classified as emotionally disturbed. Summitview treats a wide variety of psychological disorders, but many of the adolescents admitted meet criteria for or demonstrate traits of BPD. County departments of social services, mental health, and adoption services make most placements into the residential treatment program. The primary treatment approach used in the residential treatment program is DBT.

Vista Del Mar Psychiatric Residential Treatment Program

www.vistadelmar.org/frameindex.html

This program serves children ages ten to seventeen and offers a skilled staff of social workers, psychiatrists, psychologists, youth development counselors, and recreational therapists. The average stay is twelve months.

Massachusetts
Grove Street Adolescent Residence

www.thebridgecm.org/programs.htm

This highly structured residential program provides comprehensive residential clinical services to males and females ages thirteen to nineteen and uses the principles of DBT to treat individuals with impulsive and self-destructive behaviors.

The Chamberlain School

www.chamberlainschool.org

This program offers DBT treatment and works with boys and girls ages eleven to twenty who suffer from a variety of mental health disorders.

Utah
Moonridge Academy

www.moonridgeacademy.com

This school offers a specialized learning and healing environment for girls ages twelve to fifteen who begin to experiment with high-risk behaviors.

Kolob Canyon Residential Treatment Center

www.kolobcanyonrtc.com

This center treats girls ages twelve to seventeen suffering from depression or low self-esteem. According to their website, it offers a "clinically intense blend of traditional and non-traditional therapy delivered in a safe and nurturing environment."

Vermont
Bromley Brook School

www.bromleybrook.com/about.html

Bromley Brook is a therapeutic boarding school for girls age thirteen to seventeen. The school treats young woman who might be depressed, anxious, confused, isolating socially, in conflict with the family, behaving in contradiction to known family values, underachieving academically, and/or giving up and withdrawing. Others may be overachieving or over performing academically and/or athletically, causing unhealthy stress or physical problems, having personal identity or self-image issues, and/or taking unnecessary and unhealthy risks.

BOOKS RECOMMENDED BY OUR ADOLESCENTS WITH BPD AND THEIR FAMILIES

Borderline Personality Disorder Demystified: An Essential Guide for Understanding and Living with BPD by Robert Friedel, M.D.

By Their Own Young Hand: Deliberate Self-Harm and Suicidal Ideas in Adolescents by Keith Hawton, Karen Rodham, and Emma Evans

Understanding and Treating Borderline Personality Disorder: A Guide for Professionals and Families edited by John G. Gunderson, M.D. and Perry D. Hoffman, Ph.D.

Dialectical Behavior Therapy with Suicidal Adolescents by Alec L. Miller, Jill H. Rathus, and Marsha M. Linehan

Surviving a Borderline Parent: How to Heal Your Childhood Wounds & Build Trust, Boundaries, and Self-Esteem by Kimberlee Roth and Freda B. Friedman, Ph.D., LCSW

Get Me Out of Here: My Recovery from Borderline Personality Disorder by Rachel Reiland

Siren's Dance: My Marriage to a Borderline: A Case Study by Anthony Walker, M.D.

Stop Walking on Eggshells: Taking Your Life Back When Someone You Care About Has Borderline Personality Disorder by Randi Kreger and Paul T. Mason

Lost in the Mirror: An Inside Look at Borderline Personality Disorder, Second Edition by Richard Moskovitz, M.D.

Acting out: Expressing unconscious emotional conflicts or feelings, such as hostility or love, through behavior rather than becoming aware of and experiencing the feelings.

Adrenaline: A hormone, which is also known as epinephrine, that also acts as a neurotransmitter. It is extremely important in the fight-or-flight response because it signals the heart to pump harder, to get ready for action.

Acetylcholine: A neurotransmitter that appears to be involved in learning and memory.

Affect: A subjectively experienced feeling state (emotion) and the observable behavior that represents it.

Alexithymia: The inability to describe emotions in a verbal manner.

Allele: An alternate form of a gene. Variations in hair color and other inherited characteristics are due to different alleles.

Amygdala: The part of the brain whose primary role is in the formation and storage of memories associated with emotional events (such as fear and anger).

Anhedonia: The inability to experience pleasure from activities that usually produce pleasurable feelings.

Anorexia nervosa: An eating disorder characterized by a misperception of body image. Patients with anorexia nervosa often believe they are overweight even when they are grossly underweight and take extreme measures to lose weight, including restricting food intake and exercising excessively, often putting themselves at serious physical harm.

Antipsychotic medication: A type of drug used to treat psychosis. This class of drugs is frequently used in conditions such as schizophrenia, mania, and delusional disorder. Further, because antipsychotics also have some effects as mood stabilizers, they are sometimes used to treat mood disorders.

Attachment: The emotional connection that infants and children develop toward their parents and others who care for them.

Avoidance: A defense mechanism consisting of refusal to deal with situations, objects, or activities.

Co-morbidity: The presence of coexisting illnesses that occur together with the targeted diagnosis. Co-morbidity may adversely affect the ability of people to function and may complicate their overall treatment plans.

Cyclothymia: Cyclothymia is a condition characterized by repetitive periods of mild depression followed by periods of normal or slightly elevated mood.

Declarative memory: The aspect of memory that stores facts and experiences.

Delusion: A false belief based on incorrect inferences about the external reality that is firmly believed despite what almost everyone else believes and despite obvious proof or evidence to the contrary. Also, the belief is not one ordinarily accepted by other members of the person's culture or faith.

Denial: Failing to recognize the obvious implications or consequences of a thought, act, or situation.

Dissociation: A psychological state in which certain thoughts, emotions, sensations, or memories are separated from the rest of a person's experience. During a dissociative episode, these thoughts, emotions, and memories are not associated with other current information as they normally would be. A dissociative episode generally serves to create a temporary mental escape from the fear and pain of a traumatic recollection and at times may lead to a complete loss of memory of the traumatic event.

Dopamine: A neurotransmitter that regulates movement, emotion, attention, motivation, and feelings of pleasure.

Emotional maltreatment: Preventing a child from attaining basic emotional needs such as psychological safety, acceptance, love, self-esteem, and age-appropriate autonomy.

Episodic memory: A sub-category of declarative memory, which deals more with the recollection of events.

Etiology: The causes or origins of a medical or psychiatric disorder.

Flashback: The recurrence of a memory, feeling, or perceptual experience from the past. The past event would generally have elicited powerful feelings and emotions.

GABA (Gamma-aminobutyric acid): A neurotransmitter responsible for slowing the brain down. Drugs that act to increase GABA are used as anti-anxiety drugs and anti-seizure drugs.

Gender identity: A person's inner conviction of being either male or female. Their gender identity may be the same as or different from their actual gender. For instance, a man may have an inner conviction that he is female.

Hallucination: A false sensory experience that has no external stimulus and can affect sight, smell, taste, touch, and hearing. Typically patients describe seeing things or hearing things that others cannot see or hear.

Hippocampus: The part of the brain that is critical for declarative memory— that is, the memory of persons, places, and things.

Idealization: A mental mechanism in which the person attributes exaggeratedly positive qualities to the self or others.

Leptin: A hormone produced by fat cells that suppresses appetite and encourages the burn of fat stored in adipose tissue.

Methylphenidate: A stimulant drug used to treat attention deficit hyperactivity disorder. This is the generic name of Ritalin.

Neglect: The failure to provide for a child's basic physical needs for adequate food, clothing, shelter, and medical treatment.

Neuroleptic: A synonym for antipsychotic.

Object relations: A school of thought that emphasizes the importance of mental representation of the self and of others.

Obsession: Recurrent and persistent thought, impulse, or image experienced as intrusive and distressing. They are recognized as being excessive and unreasonable even though they are recognized as the product of one's mind, and they cannot be expunged by logic or reasoning.

Panic attacks: Episodes of severe anxiety associated with symptoms such as shortness of breath, heart palpitations, chest pain, sweating, nausea, dizziness light-headedness, and hyperventilation. During panic attacks, sufferers often believe they are dying, going insane, or having heart attacks.

Prefrontal cortex: A part of the frontal lobes of the brain used in planning complex cognitive behaviors, expressing personality, and evaluating correct social behavior.

Primary emotions: Emotions that we feel first, as a first response to a situation. There are considered to be eight primary emotions—guilt, anger, sadness, surprise, shame, fear, disgust, and joy.

Projection: Attributing one's own feelings or thoughts to others.

Psychoanalysis: The form of psychotherapy based on the psychoanalytic theory of Sigmund Freud. The most fundamental concept of psychoanalysis is the notion of the unconscious mind as a reservoir of repressed memories of traumatic events, which continuously influence conscious thought and behavior.

Psychotic: Although there are a few different definitions for this term, in this book I use it to mean delusions, hallucinations, paranoia, and severely bizarre behavior.

Regression: Behavior in which a person returns to earlier (or younger) patterns of reacting or thinking.

Reflective awareness: An awareness of being aware.

Reinforcement: The increasing of a desired behavior by reward or avoidance of punishment. This process is central in operant conditioning.

Risk factors: Biological, genetic, developmental, and environmental exposures that increase the chance of developing an illness.

Secondary emotions: Secondary emotions appear after primary emotions. For example, the fear of a threat turns to anger.

Serotonin: A neurotransmitter that affects emotions, behavior, and thought.

Splitting: A psychological defense in which the self or others are seen as all good or all bad, and where a person is unable to integrate the positive and negative qualities of self and others into cohesive images. Often the person alternately idealizes and devalues the same person.

Validation: The act of affirming that a person's experience, feeling, or perspective is valid. It does not necessarily mean that the affirming person agrees with the other's perspective.

JOURNAL ARTICLES

Abbar, M., P. Courtet, F. Bellivier, M. Leboyer, J. P. Boulenger, D. Castelhau, M. Ferreira, C. Lambercy, D. Mouthon, A. Paoloni-Giacobino, M. Vessaz, A. Malafosse, and C. Buresi. "Suicide Attempts and the Tryptophan Hydroxylase Gene," *Nature*, May 2001, 6(3):268–73.

Adachi, T., T. Masumura, M. Arai, N. Adachi, S. Akazawa, H. Arai. "Self-Administered Electroconvulsive Treatment With a Homemade Device," *Journal of ECT*, 2006, 22(3):226–27.

Agrawal, H. R., J. Gunderson, B. M. Holmes, K. Lyons-Ruth. "Attachment Studies with Borderline Patients: A Review," *Harvard Review of Psychiatry*, 2004, 12(2):94–104.

Akiskal, H. S., M. L. Bourgeois, J. Angst, R. Post, H. Moller, R. Hirschfeld. "Re-evaluating the Prevalence of and Diagnostic Composition within the Broad Clinical Spectrum of Bipolar Disorders," *Journal of Affective Disorders*, 2000, 59, Suppl. 1:S5–S30.

Anderson, S. W., A. Bechara, H. Damasio, et al. "Impairment of Social and Moral Behavior Related to Early Damage in Human Prefrontal Cortex," *National Neuroscience*, 1999, 2:1,032–37.

Archer, R. P., J. D. Ball, and J. A. Hunter. "MMPI Characteristics of Borderline Psychopathology in Adolescent Inpatients," *Journal of Personality Assessment*, 1985, 49(1):47–55.

Arranz, B., A. Eriksson, E. Mellerup, P. Plenge, and J. Marcusson. "Brain 5-HT1A, 5-HT1D and 5-HT2 Receptors in Suicide Victims," *Biological Psychiatry*, 1994, 35(7):457–63.

Asaad, T., T. Okasha, and A. Okasha. "Sleep EEG findings in ICD-10 Borderline Personality Disorder in Egypt," *Journal of Affective Disorders*, 2002, 71(1–3):11–18.

Asberg, M. "Neurotransmitters and Suicidal Behavior: The Evidence from Cerebrospinal Fluid Studies," *Annals of the New York Academy of Sciences*, 1997, 836:158–81.

Asnis, G. M., J. Eisenberg, H. M. van Praag, C. Z. Lemus, J. M. Harkvay Friedman, and A. H. Miller. "The Neuroendocrine Response to Fenfluramine in Depressive and Normal Controls," *Biological Psychiatry*, 1988, 24:117–20.

Atmaca, M., M. Kuloglu, E. Tezcan, O. Gecici, and B. Ustundag. "Serum Cholesterol and Leptin Levels in Patients with Borderline Personality Disorder," *Neuropsychobiology*, 2002, 45(4):167–71.

Avdibegovic, E. and O. Sinanovic. "Consequences of Domestic Violence on Women's Mental Health in Bosnia and Herzegovina," *Croatian Medical Journal*, 2006, 47(5):730–41.

Bargh, J. A. and K. Y. McKenna. "The Internet and Social Life," *Annual Review of Psychology*, 2004, 55:573–90.

Barnow, S., C. Spitzer, H. J. Grabe, C. Kessler, and H. J. Freyberger. "Individual Characteristics, Familial Experience, and Psychopathology in Children of Mothers with Borderline Personality Disorder," *Journal of the American Academy of Child and Adolescent Psychiatry*, 2006, 45(8):965–72.

Bateman, A. and P. Fonagy. "Effectiveness of Partial Hospitalization in the Treatment of Borderline Personality Disorder: A Randomized Controlled Trial," *American Journal of Psychiatry*, 1999, 156:1,563–69.

Battle, C. L., M. T. Shea, D. M. Johnson, S. Yen, C. Zlotnick, M. C. Zanarini, C. A. Sanislow, A. E. Skodol, J. G. Gunderson, C. M. Grilo, T. H. McGlashan, and L. C. Morey. "Childhood Maltreatment Associated with Adult Personality Disorders: Findings from the Collaborative Longitudinal Personality Disorders Study," *Journal of Personality Disorders*, 2004, 18(2):193–211.

Becker, D. F., C. M. Grilo, W. S. Edell, and T. H. McGlashan. "Comorbidity of Borderline Personality Disorder with Other Personality Disorders in Hospitalized Adolescents and Adults," *American Journal of Psychiatry*, 2000, 157(12):2,011–16.

Becker, D. F., C. M. Grilo, W. S. Edell, and T. H. McGlashan. "Diagnostic Efficiency of Borderline Personality Disorder Criteria in Hospitalized Adolescents: Comparison with Hospitalized Adults," *American Journal of Psychiatry*, 2002, 159(12):2,042–47.

Becker, D. F., T. H. McGlashan, and C. M. Grilo. "Exploratory Factor Analysis of Borderline Personality Disorder Criteria in Hospitalized Adolescents," *Comprehensive Psychiatry*, 2006, 47(2):99–105.

Bellino, S., L. Patria, E. Paradiso, R. Di Lorenzo, C. Zanon, M. Zizza, and F. Bogetto. "Major Depression in Patients with Borderline Personality Disorder: A Clinical Investigation," *Canadian Journal of Psychiatry*, 2005, 50(4):234–38.

Bellino, S., E. Paradiso, and F. Bogetto. "Oxcarbazepine in the Treatment of Borderline Personality Disorder: A Pilot Study," *Journal of Clinical Psychiatry*, 2005, 66(9):1,111–15.

Berk, M. S., E. Jeglic, G. K. Brown, G. R. Henriques, and A. T. Beck. "Characteristics of Recent Suicide Attempters with and without Borderline Personality Disorder," *Archives of Suicide Research*, 2007, 11(1):91–104.

Berlin, H. A., E. T. Rolls, and S. D. Iversen. "Borderline Personality Disorder, Impulsivity, and the Orbitofrontal Cortex," *American Journal of Psychiatry*, 2005, 162(12):2,360–73.

Bolton, E. E., K. T. Mueser, and S. D. Rosenberg. "Symptom Correlates of Posttraumatic Stress Disorder in Clients with Borderline Personality Disorder," *Comprehensive Psychiatry*, 2006, 47(5):357–61.

Bradley, R., C. Zittel Conklin, and D. Westen. "The Borderline Personality Diagnosis in Adolescents: Gender Differences and Subtypes," *Journal of Child Psychology and Psychiatry*, 2005, 46(9):1006–19.

Brambilla, P., P. H. Soloff, M. Sala, M. A. Nicoletti, M. S. Keshavan, and J. C. Soares. "Anatomical MRI Study of Borderline Personality Disorder Patients," *Psychiatry Research*, 2004, 131(2):125–33.

Brassington, J. and R. Krawitz. "Australasian Dialectical Behaviour Therapy Pilot Outcome Study: Effectiveness, Utility and Feasibility," *Australasian Psychiatry*, 2006, 14(3):313–19.

Brodsky, B. S., K. M. Malone, S. P. Ellis, R. A. Dulit, and J. J. Mann. "Characteristics of Borderline Personality Disorder Associated with Suicidal Behavior," *American Journal of Psychiatry*, 1997, 154(12):1,715–19.

Brown, J. D., K. W. Childers, and C. S. Waszak. "Television and Adolescent Sexuality," *Journal of Adolescent Health Care*, 1990, 11(1):62–70.

Chabrol, H., K. Chouicha, A. Montovany, S. Callahan, E. Duconge, and H. Sztulman. "Personality Disorders in a Nonclinical Sample of Adolescents," *L'Encephale*, 2002, 28(6 Pt 1):520–24.

Chanen, A. M., H. J. Jackson, P. D. McGorry, K. A. Allot, V. Clarkson, and H. P. Yuen. "Two-Year Stability of Personality Disorder in Older Adolescent Outpatients," *Journal of Personality Disorders*, 2004, 18(6):526–41.

Chen, E. Y., M. Z. Brown, T. T. Lo, and M. M. Linehan. "Sexually Transmitted Disease Rates and High-Risk Sexual Behaviors in Borderline Personality Disorder versus Borderline Personality Disorder with Substance Use Disorder," *Journal of Nervous and Mental Disease*, 2007, 195(2):125–29.

Coccaro, E. F., L. J. Siever, H. M. Klar, G. Mauer, K. Cochrane, T. B. Cooper, et al. "Serotonin Studies in Patients with Affective and Personality Disorders," *Archives of General Psychiatry*, 1989, 46:587–99.

Cohen, P., H. Chen, T. N. Crawford, J. S. Brook, and K. Gordon. "Personality Disorders in Early Adolescence and the Development of Later Substance Use Disorders in the General Population," *Drug and Alcohol Dependence*, 2007, 88, Suppl. 1:S71–S84.

Crandell, L. E., M. P. H. Patrick, and R. P. Hobson, "Still-Face Interactions between Mothers with Borderline Personality Disorder and Their 2-Month-Old Infants," *The British Journal of Psychiatry*, 2003, 183:239–47.

Crawford, T. N., P. Cohen, and J. S. Brook. "Dramatic-Erratic Personality Disorder Symptoms: I. Continuity from Early Adolescence into Adulthood," *Journal of Personality Disorders*, 2001, 4:319–35.

Crick, N. R., D. Murray-Close, and K. Woods. "Borderline Personality Features in Childhood: A Short-Term Longitudinal Study," *Developmental Psychopathology*, 2005, 17:1,051–570.

Crowell, S. E., T. P. Beauchaine, E. McCauley, C. J. Smith, A. L. Stevens, and P. Sylvers. "Psychological, Autonomic, and Serotonergic Correlates of Parasuicide among Adolescent Girls," *Developmental Psychopathology*, 2005, 17(4):1,105–27.

Crumley, F. E. "Adolescent Suicide Attempts and Borderline Personality Disorder: Clinical Features," *Southern Medical Journal*, 1981, 74(5):546–49.

Davidson, K. J. Norrie, P. Tyrer, A. Gumley, P. Tata, H. Murray, and S. Palmer. "The Effectiveness of Cognitive Behavior Therapy for Borderline Personality Disorder: Results from the Borderline Personality Disorder Study of Cognitive Therapy Trial," *Journal of Personality Disorders*, 2006, 20(5):450–65.

Davidson, M. R. Mohs, and L. J. Siever. "Affective and Impulsive Personality Traits in the Relatives of Patients with Borderline Personality Disorder," *American Journal of Psychiatry*, 1991, 148(10):1,378–85.

Deans, C. and E. Meocevic. "Attitudes of Registered Psychiatric Nurses Towards Patients Diagnosed with Borderline Personality Disorder," *Contemporary Nurse*, 2006, 21(1):43–49.

De la Fuente, J. M., P. Tugendhaft, and N. Mavroudakis. "Electroencephalographic Abnormalities in Borderline Personality Disorder," *Psychiatry Research*, 1998, 77(2):131–38.

Deltito, J., L. Martin, J. Riefkohl, B. Austria, A. Kissilenko, C. Corless, and P. Morse. "Do Patients with Borderline Personality Disorder Belong to the Bipolar Spectrum?" *Journal of Affective Disorders*, 2001, 67(1–3):221–28.

Dinn, W. M., C. L. Harris, A. Aycicegi, P. B. Greene, S. M. Kirkley, and C. Reilly. "Neurocognitive Function in Borderline Personality Disorder," *Progress in Neuropsychopharmacology*, 2004, 28(2):329–41.

Donegan, N. H., C. A. Sanislow, H. P. Blumberg, R. K. Fulbright, C. Lacadie, P. Skudlarski, J. C. Gore, I. R. Olson, T. H. McGlashan, and B. E. Wexler. "Amygdala Hyperreactivity in Borderline Personality Disorder: Implications for Emotional Dysregulation," *Biological Psychiatry*, 2003, 54(11):1,284–93.

Dubo, E. D., M. C. Zanarini, R. E. Lewis, and A. A. Williams. "Childhood Antecedents of Self-Destructiveness in Borderline Personality Disorder," *Canadian Journal of Psychiatry*, 1997, 42(1):63–69.

Dulit, R. A., M. R. Fyer, A. C. Leon, B. S. Brodsky, and A. J. Frances. "Clinical Correlates of Self-Mutilation in Borderline Personality Disorder," *American Journal of Psychiatry*, 1994, 151:1,305–11.

Ebner-Priemer, U.W., S. Badeck, C. Beckmann, A. Wagner, B. Feige, I. Weiss, K. Lieb, and M. Bohus. "Affective Dysregulation and Dissociative Experience in Female Patients with Borderline Personality Disorder: A Startle Response Study," *Journal of Psychiatric Research*, 2005, 39(1):85–92.

Engel, M. "Psychological Testing of Borderline Children," *Archives of General Psychiatry*, 1963, 8:426.

Fallon, P. "Traveling Through the System: The Lived Experience of People with Borderline Personality Disorder in Contact with Psychiatric Services," *Journal of Psychiatric and Mental Health Nursing*, 2003, 10(4):393–401.

Feske, U., B. Mulsant, P. Pilkonis, P. Soloff, D. Dolata, H. Sackeim, and R. F. Haskett. "Clinical Outcome of ECT in Patients with Major Depression and Comorbid Borderline Personality Disorder," *American Journal of Psychiatry*, 2004, 161:2,073–80.

Fleischhaker, C., M. Munz, R. Bohme, B. Sixt, and E. Schulz. "Dialectical Behaviour Therapy for Adolescents (DBT-A)—A Pilot Study on the Therapy of Suicidal, Parasuicidal, and Self-Injurious Behaviour in Female Patients with a Borderline Disorder," *Zeitschrift fur Kinder- und Jugendpsychiatrie und Psychotherapie*, 2006, 34(1):15–25.

Fossati, A., L. Novella, D. Donati, M. Donini, and C. Maffei. "History of Childhood Attention Deficit/Hyperactivity Disorder Symptoms and Borderline Personality Disorder: A Controlled Study," *Comprehensive Psychiatry*, 2002, 43(5):369–77.

Frankenburg, F. R. and M. C. Zanarini. "Divalproex Sodium Treatment of Women with Borderline Personality Disorder and Bipolar II Disorder: A Double-Blind Placebo-Controlled Pilot Study," *Journal of Clinical Psychiatry*, 2002, 63(5):442–46.

Gardner, D. L. and R. W. Cowdry. "Alprazolam-Induced Dyscontrol in Borderline Personality Disorder," *American Journal of Psychiatry*, 1985, 142(1):98–100.

Gest, S. "Behavioral Inhibition: Stability and Associations with Adaptation from Childhood to Early Adulthood," *Journal of Personality and Social Psychology*, 1997, 72:467–75.

Giesen-Bloo, J., R. van Dyck, P. Spinhoven, W. van Tilburg, C. Dirksen, T. van Asselt, I. Kremers, M. Nadort, and A. Arntz. "Outpatient Psychotherapy for Borderline Personality Disorder: A Randomized Trial of Schema Focused Therapy versus Transference Focused Therapy," *Archives of General Psychiatry*, 2006, 63(6):649–58.

Golier, J. A., R. Yehuda, L. M. Bierer, V. Mitropoulou, A. S. New, J. Schmeidler, J. M. Silverman, and L. J. Siever. "The Relationship of Borderline Personality Disorder to Posttraumatic Stress Disorder and Traumatic Events," *American Journal of Psychiatry*, 2003, 160(11):2,018–24.

Goodman, M. and A. S. New. "Impulsive Aggression in Borderline Personality Disorder," *Current Psychiatry Reports*, 2000, 2(1):56–61.

Grilo, C. M., D. F. Becker, D. C. Fehon, M. L. Walker, W. S. Edell, and T. H. McGlashan. "Gender Differences in Personality Disorders in

Psychiatrically Hospitalized Adolescents," *American Journal of Psychiatry*, 1996, 153(8):1,089–91.

Grilo, C. M., C. A. Sanislow, A. E. Skodol, J. G. Gunderson, R. L. Stout, M. T. Shea, M. C. Zanarini, D. S. Bender, L. C. Morey, I. R. Dyck, and T. H. McGlashan. "Do Eating Disorders Co-Occur with Personality Disorders? Comparison Groups Matter," *International Journal of Eating Disorders*, 2003, 33(2):155–64.

Gross, E. F. "Adolescent Internet Use: What We Expect, What Teens Report," *Journal of Applied Developmental Psychology*, 2004, 25:633–49.

Gunderson, J., I. Weinberg, M. Daversa, K. Kueppenbender, M. Zanarini, M. T. Shea, A. E. Skodol, C. A. Sanislow, S. Yen, L. C. Morey, C. M. Grilo, T. H. McGlashan, R. L. Stout, and I. Dyck. "Descriptive and Longitudinal Observations on the Relationship of Borderline Personality Disorder and Bipolar Disorder," *American Journal of Psychiatry*, 2006, 163:1,173–78.

Gurvits, I. G., H. W. Koenigsberg, and L. J. Siever. "Neurotransmitter Dysfunction in Patients with Borderline Personality Disorder," *Psychiatric Clinics of North America*, 2000, 23(1):27–40.

Guzder, J., J. Paris, P. Zelkowitz, and R. Feldman. "Psychological Risk Factors for Borderline Pathology in School-Age Children," *Journal of the American Academy of Child and Adolescent Psychiatry*, 1999, 38(2):206–12.

Helgeland, M. I., E. Kjelsberg, and S. Torgersen. "Continuities between Emotional and Disruptive Behavior Disorders in Adolescence and Personality Disorders in Adulthood," *American Journal of Psychiatry*, 2005, 162:1,941–47.

Henry, C., V. Mitropoulou, A. S. New, H. W. Koenigsberg, J. Silverman, and L. J. Siever. "Affective Instability and Impulsivity in Borderline Personality and Bipolar II Disorders: Similarities and Differences," *Journal of Psychiatric Research*, 2001, 35(6):307–12.

Hollander, E., A. C. Swann, E. F. Coccaro, P. Jiang, and T. B. Smith. "Impact of Trait Impulsivity and State Aggression on Divalproex versus Placebo Response in Borderline Personality Disorder," *American Journal of Psychiatry*, 2005, 162(3):621–24.

Houston, R. J., N. A. Ceballos, V. M. Hesselbrock, and L. O. Bauer. "Borderline Personality Disorder Features in Adolescent Girls: P300

Evidence of Altered Brain Maturation," *Clinical Neurophysiology*, 2005, 116(6):1,424–32.

Ikuta, N., M. C. Zanarini, K. Minakawa, Y. Miyake, N. Moriya, and A. Nishizono-Maher. "Comparison of American and Japanese Outpatients with Borderline Personality Disorder," *Comprehensive Psychiatry*, 1994, 35(5):382–85.

Iribarren, C., J. H. Markovitz, D. R. Jacobs Jr., P. J. Schreiner, M. Daviglus, and J. R. Hibbeln. "Dietary Intake of n-3, n-6 Fatty Acids and Fish: Relationship with Hostility in Young Adults—The CARDIA Study," *European Journal of Clinical Nutrition*, 2004, 58(1):24–31.

Irle, E., C. Lange, and U. Sachsse. "Reduced Size and Abnormal Asymmetry of Parietal Cortex in Women with Borderline Personality Disorder," *Biological Psychiatry*, 2005, 57(2):173–82.

Jacobsen, T. and V. Hofmann. "Children's Attachment Representations: Longitudinal Relations to School Behavior and Academic Competency in Middle Childhood and Adolescence." *Developmental Psychology*, 1997, 33:703–10.

Joyce, P. R., P. C. McHugh, J. M. McKenzie, P. F. Sullivan, R. T. Mulder, S. E. Luty, J. D. Carter, C. M. Frampton, C. Robert Cloninger, A. M. Miller, and M. A. Kennedy. "A Dopamine Transporter Polymorphism Is a Risk Factor for Borderline Personality Disorder in Depressed Patients," *Psychological Medicine*, 2006, 36(6):807–13.

Joyce, P. R., J. M. McKenzie, R. T. Mulder, S. E. Luty, P. F. Sullivan, A. L. Miller, and M. A. Kennedy. "Genetic, Developmental and Personality Correlates of Self-Mutilation in Depressed Patients," *Australian and New Zealand Journal of Psychiatry*, 2006, 40:225–29.

Juengling, F. D., C. Schmahl, B. Hesslinger, D. Ebert, J. D. Bremner, J. Gostomzyk, M. Bohus, and K. Lieb. "Positron Emission Tomography in Female Patients with Borderline Personality Disorder," *Journal of Psychiatric Research*, 2003, 37(2):109–15.

Kagan, J. and N. Snidman. "Temperamental Factors in Human Development," *American Psychologist*, 1991, 46:856–62.

Kasen, S., P. Cohen, A. E. Skodol, J. G. Johnson, and J. S. Brook. "Influence of Child and Adolescent Psychiatric Disorders on Young Adult Personality Disorder," *American Journal of Psychiatry*, 1999, 156(10):1,529–35.

Katz, L. Y., S. Gunasekara, and A. L. Miller. "Dialectical Behavior Therapy for Inpatient and Outpatient Parasuicidal Adolescents," *Adolescent Psychiatry*, 2002, 26:161–78.

Kellner, C. H., R. M. Post, F. Putnam, R. Cowdry, D. Gardner, M. A. Kling, M. D. Minichiello, J. R. Trettau, and R. Coppola. "Intravenous Procaine as a Probe of Limbic System Activity in Psychiatric Patients and Normal Controls," *Biological Psychiatry*, 1987, 22(9):1,107–26.

Koenigsberg, H. "Integrating Psychotherapy and Pharmacotherapy in the Treatment of Borderline Personality Disorder," *In Session: Psychotherapy in Practice*, 1997, 3(2):39–56.

Kooimana, C. G., S. van Rees Vellingaa, P. Spinhovenb, N. Draijerc, R. W. Trijsburgd, and H. G. M. Rooijmansa "Childhood Adversities as Risk Factors for Alexithymia and Other Aspects of Affect Dysregulation in Adulthood," *Psychotherapy and Psychosomatics*, 2004, 73:107–116.

Kullgren, G. "Factors Associated with Completed Suicide in Borderline Personality Disorder," *The Journal of Nervous and Mental Disorders*, 1998, 76(1):40–44.

Kutcher, S., G. Papatheodorou, S. Reiter, and D. Gardner. "The Successful Pharmacological Treatment of Adolescents and Young Adults with Borderline Personality Disorder: A Preliminary Open Trial of Flupenthixol," *Journal of Psychiatry and Neuroscience*, 1995, 2(2):113–18.

Lange, C., L. Kracht, K. Herholz, U. Sachsse, and E. Irle. "Reduced Glucose Metabolism in Temporo-Parietal Cortices of Women with Borderline Personality Disorder," *Psychiatry Research*, 2005, 139(2):115–26.

Lee, R., T. D. Geracioti, J. W. Kasckow, and E. F. Coccaro. "Childhood Trauma and Personality Disorder: Positive Correlation with Adult CSF Corticotropin-Releasing Factor Concentrations," *American Journal of Psychiatry*, 2005, 162:995–97.

Lewinsohn, P. M., P. Rohde, J. R. Seeley, and D. N. Klein. "Axis II Psychopathology as a Function of Axis I Disorders in Childhood and Adolescence," *Journal of the American Academy of Child and Adolescent Psychiatry*, 1997, 36(12): 1,752–59.

Leyton, M., H. Okazawa, M. Diksic, J. Paris, P. Rosa, S. Mzengeza, S. N. Young, P. Blier, and C. Benkelfat. "Brain Regional-[11C]Methyl-L-Tryptophan Trapping in Impulsive Subjects with Borderline Personality Disorder," *American Journal of Psychiatry*, 2001, 158:775–82.

Linehan, M. M., H. E. Armstrong, A. Suarez, D. Allmon, and H. L. & Heard. "Cognitive-Behavioral Treatment of Chronically Parasuicidal Borderline Patients," *Archives of General Psychiatry*, 1991, 48:1,060–64.

Lofgren, D. P., J. Bemporad, J. King, K. Lindem, and G. O'Driscoll. "A Prospective Follow-Up Study of So-Called Borderline Children," *American Journal of Psychiatry*, 1991, 148:1,541–47.

Lyons-Ruth, K., B. Repacholi, S. McLeod, and E. Silva. "Disorganized Attachment Behavior in Infancy: Short-Term Stability, Maternal and Infant Correlates, and Risk-Related Subtypes," *Developmental Psychopathology*, 1991, 3:377–96.

Mahler, M. "Clinical Studies in Benign and Malignant Cases of Childhood Psychosis—Schizophrenia-Like," *American Journal of Orthopsychiatry*, 1949, vol 19:s297, footnote.

Miller, A. L. "Dialectical Behavior Therapy: A New Treatment Approach for Suicidal Adolescents," *American Journal of Psychotherapy*, 1999, 53(3):413–17.

Miller, F. T., T. Abrams, R. Dulit, and M. Fyer. "Substance Abuse in Borderline Personality Disorder," *American Journal of Drug and Alcohol Abuse*, 1993, 19(4):491–97.

Minzenberg, M. J., J. H. Poole, and S. Vinogradov. "Adult Social Attachment Disturbance Is Related to Childhood Maltreatment and Current Symptoms in Borderline Personality Disorder," *The Journal of Nervous and Mental Disorders*, 2006, 194(5):341-48.

Minzenberg, M. J., J. H. Poole, and S. Vinogradov. "Social-Emotion Recognition in Borderline Personality Disorder," *Comprehensive Psychiatry*, 2006, 47(6):468–74.

Nehls, N. "Being a Case Manager for Persons with Borderline Personality Disorder: Perspectives of Community Mental Health Center Clinicians," *Archives of Psychiatric Nursing*, 2000, 14(1):12–18.

Nehls, N. "Borderline Personality Disorder: The Voice of Patients," *Research in Nurses and Health*, 1999, 22(4):285–93.

New, A. S., R. L. Trestman, and V. Mitropoulou. "Serotonergic Function and Self-Injurious Behavior in Personality Disorder Patients," *Psychiatry Research*, 1997, 69:17–26.

Nickel, C., M. Simek, A. Moleda, M. Muehlbacher, W. Buschmann, R. Fartacek, E. Bachler, C. Egger, W. K. Rother, T. H. Loew, and M. K.

Nickel. "Suicide Attempts versus Suicidal Ideation in Bulimic Female Adolescents," *Pediatrics International*, 2006, 48(4):374–81.

Nickel, M. K. "Aripiprazole in the Treatment of Patients with Borderline Personality Disorder: A Double-Blind, Placebo-Controlled Study," *American Journal of Psychiatry*, May 2006, 163(5):833–38.

Nickel, M. K. "Topiramate Treatment of Aggression in Female Borderline Personality Disorder Patients: A Double-Blind, Placebo-Controlled Study," *Journal of Clinical Psychiatry*, Nov 2004, 65(11):1,515–19.

Nixon, M. K., P. F. Cloutier, and S. Aggarwal. "Affect Regulation and Addictive Aspects of Repetitive Self-Injury in Hospitalized Adolescents," *Journal of the American Academy of Child and Adolescent Psychiatry*, 2002, 41:1,333–41.

Nock, M. K., T. E. Joiner, K. H. Gordon, E. Lloyd-Richardson, and M. J. Prinstein. "Non-Suicidal Self-Injury among Adolescents: Diagnostic Correlates and Relation to Suicide Attempts," *Psychiatry Research*, 2006, 144(1):65–72.

Norra, C., M> Mrazeka, F. Tuchtenhagena, R. Gobbeléb, H. Buchnerb, H. Saßa, and S. C. Herpertza. "Enhanced Intensity Dependence as a Marker of Low Serotonergic Neurotransmission in Borderline Personality Disorder," *Journal of Psychiatric Research*, 2003, 37 (1):23–33.

Oldham, J. M., A. E. Skodol, H. D. Kellman, S. E. Hyler, L. Rosnick, and M. Davies. "Diagnosis of DSM-III-R Personality Disorders by Two Structured Interviews: Patterns of Comorbidity," *American Journal of Psychiatry*, 1992, 149:213–20.

Palmer, S., K. Davidson, P. Tyrer, A. Gumley, P. Tata, J. Norrie, H. Murray, and H. Seivewright. "The Cost Effectiveness of Cognitive Behavior Therapy for Borderline Personality Disorder: Results from the BOSCOT Trial," *Journal of Personality Disorders*, 2006, 20(5):466–81.

Paris, J. "Is Hospitalization Useful for Suicidal Patients with Borderline Personality Disorder?" *Journal of Personality Disorders*, 2004, 18(3):240–47.

Perrella, C., D. Carrus, E. Costa, and F. Schifano. "Quetiapine for the Treatment of Borderline Personality Disorder; an Open-Label Study," *Progress in Neuro-Psychopharmacology & Biological Psychiatry*, 2007, 31(1):158–63.

Philipsen, A., H. Richter, C. Schmahl, J. Peters, N. Rusch, M. Bohus, and K. Lieb. "Clonidine in Acute Aversive Inner Tension and Self-Injurious Behavior in Female Patients with Borderline Personality Disorder," *Journal of Clinical Psychiatry*, 2004, 65(10):1,414–19.

Philipsen, A., C. Schmahl, and K. Lieb. "Naloxone in the Treatment of Acute Dissociative States in Female Patients with Borderline Personality Disorder," *Pharmacopsychiatry*, 2004, 37(5):196–99.

Pinto, A., W. L. Grapentine, G. Francis, and C. M. Picariello. "Borderline Personality Disorder in Adolescents: Affective and Cognitive Features," *Journal of the American Academy of Child and Adolescent Psychiatry*, 1996, 35(10):1,338–43.

Pooley, E. C., K. Houston, K. Hawton, and P. J. Harrison. "Deliberate Self-Harm Is Associated with Allelic Variation in the Tryptophan Hydroxylase Gene (TPH A779C), but not with Polymorphisms in Five Other Serotonergic Genes," *Psychological Medicine*, 2003, 33(5):775–83.

Prado, C. "Functional Impairments in Patients with Borderline Personality Disorders Demonstrated by NeuroSPECT HMPAO Tc 99 m in Basal Conditions and Under Frontal Activation," *Alasbimn Journal*, 2002, 2(7): Article No. AJ07-1.

Preston, G. A., B. K. Marchant, F. W. Reimherr, R. E. Strong, and D. W. Hedges. "Borderline Prsonality Disorder in Patients with Bipolar Disorder and Response to Lamotrigine," *Journal of Affective Disorders*, 2004, 79(1–3): 297–303.

Raine, A., M. Buchsbaum, and L. LaCasse. "Brain Abnormalities in Murderers Indicated by Positron Emission Tomography," *Biological Psychiatry*, 1997, 42:495–508.

Raine, A., T. Lencz, and S. Bihrle. "Reduced Prefrontal Gray Volume and Autonomic Deficits in Antisocial Personality Disorder," *Archives of General Psychiatry*, 2000, 57(2):119–27.

Raine, A., J. Stoddard, and S. Bihrle. "Prefrontal Glucose Deficits in Murderers Lacking Psychosocial Deprivation," *Neuropsychology and Behavioral Neurology*, 1998, 11:1–7.

Rey, J. M., A. Morris-Yates, M. Singh, G. Andrews, and G. W. Stewart. "Continuities between Psychiatric Disorders in Adolescents and Personality Disorders in Young Adults," *American Journal of Psychiatry*, 1995, 152(6):895–900.

Rey, J. M., M. Singh, A. Morris-Yates, and G. Andrews. "Referred Adolescents as Young Adults: The Relationship between Psychosocial Functioning and

Personality Disorder," *Australia and New Zealand Journal of Psychiatry*, 1997, 31(2):219–26.

Rinne, T., W. van den Brink, L. Wouters, and R. van Dyck "SSRI Treatment of Borderline Personality Disorder: A Randomized, Placebo-Controlled Clinical Trial for Female Patients with Borderline Personality Disorder," *American Journal of Psychiatry*, 2002, 159:2,048–54.

Rinne, T., W. van den Brink, L. Wouters, and R. van Dyck. "SSRI Treatment of Borderline Personality Disorder: A Randomized, Placebo-Controlled Clinical Trial for Female Patients with Borderline Personality Disorder," *Current Psychiatry Reports*, 2003, 5(3):176–77.

Rocca, P., L. Marchiaro, E. Cocuzza, and F. Bogetto. "Treatment of Borderline Personality Disorder with Risperidone," *Journal of Clinical Psychiatry*, 2002, 63:241–44.

Rogosch, F. A. and D. Cicchetti. "Child Maltreatment, Attention Networks, and Potential Precursors to Borderline Personality Disorder," *Developmental Psychopathology*, 2005, 17(4):1,071–89.

Russ, M. J., S. D. Roth, A. Lerman, T. Kakuma, K. Harrison, R. D. Shindledecker, J. Hull, and S. Mattis. "Pain Perception in Self-Injurious Patients with Borderline Personality Disorder," *Biological Psychiatry*, 1992, 32(6):501–11.

Sakai, J. T., S. E. Young, M. C. Stallings, D. Timberlake, A. Smolen, G. L. Stetler, and T. J. Crowley. "Case-Control and Within-Family Tests for an Association between Conduct Disorder and 5HTTLPR," *American Journal of Medical Genetics Part B Neuropsychiatric Genetics*, 2006, 141(8):825–32.

Salzman, C., A. N. Wolfson, A. Schatzberg, J. Looper, R. Henke, M. Albanese, J. Schwartz, and E. Miyawaki. "Effect of Fluoxetine on Anger in Symptomatic Volunteers with Borderline Personality Disorder," *Journal of Clinical Psychopharmacology*, 1995, 15:23–29.

Sansone, R. A., J. L. Levitt, and L. A. Sansone. "The Prevalence of Personality Disorders among Those with Eating Disorders," *Eating Disorders*, 2005, 13(1):7–21.

Schafer, M., B. Schnack, and M. Soyka. "Sexual and Physical Abuse During Early Childhood or Adolescence and Later Drug Addiction," *Psychotherapie Psychosomatik Medizinische Psychologie*, 2000, 50(2):38–50.

Schmahl, C., M. Bohus, F. Esposito, R. D. Treede, F. Di Salle, W. Greffrath, P. Ludaescher, A. Jochims, K. Lieb, K. Scheffler, J. Hennig, and E. Seifritz. "Neural Correlates of Antinociception in Borderline Personality Disorder," *Archives of General Psychiatry*, 2006, 6:659–67.

Schmahl, C., W. Greffrath, U. Baumgartner, T. Schlereth, W. Magerl, A. Philipsen, K. Lieb, M. Bohus, and R. D. Treede. "Differential Nociceptive Deficits in Patients with Borderline Personality Disorder and Self-Injurious Behavior: Laser-Evoked Potentials, Spatial Discrimination of Noxious Stimuli, and Pain Ratings," *Pain*, 2004, 110(1–2):470–79.

Schmahl, C. and J. D. Bremner. "Neuroimaging in Borderline Personality Disorder," *Journal of Psychiatric Research*, 2006, 40(5):419–27.

Schmahl, C. G., E. Vermetten, B. M. Elzinga, and J. D. Bremner. "A Positron Emission Tomography Study of Memories of Childhood Abuse in Borderline Personality Disorder," *Biological Psychiatry*, 2004, 55(7):759–65.

Schnell, K. and S. C. Herpertz. "Effects of Dialectic Behavioral Therapy on the Neural Correlates of Affective Hyperarousal in Borderline Personality Disorder," *Journal of Psychiatric Research*, 2006, 8(3):133–142.

Segal-Trivitz, Y., Y. Bloch, Y. Goldburt, D. Sobol-Havia, Y. Levkovitch, and G. Ratzoni. "Comparison of Symptoms and Treatments of Adults and Adolescents with Borderline Personality Disorder," *International Journal of Adolescent Medicine and Health*, 2006, 18(2):215–20.

Silverman, J. M., L. Pinkham, T. B. Horvath, E. F. Coccaro, K. Howard, S. Schear, S. Apter, M. Davidson, R. Mohs, and L. J. Siever. "Affective and Impulsive Personality Disorder Traits in the Relatives of Patients with Borderline Personality Disorder," *American Journal of Psychiatry*, 1991, 148(10):1,378–85.

Slap, G., E. Goodman, and B. Huang. "Adoption as a Risk Factor for Attempted Suicide During Adolescence," *Pediatrics*, 2001, 108(2):E30.

Smith, D. J., W. J. Muir, and D. H. Blackwood. "Borderline Personality Disorder Characteristics in Young Adults with Recurrent Mood Disorders: A Comparison of Bipolar and Unipolar Depression," *Journal of Affective Disorders*, 2005, 87(1):17–23.

Soloff, P. H., A. Fabio, T. M. Kelly, K. M. Malone, and J. J. Mann. "High-Lethality Status in Patients with Borderline Personality Disorder," *Journal of Personality Disorders*, 2005, 19(4):386–99.

Soloff, P. H., K. G. Lynch, T. M. Kelly, K. M. Malone, and J. J. Mann. "Characteristics of Suicide Attempts of Patients with Major Depressive Episode and Borderline Personality Disorder: A Comparative Study," *American Journal of Psychiatry*, 2000, 157:601–608.

Soloff, P. H., C. C. Meltzer, C. Becker, P. J. Greer, T. M. Kelly, and D. Constantine. "Impulsivity and Prefrontal Hypometabolism in Borderline Personality Disorder," *Psychiatry Research*, 2003, 123(3):153–63.

Steinberg, B. J., R. Trestman, V. Mitropoulou, M. Serby, J. Silverman, E. Coccaro, S. Weston, M. de Vegvar, and L. J. Siever. "Depressive Response to Physostigmine Challenge in Borderline Personality Disorder Patients," *Neuropsychopharmacology*, 1997, 17(4):264–73.

Stone, M. H., S. W. Hurt, and D. K. Stone. "The PI-500: Long-Term Follow-Up of Borderline In-Patients Meeting DSMIII Criteria I: Global Outcome," *Journal of Personality Disorders*, 1987:1,291–98.

Stone, M. H., D. K. Stone, and S. W. Hurt. "Natural History of Borderline Patients Treated by Intensive Hospitalization," *Psychiatric Clinics of North America*, 1987, 10:185–206.

Swartz, H. A., P. A. Pilkonis, E. Frank, J. M. Proietti, and J. Scott. "Acute Treatment Outcomes in Patients with Bipolar I Disorder and Co-Morbid Borderline Personality Disorder Receiving Medication and Psychotherapy," *Bipolar Disorders*, 2005, 7(2):192–97.

Tanskanen, A., J. R. Hibbeln, J. Hintikka, K. Haatainen, K. Honkalampi, and H. Viinamaki. "Fish Consumption, Depression, and Suicidality in a General Population," *Archives of General Psychiatry*, 2001, 58(5):512–13.

Tebartz van Elst, L., B. Hesslinger, T. Thiel, E. Geiger, K. Haegele, L. Lemieux, K. Lieb, M. Bohus, J. Hennig, and D. Ebert. "Frontolimbic Brain Abnormalities in Patients with Borderline Personality Disorder: A Volumetric Magnetic Resonance Imaging Study," *Biological Psychiatry*, 2003, 54(2):163–71.

Thatcher, D. L., J. R. Cornelius, and D. B. Clark. "Adolescent Alcohol Use Disorders Predict Adult Borderline Personality," *Addictive Behaviors*, 2005, 30(9):1,709–24.

Thompson, R., E. Briggs, D. J. English, H. Dubowitz, L. C. Lee, K. Brody, M. D. Everson, and W. M. Hunter. "Suicidal Ideation among 8-Year-Olds Who Are Maltreated and at Risk: Findings from the LONGSCAN Studies," *Child Maltreatment*, 2005, 10(1):26–36.

Torgersen, S. "Genetics of Patients with Borderline Personality Disorder," *Psychiatric Clinics of North America*, 2000, 23(1):1–9.

Valkenburg, P. M., J. Peter, and A. P. Schouten. "Friend Networking Sites and Their Relationship to Adolescents' Well-Being and Social Self-Esteem," *Cyberpsychology and Behavior*, 2006, 9(5):584–90.

Van Den Bosch, L. M., M. W. Koeter, T. Stijnen, R. Verheul, and W. Van Den Brink. "Sustained Efficacy of Dialectical Behaviour Therapy for Borderline Personality Disorder," *Behaviour Research and Therapy*, 2005, 43(9):1,231–41.

Van Den Bosch, L. M., R. Verheul, W. Langeland, and W. Van Den Brink. "Trauma, Dissociation, and Posttraumatic Stress Disorder in Female Borderline Patients with and without Substance Abuse Problems," *Australia and New Zealand Journal of Psychiatry*, 2003, 37(5):549–55.

Van Wel, B., I. Kockmann, N. Blum, B. Pfohl, D. W. Black, and W. Heesterman. "STEPPS Group Treatment for Borderline Personality Disorder in The Netherlands," *Annals of Clinical Psychiatry*, 2006, 18(1):63–7.

Weiger, W. A. and D. M. Bear. "An Approach to the Neurology of Aggression," *Journal of Psychiatric Research*, 1988, 22:85–98.

Westen, D., J. Shedler, C. Durrett, S. Glass, and A. Martens. "Personality Diagnoses in Adolescence: DSM-IV Axis II Diagnoses and an Empirically Derived Alternative," *American Journal of Psychiatry*, 2003, 160:952–66.

Whitlock, J. L., J. L. Powers, and J. Eckenrode. "The Virtual Cutting Edge: The Internet and Adolescent Self-Injury," *Developmental Psychology*, 2006, 42(3):407–17.

Wilson, S. T., E. A. Fertuck, A. Kwitel, M. C. Stanley, and B. Stanley. "Impulsivity, Suicidality and Alcohol Use Disorders in Adolescents and Young Adults with Borderline Personality Disorder," *International Journal of Adolescent Medicine and Health*, 2006, 18(1):189–96.

Wingenfeld, K., M. Driessen, B. Adam, and A. Hill. "Overnight Urinary Cortisol Release in Women with Borderline Personality Disorder Depends on Comorbid PTSD and Depressive Psychopathology," *European Psychiatry*, 2006, 194(12):967–970.

Yoshida, K., E. Tonai, H. Nagai, K. Matsushima, M. Matsushita, J. Tsukada, Y. Kiyohara, and R. Nishimura. "Long-Term Follow-Up Study of

Borderline Patients in Japan: A Preliminary Study," *Comprehensive Psychiatry*, 2006, 47(5):426–32.

Zanarini, M. C. and F. R. Frankenburg. "Olanzapine Treatment of Female Borderline Personality Disorder Patients: A Double-Blind, Placebo-Controlled Pilot Study," *Journal of Clinical Psychiatry*, 2001, 62(11):849–54.

Zanarini, M. C. and F. R. Frankenburg. "Omega-3 Fatty Acid Treatment of Women with Borderline Personality Disorder: A Double-Blind, Placebo-Controlled Pilot Study," *American Journal of Psychiatry*, 2003, 160(1):167–69.

Zanarini, M. C., F. R. Frankenburg, and E. A. Parachini. "A Preliminary, Randomized Trial of Fluoxetine, Olanzapine, and the Olanzapine-Fluoxetine Combination in Women with Borderline Personality Disorder," *Journal of Clinical Psychiatry*, 2004, 65(7):903–907.

Zanarini, M. C., F. R. Frankenburg, J. Hennen, D. B. Reich, and K. Silk. "Axis I Comorbidity in Patients with Borderline Personality Disorder: 6-Year Follow-Up and Prediction of Time to Remission," *American Journal of Psychiatry*, 2004, 161:2,108–14.

Zanarini, M. C., F. R. Frankenburg, J. Hennen, D. B. Reich, and K. R. Silk. "The McLean Study of Adult Development: Overview and Implications of the First Six Years of Prospective Follow-Up," *Journal of Personality Disorders*, 2005, 19(5):505–23.

Zanarini, M. C., F. R. Frankenburg, M. E. Ridolfi, S. Jager-Hyman, J. Hennen, and J. G. Gunderson. "Reported Childhood Onset of Self-Mutilation among Borderline Patients," *Journal of Personality Disorders*, 2006, 20(1):9–15.

Zanarini, M. C., F. R. Frankenburg, L. Yong, G. Raviola, D. B. Reich, J. Hennen, J. I. Hudson, and J. G. Gunderson. "Borderline Psychopathology in the First-Degree Relatives of Borderline and Axis II Comparison Probands," *Journal of Personality Disorders*, 2004, 18(5):439–47.

Zanarini, M. C., A. A. Williams, R. E. Lewis, R. B. Reich, S. C. Vera, M. F. Marino, A. Levin, L. Yong, and F. R. Frankenburg "Reported Pathological Childhood Experiences Associated with the Development of Borderline Personality Disorder," *American Journal of Psychiatry*, 1997, 154(8):1,101–1,106.

Zanarini, M. C., L. Yong, F. R. Frankenburg, J. Hennen, D. B. Reich, M. F. Marino, and A. A. Vujanovic. "Severity of Reported Childhood Sexual Abuse and Its Relationship to Severity of Borderline Psychopathology and Psychosocial Impairment among Borderline Inpatients," *The Journal of Nervous and Mental Disorders*, 2002, 190(6):381–87.

Zeanah, C. H. "Beyond Insecurity: A Reconceptualization of Attachment Disorders of Infancy," *Journal of Consulting and Clinical Psychology*, 1996, 64:42–52.

Zeanah, C. H. and N. A. Fox. "Temperament and Attachment Disorders," *Journal of Clinical Child and Adolescent Psychology*, 2004, 33:32–41.

Zeanah, C. H., A. Keyes, and L. Settles. "Attachment Relationship Experiences and Childhood Psychopathology," *Annals of the New York Academy of Science*, 2003, 1008:22–30.

Zeanah, C. H., M. Scheeringa., N. W. Boris, S. S. Heller, A. T. Smyke, and J. Trapani. "Reactive Attachment Disorder in Maltreated Toddlers," *Child Abuse and Neglect*, 2004, 28:877–88.

Zelkowitz, P., J. Paris, J. Guzder, and R. Feldman. "Diatheses and Stressors in Borderline Pathology of Childhood: The Role of Neuropsychological Risk and Trauma," *Journal of the American Academy of Child and Adolescent Psychiatry*, 2001, 40(1):100–105.

Zimmerman, M. and J. I. Mattia. "Axis I Diagnostic Comorbidity and Borderline Personality Disorder," *Comprehensive Psychiatry*, 1999, 40(4):245–52.

Zimmerman, M., L. Rothschild, and I. Chelminski. "The Prevalence of DSM-IV Personality Disorders in Psychiatric Outpatients," *American Journal of Psychiatry*, 2005, 162:1,911–18.

Zweig-Frank, H., J. Paris, and J. Guzder. "Psychological Risk Factors for Dissociation and Self-Mutilation in Female Patients with Borderline Personality Disorder," *Canadian Journal of Psychiatry*, 1994, 39(5):259–64.

BOOKS

Ainsworth, M., M. C. Blehar, E. Waters, and S. Wall. *Patterns of Attachment: A Psychological Study of the Strange Situation*. Hillsdale, N.J.: Erlbaum, 1978.

Alderman, T. *The Scarred Soul: Understanding and Ending Self-Inflicted Violence*. Oakland, CA: New Harbinger, 1997.

American Psychiatric Association. *Diagnostic and Statistical Manual of Mental Disorders*, Fourth Edition, Text Revision (DSM-IV-TR). American Psychiatric Association, 2000.

Chethik, M. *The Borderline Child. In: Basic Handbook of Child Psychiatry*, Noshpitz J, ed. New York: Basic Books, 1979.

Fruzzetti, A.E., P.D Hoffman, and M. Linehan. *Dialectical Behavior Therapy with Couples and Families*. New York: Guilford Publications, in press.

Linehan, M. *Cognitive Behavioral Treatment of Borderline Personality Disorder*. New York: Guilford Press, 1993.

Linehan, M. *Skills Training Manual for Treating Borderline Personality Disorder*. New York: Guilford Press, 1993.

Wurtzel, E. *Prozac Nation: Young and Depressed in America*. Boston: Houghton Mifflin, 1994.

OTHER RESEARCH AND CITATIONS

Batty, D. "Transsexual expert 'put patients at risk,'" *Guardian Unlimited*, Friday, November 3, 2006.

BBC Interview with Princess Diana, November 1995.

Bohart A.C. and L. Greenberg (eds.), "Empathy Reconsidered: New Directions in Psychotherapy," Washington DC: American Psychological Association, May 2000.

Brodzinsky, D. M. "Long-Term Outcomes in Adoption," *Adoption*, 1993, 3(1).

Caspi, A. "Personality Development across the Lifespan," In *Handbook of Child Psychology*, 1998, vol. 3, *Social, Emotional, and Personality Development*, ed. W. Damon. New York: Wiley, pp. 311–388.

Caspi, A. and R. L. Shiner. "Personality Development." In *Handbook of Child Psychology*, 2006, vol. 3., *Social, Emotional, and Personality Development*, 6th ed., W. Damon & R. Lerner (series eds.) & N. Eisenberg (vol. ed.). 6th ed. New York: Wiley, pp. 300-365.

Chanen, A. ORYGEN Research Center, Department of Psychiatry, The University of Melbourne, Australia: "An MRI Study of the Orbitofrontal Cortex and Medial Temporal Lobe in Adolescent Borderline Personality Disorder."

Freud, A. "The Assessment of Borderline Cases." In *The Writings of Anna*

Freud, vol. 5. New York, NY: International Universities Press, 1969.

Fruzzetti, A. E. "Couples and Family Dialectical Behavior Therapy: Brief Intervention Outcomes." Paper presented at the 3rd Annual Convention of the International Society for Dialectical Behavior Therapy, Washington DC, 1998.

Fruzzetti, A. E., A. Rubio, and S. R Thorp. "DBT as an Alternative to Anger Management for Male Batterers." Paper presented at the 3rd Annual Convention of the International Society for Dialectical Behavior Therapy, Washington DC, 1998.

The Grove Street Adolescent Residence of The Bridge of Central Massachusetts, Inc. 2004 APA Gold Award: "Using Dialectical Behavior Therapy to Help Troubled Adolescents Return Safely to Their Families and Communities," *Psychiatric Services*, 2004, 55:1,168–70.

Lyons-Ruth, K. "Maternal Depressive Symptoms, Disorganized Infant-Mother Attachment Relationships and Hostile-Aggressive Behavior in the Pre-School Classroom," In *Rochester Symposium on Developmental Psychology*, 1992, vol. 4. Rochester, NY: University of Rochester Press, pp. 131–71.

U.S. Food and Drug Administration. *FDA Public Health Advisory: Suicidality in Children and Adolescents Being Treated with Antidepressant Medications.* October 15, 2004.

Vela, R. M., E. H. Gottlieb E. H., and H. P. Gottlieb. "Borderline Syndromes in Childhood: A Critical Review," In *The Borderline Child*, 1983, ed. Robson K. S., New York: McGraw-Hill, pp. 32–48.

Whitlock, J. L., J. L. Powers, and J. Eckenrode. "The Virtual Cutting Edge: The Internet and Adolescent Self-Injury" from "Children, Adolescents, and the Internet," special section of *Developmental Psychology*, 42(3).

ACKNOWLEDGMENTS

I COULD NOT HAVE WRITTEN THIS BOOK without the support and input of many people, but it would have been pointless were it not for the kids and families who struggle daily with the impact of BPD. In particular Eric, Peter, Nancy, Helen, Addie, Lauren, Ashley, Alexis, Casey, Allie, Jen, and Emma have taught me more about adolescent BPD in a few years than many lifetimes of book learning could ever teach.

At McLean Hospital, Cynthia Kaplan, Joe Gold, and Phil Levendusky have strongly supported the dedicated treatment of adolescents with BPD. Paul Jay and his excellent mental health staff, Sue Mandelbaum, Michael Hollander, Janna Hobbs, Peg Polomsky, Jessica Feinberg, Prim Sawyer, Dominique Vo, Jennifer Mehrtens, and Erin Clement all provide tremendous support on our DBT consultation team.

Mike Rater's skepticism has kept me clinically honest. Ginny Wedge, Jim Holsomback, and K. C. Chiappa have for years been dedicated to the cause of adolescents with BPD. Sarah Hunt and Sequina Taylor continue to work tirelessly to interface with emergency rooms, insurance companies, and all levels of administrative challenges to make sure that kids are helped in a timely fashion.

John Gunderson has provided years of wisdom and supervision. Mary Zanarini is currently conducting a study to better define the nature of BPD in adolesents.

Marsha Linehan has truly underscored the role of mindfulness in treating BPD, and she has helped change the course, prognosis, and dialogue of BPD.

Kiera van Gelder has bravely put a face on the condition when few others would do so and reached out to countless people in offering hope from firsthand experience.

Perry Hoffman is slowly educating the world about BPD through the NEA-BPD foundation.

Finally, had my original manuscript made any sense, my editor Cara Connors probably would not have learned as much about BPD as she was forced to through hours of micro-editing the thousands of words and thoughts I threw at her. Thank you!

Blaise A. Aguirre, M.D., is the medical director of the Adolescent Dialectical Behavioral Therapy Center at McLean Hospital in Belmont, Massachusetts, which opened in 2007. He is a co-author of *Helping Your Troubled Teen: Learn to Recognize, Understand, and Address the Destructive Behavior of Today's Teens,* published in 2007 by Fair Winds Press. He attended medical school at the University of the Witwatersrand, Johannesburg, South Africa. He completed his residency and fellowship in adult and child psychiatry at Boston University School of Medicine. He served as a staff psychiatrist at the New England Home for Little Wanderers in Boston from 1996 to 1998 and was then medical director at the Lowell Youth Treatment Center in Lowell, Massachusetts, from 1998 to 2000. He has been a staff psychiatrist at McLean Hospital since 2000 and is an instructor in psychiatry at Harvard Medical School.

INDEX